BOILING POINT

212°

IT ONLY TAKES ONE DEGREE

Monitoring Cultural Shifts in the 21st Century

GEORGE BARNA
& MARK HATCH

Regal

A Division of Gospel Light
Ventura, California, U.S.A.

Published by Regal Books
From Gospel Light
Ventura, California, U.S.A.
Printed in the U.S.A.

Regal Books is a ministry of Gospel Light, an evangelical Christian publisher dedicated to serving the local church. We believe God's vision for Gospel Light is to provide church leaders with biblical, user-friendly materials that will help them evangelize, disciple and minister to children, youth and families.

It is our prayer that this Regal book will help you discover biblical truth for your own life and help you meet the needs of others. May God richly bless you.

For a free catalog of resources from Regal Books/Gospel Light, please call your Christian supplier or contact us at 1-800-4-GOSPEL or www.regalbooks.com.

Cover and Interior Design by Rob Williams
Edited by Wil Simon

LIBRARY OF CONGRESS CATALOGING-IN-PUBLICATION DATA
Barna, George
Boiling point/George Barna and Mark Hatch.
p. cm.
Includes bibliographical references (p.).
ISBN 0-8307-2651-9 (trade paper)
1. Christianity—United States. 2. Twenty-first century—Forecasts. 3. United States—Church history. 4. Church growth—United States. I. Hatch, Mark, 1960 – II. Title.

BR526 .B335 2001
277.3'083'0112—dc21

2 3 4 5 6 7 8 9 10 11 12 13 14 15 16 17 18 19 20 / 10 11 09 08 07 06 05 04 03 02

Rights for publishing this book in other languages are contracted by Gospel Light Worldwide, the international nonprofit ministry of Gospel Light. Gospel Light Worldwide also provides publishing and technical assistance to international publishers dedicated to producing Sunday School and Vacation Bible School curricula and books in the languages of the world. For additional information, visit www.gospellightworldwide.org; write to Gospel Light Worldwide, P.O. Box 3875, Ventura, CA 93006; or send an e-mail to info@gospellightworldwide.org.

Contents

ACKNOWLEDGMENTS

My sincere thanks go to Mark Hatch for lending his expertise in technology, medicine and health care, and international business and politics to this effort. I could not have worked on this book had it not been for the stellar efforts of my colleagues at the Barna Research Group, who ran the company in my absence. The core unit included Rachel Ables, Pam Jacob, David Kinnaman, Jill Kinnaman, Carmen Moore, Sarah Polley, Irene Robles, Celeste Rivera and Meg Wells. My partner in The Barna Institute, Kim Wilson, endured being ignored for weeks as I wrestled with the writing of this book.

Our friends at Gospel Light have been helpful and encouraging, as always. In particular, thanks must go to Bill Greig III, Kyle Duncan, David Webb, Bill Denzel, Wil Simon—and the other 200 or so GL partners who will make this book a ministry resource.

Most of all I thank my family for letting me abandon them for three weeks while I hibernated to write this book. My wife, Nancy, did everything required—included major sacrificing—to keep things afloat and copacetic. My daughters, Samantha and Corban, were also understanding and supportive, asking me daily how the book was progressing and praying for the book and me every night during this process. I am grateful that God has surrounded me with such tangible representatives of His love and encouragement and that He provided this incredible opportunity to try to help the Church. I pray that this book will serve Him and His Church well.

George Barna

First, for this amazing journey that He leads me on, I must thank my Lord. Then, thanks to George Barna for inviting me to participate in this project as well as for providing all the help in making it work. I thank Bill Greig III, whose question over lunch, "Have you ever thought of writing a Christian book about the future?" started this adventure for me.

I am grateful to the folks at the Barna Research Group that helped and to Marcia Zimmermann and Ron Archer who slogged through noisy transcription duties. To the staff at Gospel Light, particularly Kyle Duncan, David Webb, Bill Denzel and Wil Simon, a special debt of gratitude is owed for pulling the book together.

To those I owe the most gratitude, my family, a special thanks. A great debt is owed to my helpmate, Cindy, who makes the amazing journey possible through her unending support, encouragement and prayers. I could not do what I do without her, and for that I am eternally grateful. To my boys, Luke and Christopher, who often waited to see their dad until he was done writing and who lifted me up in their prayers—thanks guys.

Mark Hatch

PROLOGUE

A DAY IN THE LIFE OF JILL

In 1990, when I wrote *The Frog in the Kettle*, I opened and closed the book with a description of the life of Jill, a composite character. In the beginning I described what her life would be like in the year 2000. I closed the book with a revised depiction of her life, assuming the Church would heed the warnings about the coming changes in society and minister strategically during the '90s. The tale you will read below picks up Jill's life 10 years hence, in 2010, again assuming that the trends on the horizon occur without significant reshaping by the Church. The intent of this fictionalized account is to provide you with a feel for what a typical person's story will most likely be at the close of the current decade. The rest of this book will fill you in on how Jill got there.—George Barna

The bedroom lights suddenly spring to action and the room is illuminated with a dim glow. Simultaneously, the stereo system begins to serenade the sleeping couple with tunes from a favorite CD while water, at just the right temperature, gurgles into the bathtub. It is 7:00 A.M., Thursday, and Jill Moore's "smart house" is doing its part to rouse her and her husband out of bed. Groggily, Jill and Carl roll off opposite sides of their king-sized bed and begin their unsynchronized morning stumble toward various parts of the master bedroom in preparation for the day ahead.

Carl reaches the bathroom vanity and rubs the vestiges of sleep from his eyes. Next to the medicine cabinet, the TV screen recessed into the wall automatically turns on, providing a specialty news channel—his choice is Digitas, commonly known as the Techie Channel—to bring him the latest moment-by-moment developments and emerging challenges in the world of technology. While he brushes his teeth, Carl calls out a command to the TV set and the program dissolves into a screen that displays e-mail messages and significant news headlines of personal interest. Standing before the mirror with his eyes three-quarters open, Carl does a double take at one particular line of text and immediately gives another verbal command that produces a video clip related to that news story. During the night the computer firm he works for was involved in a major deal; the video relays the key points of the saga to the dismayed man of the house. Disgusted by the news, Carl barks another order at the wall, and the screen shifts to a music channel, featuring gyrating dancers and guitar-waving musicians harmonizing to multilayered rock rhythms. In the upper right-hand corner of the screen is a scrolling menu of the day's events around the world that might be of particular interest to Carl. He ignores it all and begins shaving.

Meanwhile, Jill leisurely slips into the tub and luxuriates in her morning bath—a habit she initiated three years ago just after her marriage to Carl. Following her divorce, Jill, as a single parent, had raised her son, Jackson, until he had decided to leave for college. Shortly after her son's departure, she married Carl, with whom she had been living for several years. She celebrated her marriage to Carl by leaving her job; Jill wanted to enjoy her empty nest and the relief from the pressure of single parenting. But after seven months of puttering around the house, she was bored and quickly decided to go back to work, taking a respectable but low-stress, part-time job as an assistant hotel manager. Now she had settled into a daily routine that combined her desire to lead a more comfortable life with a job that presented some much-needed mental challenges.

Yet, as she soaked in the tub and watched Carl prepare for work, Jill thought, *I wonder what brought us together? Why did we marry?* She quickly recalled her divorce, the subsequent time of depression, the string of men that followed. She had hoped these relationships would provide emotional stability for her and a male role model for Jackson. Each live-in relationship—there had been three—lasted for several years.

Then she met Carl through an on-line therapy group for divorced parents. Following several months of cyberchat, they both attended a live, in-person event with the group and discovered that they hit it off in person as well. They dated casually for several months, and as the relationship became serious, the natural step for them was to live together, which they did for a couple of years before agreeing to get married.

Remarriage was a common thing in the United States, but it was still a big step for both of them. Carl, in particular, demurred. Besides the demands of his international consulting work, the memories of his sour first marriage and the challenge of making ends meet without Jill's salary fueled his anxiety over how he thought his daughters would react to having a stepmother and being part of a blended family. The girls were still close to their natural mother, even though they lived nine months of the year with him. It was only after his girls reached their teen years (when Allie was 17 and Brittany had reached 13) that Carl felt the freedom to take the next step—to remarry and enter, as he labeled it, "phase 3" of his adult life.

The marriage, however, had proved to be more of an adjustment than they had anticipated. Unexpectedly, prior to their wedding, Jill's son decided to move back and live at home. He had just turned 21 and had completed the number of credits required to finish what used to be known as the sophomore year in college. (Jill never quite understood why it took kids an average of six years to finish a four-year college program.) Over the next two years, Jackson's presence, along with Allie's and Brittany's, created new tensions and bonds in the household as each one tested the others to figure out the roles and turf that could be claimed as his or her own in this new physical and emotional arrangement. In short, they had become the quintessential blended family.

Other challenges for Jill and Carl included her change in career and their move from Dallas to Denver. People moved regularly—one out of every six households changed homes each year—but moving 800 miles away from her longtime hometown had been a major adjustment for Jill. The primary reason for the move was to improve their quality of life. Carl and Jill found a great midsized home in a gated community not far from the mountains, just north of Denver. As a computer engineer, Carl worked from his home, connecting with clients around the world via the Internet and videophone. Subsequent to the marriage, having left behind her lucrative job at an insurance company, Jill took a few months to get the new house in order, get acquainted with the area and help the kids adjust to their new surroundings. Within a few months she drove herself (and Carl) crazy around the house and happily took the hotel position.

Denver, it turned out, was similar to Dallas in terms of people's behavior. She assumed that every place in the country was pretty much this way these days. People barely gave a second thought to lying and cheating anymore; it was assumed that you'd do whatever you had to do to enjoy the outcomes you desired. People lied all the time, whether it was on job applications, in conversations with friends or at a store to get a few cents off a product. Cheating was normal, and you needed eyes in the back of your head to protect yourself against being taken advantage of. Rudeness was widespread, whether it was cutting people off on the freeway, parking in spaces designated for others, using crude language in public or saying impolite things to people who caused a moment of inconvenience. Even though Jill hadn't been raised that way, she had adapted to this unfortunate deterioration of society; after all, she figured, those who didn't play by the new rules would die by them. She didn't necessarily like the kind of person that such underhanded and selfish behaviors had turned her into, but what else could she do? If she didn't look out for herself, nobody else would.

By far the toughest part of the move was the abandonment of her longstanding friendships around Dallas. Their new home just north of Denver was nice, but the chance to connect with other people her age (she had turned 52 a month ago) was difficult; she felt isolated. Carl, on the phone and Net all day, six days a week, had little interest in meeting and building new friendships. She wondered if all guys were like that. But Carl's lack of interest in making new friends prompted Jill to shoulder that challenge alone. She knew that Baby Boomers were not a highly relational group, and she had little in common with most of the Baby Busters she encountered. Through the local gym, some on-line groups and other people she met at work, Jill eventually pieced together a social life that met some of her needs.

But there was one issue the move did not ameliorate. For some time Jill was aware of an inexorable sense of emptiness regarding her life. She and Carl shared a love of entertainment and frequently went to public events—concerts, movies, sporting events, theater and lectures on topics of mutual interest. They lived in a comfortable home in a respectable community and had an above-average income. Their kids had not succumbed to the usual teenage temptations—drugs, alcohol, anorexia, gambling, sexual promiscuity, TV addiction—and were doing satisfactorily in school. The move to Denver had enabled them to shed hundreds of pounds of excess stuff they had accumulated over the years. Jill and Carl exercised regularly—he engaged in tennis, she in swimming, and they took a long walk together three nights a week. For the most part, they lived the good life. But the good life just didn't seem good enough. Sometimes Jill daydreamed of pumping up their combined annual salary of $88,000—well over the national average in 2010—by another $15,000. But instinctively she knew that no matter how much they made, an increase in income would not eliminate the uneasiness she harbored deep inside.

Carl felt it, too, although his experience was different from Jill's. He realized that his job simply was not producing the fulfillment that he had hoped for. He'd been through a string of jobs in the past 15 years, jumping companies five times. Each transition brought an increase in pay and responsibility, but no commensurate rise in fulfillment. He suggested to Jill that maybe they needed a more radical lifestyle change to reach a place of inner peace. He talked about moving to Reno, Nevada, a fast-growing entertainment hub. He mentioned saving up to buy a second home on the beach, perhaps in Southern California, to give them a serious escape hatch. He discussed new hobbies, maybe one they could both learn, such as flying or (now that they lived at the foot of the Rockies) extreme climbing. They never seemed to arrive at resolution on these and many other ideas for change. They considered early retirement as one possible solution, but they could neither afford it on their meager savings nor could either of them imagine life without work.

The greatest mystery in their reflections related to spirituality. Before their marriage the nation had undergone a time of religious ferment. A decade ago, the "new millennium fever" had triggered a plethora of religious events designed to challenge people spiritually. Both Jill and Carl had paid attention to the activity and engaged in limited forays into the religious world. Neither of them had been much involved in faith communities since high school, when their parents had forced them to attend church. But the parade of high-profile celebrities who attributed their new-found inner peace to spiritual involvement had captured the attention of the two seekers.

Carl attended several large-scale Christian events at the urging of some business associates. Once or twice he found the experiences inexplicably moving but without any follow-up by churches or individuals, his interest waned as the months passed. He tried a "personal reinvention" retreat led by a popular self-help author, but he couldn't fathom the metaphysical musings and was turned off by the pushy product marketing at the retreat.

He thought about attending one of the many churches in the area, but he just never got around to it. There were so many other things vying for his energy that it was difficult to imagine integrating a regimen of religious activity into his life. Religion had become a real paradox: He couldn't afford the time to devote to spiritual exploration, but he also couldn't afford *not* to devote time to exploring his spiritual dimension; he couldn't grow spiritually without a basic spiritual foundation, but he couldn't get the foundation unless he made a commitment to something he wasn't sure he believed in. Besides, he felt confused over listening to Christian churches talk about love, forgiveness and community while the news reports exposed intense internal battles within churches over gay rights, women in leadership, medical ethics and the like.

Jill, too, dabbled in faith matters. Some evangelical Christian friends in Dallas had invited her to attend their church services, but she didn't find much of value there. She liked the music and even some of the lectures (they called them sermons) but not enough to make church attendance a habit. If her son had connected at the church it might have been different, but

Jackson told her he often felt like an outsider. Maybe it was just as well. Even when Jill talked with her evangelical friends, she realized that she had too little in common with them. Her personal convictions about divorce, wealth, the Bible, salvation, the role of women and sexuality were quite different from theirs and seemed to offend them. Church life seemed to work for her friends, and she was happy for them. But it just didn't appear to be the answer for her and Jackson or for Carl, Allie and Brittany.

To her surprise, she had encountered various groups of faith explorers while surfing the Net. She had actually found more depth and community through those ongoing interactions than she had at the physical churches she had visited. Jill maintained a presence with three on-line faith communities and found some solace and benefit there. The depth and honesty in the nightly chat-room discussions were so compelling that even Carl decided to listen in. Some of the "chatters" talked about on-line worship experiences and real-time on-line Bible studies they participated in. Neither Jill nor Carl had gone that far yet, although Jill was on the verge of checking out some of those experiences. The beauty of it, she felt, was that she remained protected from intense commitment but could still explore something that seemed significant and had obviously affected her on-line friends. The occasional chat-room squabbles about doctrinal or theological points did not bother her in the least. In fact, she found herself observing those exchanges quite carefully, reveling in the open dialogue and the opportunity to hear multiple viewpoints expressed.

What it all came down to for Jill was having a life that was worth living. Suicide was not an option, of course, although massive numbers of young people continued to take their own lives out of frustration and dissatisfaction. All she and Carl wanted were the basic necessities of life: simplicity, happiness, fulfillment, comfort, freedom, security, good health, independence and opportunities. She imagined that those needs hadn't changed for decades—what human could live without such basics?

Her reverie was shattered by the rapid flashing of the row of track lights in the ceiling above the tub. One thing about these smart houses, they certainly removed the stress of constantly having to watch the clock. She glanced at the digitally displayed time above the TV set: sure enough, 7:35 A.M., the programmed reminder for her to get out of the tub, get dressed and make breakfast for the family. Upstairs in the house, various computer programs and electronic gizmos had awakened Jackson, Allie and Brittany, too, while downstairs the programmed appliances had made coffee in time for the eight o'clock breakfast. Every home in their neighborhood had such electronic aids. She wondered, *How did we get along without them in years past?*

As Jill walked into the kitchen to prepare some food for the family, she took a small glass of water and swallowed her heart medication. She knew her being alive was as much a miracle as all the sophisticated conveniences around her. The doctors had discovered a potentially fatal heart problem before it became a major issue, thanks to the data garnered from a tiny computer chip that she ingested during a routine checkup. She had not shown any overt symptoms, but her physician had taken the precaution of checking her heart with one of the new robotic aids recently developed—and was she glad that he did! Her daily medication was relatively new—a synthetic drug tailored to her body chemistry. At her most recent appointment, her physician explained that new advances in gene research would shortly yield some new medicines and techniques that would eliminate the potential problem once and for all.

As Carl sat down to eat his breakfast, he began to check his pocket PC for the day's schedule. He and Jill then went through their daily calendar coordination routine. (To do so, Jill used the remote to shift the TV monitor in the adjoining family room to access her computerized appointment schedule for the day. The entire house was networked, so each person's computer was accessible from any room in the house—another wonderful convenience.) Carl would be unavailable most of the day due to a series of critical international conference calls linking him with countries in Europe, South America and China. None of the clients he'd be interacting with spoke English, but the voice recognition software through which they'd conduct their Internet phone call would provide real-time translation, facilitating a smooth conversation. Even though supersonic plane transportation was common and affordable, Carl remained a homebody.

One of his scheduled calls today would be with his boss, an Italian executive located in Milan whom Carl had never met with personally but whom he greatly respected and enjoyed working with. In fact, Carl's work team was truly a global cooperative of talent—specialists living in Osaka, Toronto,

London, Bombay and Sao Paulo. His team had never had a face-to-face meeting with everyone present, but the technology made their international operation seamless and normative. Carl found it stimulating to work with such people, although coordinating the time zones was sometimes the toughest task of the day!

After his teleconferences, Carl planned to retrieve and review the investment report prepared by his infobot, the personal electronic robot that roamed the Internet collecting data and analyzing it for him. Artificial intelligence had made major strides since the start of the new millennium, and as a computer consultant, Carl did his best to capitalize on software advances that would simplify his life. Before bed the previous evening, Carl had dictated an analysis request to the infobot. After reading the report, he expected to do some on-line trading to improve his portfolio position. Now that stock and bond transactions happened 24 hours a day, keeping up with the ever-changing value of his investments was another pressure. To minimize his risk—and his feelings of insecurity—his computer was programmed to alert him when each of his investments reached a certain level.

His final must-do would be his daily review of the new software that had been released earlier in the day. Americans had begun buckling under the stress of keeping up with the pace and breadth of life and the response had been a revolution in the software world—a focus on how to reduce stress by making life simpler. Carl needed to know of these innovations for his work, but he found himself relying upon an ever-greater number of home-based software remedies. Like most Americans, he needed help getting his life under control; and since so much of his life revolved around electronics, especially computers, he was willing to acquire whatever software solutions the world's best engineers had dreamed up just for him—and millions of others like him. The Moore's household budget included a healthy allocation just for such new products.

Jill outlined her schedule for Carl, and the couple agreed to have dinner at home around 6:30. After a brief negotiation they decided on chicken as the entrée; she promised to e-mail the order to a nearby chicken restaurant for home delivery. They then planned to watch the television programming that their video system had automatically recorded for them based on their specified tastes in TV programs.

Jill made a note that sometime tonight she had to vote, submitting her e-ballot for the primary election that would close in two days. This was an important election, since it contained more than 30 initiatives and referenda that would impact her pocketbook and lifestyle. She liked the power that such ballot measures gave her over her own life but often feared that she was insufficiently informed to make wise choices. Even so, she reasoned, it was better to participate as an ill-informed voter than to leave such decisions to politicians. Jill also noted that she must release her digital robot to pay the accumulated household bills via electronic funds transfer (EFT), print out a household finance report and calculate their bank account balances at the end of the day.

Yet, as the day began, both Carl and Jill found themselves haunted by the lack of fulfillment in their lives. They had the jobs, the money, the toys, the health, the diversions—yet, there had to be more. *There must be a better way.* Maybe starting a second family would help. Perhaps chucking it all and joining one of the growing network of communes. Maybe identifying a social cause and pouring their excess energy (if they could muster some) into furthering the cause. Despite the endless scenarios they were capable of conceiving, neither had figured out where to go from here.

Like most Americans, Jill and Carl Moore knew they had much to be thankful for. They were guardedly optimistic about the future, hopeful that the seemingly endless string of technological breakthroughs would eventually enable them to clarify and satisfy their true goals. Both wondered whether the answer was found in the popular notion that life simply has no greater meaning, that life is just a chance to live out one's dreams and fantasies without worrying about influence, grand purpose or a relationship with a divine being. They just didn't know. But they sure wanted to find out.

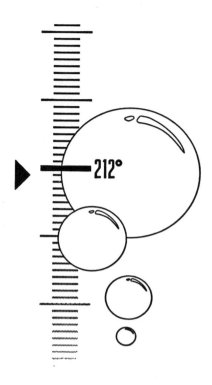

CHAPTER ONE

CHANGE IS OUR MIDDLE NAME

Count On It Being Different

You can avoid the flu, you can outrun your past, you can ignore your in-laws, you can outsmart your adversaries, and you can deny your imperfections. One thing you cannot get around, however, is change. Change will happen whether you are ready or not. Change will happen whether you like it or not. Change is inevitable. America's national motto may as well be "No change? No chance!"

Biologists provide us with a simple but powerful equation: the absence of change is death. In other words, the presence of change is a sign of life, a necessary component to being alive. You may gauge the state of a plant by ascertaining whether it is experiencing some type of transition, be it for the better or for the worse. If there is no change taking place, then the plant is dead. There is no such thing as stasis for living entities—including human beings. Intellectually, emotionally and spiritually we must either be changing or dead; there is no in-between.

Perhaps the most central of all vital signs, change is an interesting phenomenon. Visit a church meeting, a corporate stockholders' meeting, a public political forum or a family dinner where change will be discussed. The one thing that all of the players in these varied environments will share is a distaste for change. Even when a proposed change is in our best interests, people will often fight it, simply because it means the familiar will be replaced by the unknown. Change is uncomfortable, no matter how beneficial it may be or how minimal its magnitude. Sustained progress may well be the driving force behind the American system, but the old adage "we prefer the problem we know to the solution we don't" is just as true today as ever.

So, we can predict one thing about the future: You won't always like the process of getting there. Sometimes change will be a positive experience: exciting, energizing, fun, productive, interesting or astounding. Other times you will bemoan progress because of the uncertainty and insecurities that change will introduce into your life. If past experience is any guide, millions of Americans will go kicking and screaming into the future, no matter how enticing the promises may be.

But merely enduring change is not the only challenge. Not only must we look at a future existence in which curveballs and unknowns will be the norm, but we must also keep in mind that the *pace* of that change is fast—really fast! Some say our world is changing faster than ever before. Just like driving an automobile at faster and faster speeds, negotiating change these days means your reaction time must be quicker, your skill level more extensive and your self-confidence more stable.

Add to all of this the ever-broadening horizons of change, and the experience becomes even more daunting. Nothing is a given anymore. For instance, two generations ago there were some realities that you could count on not to change:

- Men proposed marriage to women.
- Children were educated in schools.
- Men ran corporations and the government.
- The courts would uphold existing legislation rather than create new laws.
- People would respect authority figures, such as clergy, the president of the country, police officers or military officials.
- Individuals would honor their contracts.
- The mass media would honor traditional norms of decency.
- Lawsuits were a means of last recourse.
- Banks never went bankrupt.
- National heroes were upstanding citizens.
- Americans appreciated their country and respected its symbols, such as the flag and national anthem.
- Public courtesy was the norm.

Wow! Where did *that* country go? Certainly that does not describe the United States we live in today. Without passing judgment on whether the changes over the last 50 years have made America a better or worse place, we can agree that our nation is a much different place and that every dimension of our lives continues to evolve. Nothing is exempt from change these days; everything, it seems, is up for grabs, almost every day. Surveys reveal that Americans are the most stressed-out people on earth, largely due to the range and degree of instability and uncertainty we constantly juggle. There is a high probability that if you lead a normal life (whatever that is), during a single day you will have to negotiate at least one significant emotional, intellectual, moral, spiritual, financial, relational or physical change that has never previously emerged in your life.

And there's more. Not only is change inevitable, occurring at a blistering pace and invading every dimension of our lives, but also the pace of change is *accelerating* at what seems to be a geometric rate. That's right, simply reacting to the changes you encounter will probably kill you—figuratively, at least. To make sense of tomorrow, you'll need to anticipate the future and do your best to prepare for the onslaught. Gone are the days when you could effectively respond to potential cultural transformations when you got around to it, when you had the time to think it through or whenever a good response came to mind. It's beyond "you snooze, you lose." Instead, try "to win the race, set the pace." In other words, if you can see it coming, you're too late. To successfully address the future, you must create it.

The Rate of Change

Four decades ago Everett Rogers wrote a groundbreaking book, *The Diffusion of Innovation*. After extensive study of how change works, Rogers concluded that it takes an innovation roughly 30 years to fully penetrate a target audience. He provided several well-researched examples from divergent aspects of our culture to demonstrate his point. His hypothesis was supported by the research of historian Arthur Schlesinger who also discovered that political and cultural changes are like a pendulum, swinging back and forth in 30-year cycles.[1]

More recent research, however, is showing that the blizzard of technological changes that have insinuated themselves into our world in the last decade have constricted the change cycle to somewhere on the order of three to five years. Fundamental expectations and operations are dramatically challenged by such a short fuse. Millions and millions of people struggle to make sense out of life because they continue to live under the old way of thinking—"I'll get used to this and understand it over the course of time"— without realizing that we no longer have the luxury of time to ease into new innovations. By the time you get used to working with DVDs or CDs (and finished replacing your entire collection of your favorite recordings on those new media), they'll be passé: the next iteration of technology will have pushed its way onto the scene.

Success demands anticipation. Trying to change reality after it has been established is a flawed strategy; reactionary incrementalism may stir peoples' emotions but rarely brings about meaningful, positive change. Being the first to offer true vision—that is, a compelling mental portrait of a preferable future—is the appropriate means of motivating people to embrace a new or different ideal.[2]

Does the Future Matter?

A friend once said, "I care a lot about the future. After all, it's where I'll be spending the rest of my life." But those insightful words are not matched by most people's behavior. Science fiction enthusiasts aside, Americans have an enduring love of nostalgia. We romanticize the past and fear the future.

Some people snicker at the thought of studying the future and investing precious resources in preparing for it. Many of those people are Christians—people who contend that their faith instructs them to trust God alone, to believe that He will take care of them and not to worry about tomorrow because there's enough to do today. They will cite verses such as Proverbs 3:5 ("Trust in the LORD with all your heart and lean not on your own understanding.") or Matthew 6:34 ("Therefore do not worry about tomorrow, for tomorrow will worry about itself. Each day has enough trouble of its own.") as their reference points.

But those arguments provide only half of the story. It appears that God wants us to consider the future. He sent prophets to tell us what was coming, in order for us to have a reasonable chance to change in accordance with His will. He ended Scripture with an extensive description of His perspective and His future plan—appropriately named Revelation—a narrative about the significance of the future, enabling us to understand both its nature and its importance. He gave us models in Scripture of the types of people whose efforts honor Him, such as the men of Issachar upon whom King David relied for advice. They were applauded as men "who understood the times and knew what Israel should do" (1 Chron. 12:32)—a pretty definitive endorsement of being able to look ahead and empower God's people to live responsibly in light of knowledge of the present and future. And Jesus Himself emphasized the value of future thinking by scolding the Pharisees and Sadducees for being able to predict the weather but remaining oblivious to the available signs of the significant realities to come (see Matt. 16:1-3).

So, is the Bible guilty of double-talk on the issue of predicting the future? Is it wrong to study the future? Is it wrong to ignore the future?

Our conclusion is that there is merit to both arguments but that a clear perspective emerges from Scripture regarding the future. The past, present and future all matter to God: He created them, and they involve His beloved creation, so indisputably the future matters to God. Would He prefer that we enter the future without preparation? Of course not! Certainly He demands that we put our complete faith and trust and hope in Him, but He expects us to use the gifts, skills and tools He has provided for us to engage the evil one in spiritual battle. No competent general sends his troops into battle without assessing the strengths, the weaknesses and the likely plans of the enemy. Likewise, God does not expect us to enter the spiritual battle on His behalf without adequate strategic intelligence or reasonable knowledge about what's coming; He wants us to be ready for the challenges we will face.

We must be alert and assertive in representing God in the world.

In fact, if the role of the Church is to influence all dimensions of culture rather than to be shaped by the culture, then we must be alert and assertive in representing God to the best of our ability in the world. That means serving Him with excellence, but we cannot achieve excellence without appropriate preparation. Part of that preparation is the body of experience that God enables us to have, since those experiences not only test us and improve us but also sensitize us to opportunities and challenges that will emerge in the days to come.

Yes, there is a tension between the two perspectives on the future—"let God handle it" versus "intentionally prepare for it." Our advice is simple: Never study the future for its own sake or for your own sake. If you investigate the future, do so for the expressed purpose of evaluating how you might better know, love and serve God with all your heart, mind, soul and strength, given the emerging challenges and opportunities you will likely face. The purpose of predicting future possibilities is to facilitate repentance, obedience and love in response to God.

Become like the men of Issachar: Understand your ministry context in its past, present and future forms, and base your plans and strategies for serving God upon the conclusions you draw from your insights. But make

God the center of those explorations and extrapolations: Always rely on His power, His wisdom, His guidance and His principles.

Recognize that there will be many aspects of the future that God will reveal to you—and many that He will not. Get comfortable with that; if we accept His omnipotence and His grace for us, then that is how it should be. Studying the future is not about obtaining perfect knowledge of all that is to come but about making better decisions on the basis of anticipation rather than spontaneous reaction.

Studying and preparing for the future are incredible opportunities to serve God. We have the opportunity to appreciate, learn from and build on the past; to fully inhabit and optimize our experience in the present; and to envision, prepare for and direct the future, in concert with His plans and purposes. In fact, the Church is truly the only entity on Earth that has an incontrovertible mandate to shape the future, in alignment with His purposes and for His glory. To do anything less would amount to willful disobedience. If we are to be His agents of change, we must be equipped to do the tasks at hand. The equipping function encompasses a solid, albeit imperfect and incomplete, perception of the future and the human and cultural changes that are coming.

The Danger of Predictions

Having made the argument for the importance of studying the future and preparing for it as best we can, let us now offer some disclaimers about predicting the future. "Futuring" is an art, not a science, even though it bears elements of scientific research within it. More importantly, attempting to predict the future is fundamentally a bad idea since some percentage of the time your predictions will be wrong—and, unfortunately, you never know which predictions will stray from the mark.

There are, of course, some aspects of our changing existence that are predictable with a very high degree of accuracy, such as demographic trends. For example, a demographer can quite precisely forecast how many teenagers there will be in 2010 or how many people will have graduated from college, as well as the number of people living in the United States.

What makes the task of prediction so iffy, however, are those aspects of reality that represent true breakthroughs or complete deviations from the expected. Many of the turning points of human history were "discontinuities"—events, ideas or behaviors so unrelated to all that preceded them that even the best futurists could not have foreseen them. For example, who could have predicted the HIV virus and AIDS? Or what about foretelling John Kennedy's assassination, Watergate and the Nixon resignation, the realities of the war in Vietnam, the tragic killings at Columbine High School or even the incredible impact of the Internet? These types of realities emerge, seemingly from out of nowhere, radically altering the world. There have been enough of these types of discontinuities over the years that any sane person should be discouraged from making predictions about the future.

However, as neither of the authors has been accused of being sane, we will endeavor to provide a portrait of what America may be like a decade down the road. Granted, a 10-year forecast is longer than most people plan for these days; "long-term plan" and "today's calendar" are interchangeable expressions for most Americans. This 10-year projection is short enough to facilitate reasonable accuracy and hopefully disturbing enough to trigger deeper reflection about your preparedness to fight the good fight of faith in the ministry context given to you by God.

We make no claims to complete revelation from God nor harbor any illusions to absolute accuracy, but we do believe that these projections are reasonable and should prove to be helpful. Our prayer is that these research-based, carefully considered projections motivate you to develop a perspective on the likely future and how you, personally, need to prepare and act. You don't have to believe everything we say; but you have to believe *something* about the future, and we hope that if you have not done your homework yet, *Boiling Point* will assist you in strategically anticipating and addressing the future.

The Road Map

Sadly, we did not have any Global Positioning System (GPS),[3] a navigational system that tracks your location and can instantly provide you with directions and best routes to arrive at your desired destination, for plotting the route to the future. The least we can do, however, is explain the journey we're about to take you on as we foretell the "triple-zero decade" (i.e., the 2000 through 2010 period).

The first portion of the book will take a look at things you can most easily relate to: demographics, generations, values, lifestyles, health and business. These are elements that intimately touch our lives every day. We will describe where we've been and where we seem to be headed. The second portion of the book will examine religion and spirituality in America. We've offered one chapter on our religious beliefs, another on our religious practices and a third one on corporate faith issues and the future look of the Church. The third section goes global in perspective. Since our lives will be much more intricately intertwined with those of people all over the world, we felt it would be important to delve into facets such as the global economy, environmental considerations, political power and, of course, the incessant evolution of technology. We end the book with a brief reflection on what it all means to you, a central figure in the development of your life experience.

Keep in mind that we are not asking you to like what seems about to unfold in our lives but to understand it and deal with it. You have two options: Play the victim, someone who is bulldozed by the inexorable march of progress and change; or be an innovator, someone who helps to shape his/her reality and make the most of the possibilities that emerge. Your choice of which role to play will influence both your joy in life and your value to the kingdom of God.

Now, buckle your seat belt. You're about to encounter a wild ride through the thickets of cultural change. May you thrive in its midst, and glorify God through your responses to the challenges and opportunities about to come your way.

Notes

1. Everett Rogers, *The Diffusion of Innovation* (New York: Free Press, 1962), n.p., and Arthur Schlesinger, *The Cycles of History* (Boston, MA: Houghton-Mifflin Publishers, 1986), n.p.
2. In times of change, leadership is an essential element to making sense of the upheavals and knowing how to address the opportunities and obstacles. Vision, however, is the heart of leadership; effective leadership is impossible unless a clear

and compelling vision has been cast for the people, and they have embraced that vision as their focus. For more discussion about the role of vision in leadership, in the local church and in one's personal life, see George Barna, *The Power of Vision* (Ventura, CA: Regal Books, 1991) and George Barna, *Turning Vision into Action* (Ventura, CA: Regal Books, 1994).

3. Global Positioning System. This is a satellite system that enables one to know definitively where one is on the earth. The satellite helps a GPS receiver know where it is, using triangulation and signal time calculations.

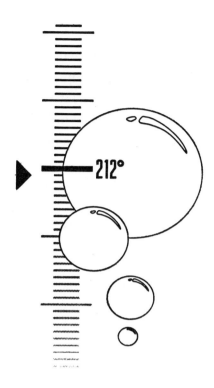

212°

CHAPTER TWO

CHANGING DEMOGRAPHICS

Future Glimpse

Although her home and the hotel where she worked were only six miles apart, sometimes it took Jill a half hour or more to get from one place to the other. *What causes traffic, anyway?* she wondered. She answered her own inquiry by reflecting on the incessant growth of the population that caused so many changes in her life. The growing number of people in America—and the ethnic and socioeconomic diversity of people—produced inconveniences, like traffic, longer lines at the checkout counter, a wider array of products to choose from, difficulty communicating in English and a declining sense of personal influence over political choices. On the other hand, population growth introduced some benefits, too: cheaper costs because goods could be mass produced and sold to a greater number of people, interesting people to meet, unusual cultures to experience, both a wider and more targeted choice of TV channels and magazines available, and much more. Like everything else, demographic change was a series of trade-offs.

As she switched lanes on the freeway to try to make up some lost time, she pondered her family life. Carl had been a solution to her need to have a male presence in the household for her son, as well as a reliable male companion and breadwinner for her. But things change, and she was feeling less drawn to him these days. Her conversation with Jackson and Brittany last evening had focused on relationships, and even though Jill felt like she didn't really connect with the kids, the conversation had been fruitful. For one thing, it reminded her how differently the various generations viewed many fundamental issues. Age meant more than years spent on Earth; it defined one's worldview, life experience, expectations, language, entertainment preferences—just about everything, it seemed. Trying to bridge the generation gap was tough.

The benefit of the talk, though, was how the rambling dialogue helped crystallize some of her uneasy feelings about her marriage. Now she realized that once Carl's children were gone, she'd probably reevaluate the relationship and decide whether or not to continue as Mrs. Moore. She just wasn't feeling as fulfilled or special as she had hoped to feel. Their communication had diminished as his job became more complex and taxing, and she wanted to have a more meaningful social life than they had developed—or were likely to develop.

But those decisions would be made in their proper time. For the moment, it was time to park the car and tackle the challenges that awaited her at the hotel, one of America's many centers of demographic heterogeneity.

The Power of Demographic Data

Four decades ago demographics were a big deal in our society. Census reports were major news items as people read about and reacted to the ways in which our population was changing. For example, if a government study predicted that the nation's black population would grow by 50 percent within the next 30 years, then people would "ooooh" and "aaaah" as if they'd just seen a fireworks display. News reports would alert people to the rising divorce rate or the fact that the average life expectancy had jumped to 64, and people would gasp at the thought. Citizens were fascinated by—and sometimes stymied or even scared by—the magnitude of growth, the pace of change and the personal implications of such transformations.

Today the rate of demographic change seems extremely tame when compared to the pace of technological changes we are witnessing. Demographic transitions may not be as dramatic as many of the other breakthroughs that are rewriting our lives—after all, which is more breathtaking, cracking the human genetic code or having more Hispanics than blacks for the first time in our history?—but demographic changes nevertheless remain a significant building block in the American experience.

Maybe you're wondering, *What are demographics, and why should I care about them?* Demographics are the statistics about the cumulative personal background characteristics of a population. The most common demographic statistics tell us the distribution of the ages, educational achievement, income, racial background, marital status and gender of the population. Knowing that the Baby Boom generation is the largest ever in the country's history—76 million people strong—is a demographic nugget. That 51 percent of all Americans are female or that the average household income today is just under $40,000 or that 12 percent of the nation's population is of Hispanic origin are examples of demographic facts.

Why should you care? Because understanding current and future demographics explains much of your daily experience. The next time you eat at your favorite Mexican or Chinese restaurant, realize that those types of food are popular because of the changing ethnic mix of the nation's population. The Internet is a cultural phenomenon in America, because we have a basic level of literacy, and that literacy depends upon educational achievement—another key demographic attribute. Crime correlates to age and income levels, which allow us to predict where crime is most likely to happen and even how much tax money we should be spending for law enforcement. If you are single and searching for a mate, demographics can tell you what parts of the country have a larger accumulation of eligible partners. The Nielsen ratings provide TV networks and their advertisers the demographic profiles of each program's viewers, helping advertisers decide if their marketing message is reaching the intended audience or not.

The personal applications of demographics are endless, powerful and largely unconscious. We integrate demographics into our thinking all the time, usually without even realizing it. We avoid looking for houses in one section of town, because people of a different social class live there. We avoid a specific church, because the congregation is comprised of people who are generally younger than those with whom we prefer to associate. If we want to reach well-educated, upper-income individuals with advertising, we might buy ad space in a magazine like the *Harvard Business Review* or *Fortune*. When you see someone driving a new-model Cadillac, you assume they have money—and respond accordingly. If you're 50 or older, you may qualify for discounts based on your senior citizen status—and thus alter your choice of products, services or activities. If you are a Hispanic immigrant, you may well choose to settle in an area of the nation that boasts a substantial population of people who are from your native culture and who speak your primary language.

> **Demographics have been integrated into our thinking.**

Demographic change is one of the more predictable forms of change we may study. The federal government spends literally billions of dollars each decade studying the changing nature of our population and providing increasingly accurate estimations of what the future will bring. The best known—and most expensive—research study in the world is our country's decennial census. The 2000 census cost taxpayers an estimated $5 billion. It will be the basis of major political decisions and the subject of endless debate and conjecture. In fact, there is an entire industry built around those numbers: companies that repackage and reanalyze the figures, organizations that help corporations convert the numbers into business models and new products, and many other value-added entities that live or die by government-derived statistical studies.

Understanding where the demographic profile of the country is going to change can help you get a grip on what the nation will be like and how to better prepare for the future. Let's take a look at some of the key demographic changes and at what the U.S. profile will be like in 2010.

Population Count

Back in 1900, the U.S. population was 76 million. During the twentieth century, the nation's population more than tripled, hitting 276 million in 2000. The growth shows signs of slowing but no sign of stopping. By the start of the next century, demographers are projecting that our population will again double, coming close to 600 million![1]

Unless there are medical advances we cannot foresee today, you probably won't be alive to verify that projection. But you probably will be here to discover that America will be home to an estimated 300 million people in 2010. That means an increase of 24 million people during this decade, which is the equivalent of adding the entire populations of New Jersey and New York to the national count. The Census Bureau expects the country to grow by about 9 percent during this decade.[2]

Starting in 2000, the number of live births is projected to begin a long-term increase. The total population will grow large enough by the end of this decade that starting in 2011, the number of live births each year thereafter will break the existing record for annual births.[3]

America's population growth does not occur uniformly across our geography. Although each region of the country will have a net increase in population by 2010, two regions—the Northeast and the Midwest—will grow less rapidly than the South and West. Roughly 80 percent of the nation's population growth will happen in the South and West. In fact, for the next quarter century you can expect the West to grow at double the national average, while the Northeast and Midwest will grow at half the rate of the U.S. (Those of you who did well in algebra may realize this means that the West will grow at four times the rate of the Northeast and Midwest between now and 2025.)[4]

One consequence is that the Northeast and Midwest will represent an ever-smaller share of the aggregate U.S. population. Another outcome is that the South will remain the most highly populated region (more than one-third of all Americans live in the southern states), and the West will pass the Midwest in size to become the second most populated region. (The Northeast will remain the smallest of the four regions.)

Certain states will lead the expansion. California, New Mexico, Arizona, Nevada, Idaho, Utah, Florida and Texas are likely to experience the greatest increases in people. The recent trend has also shown that people are moving back into cities after several decades of flight to the suburbs.

Population growth patterns differ by subgroups, too. For instance, most blacks live in the South—and two-thirds of the growth among blacks during this decade will take place in the South. Adults 65 and older are still relocating en masse to the western region, but their states of choice have shifted to Utah, North Dakota, Montana, Idaho and Arizona.

Any discussion of population growth must also include mention of immigration. During the 1990s the U.S. legally added more than 10 million internationals to the population rolls. During the present decade, as the increases attributable to the Immigration Reform and Control Act of 1986 phase out—that was a special, one-time allowance for illegal immigrants living in the U.S. to become legal citizens and then to sponsor their family members as legal entries—the immigration numbers will likely drop. However, the impact of immigration will continue to be felt for several generations. Indeed, while international migration may decline, it will continue to add several hundred thousand newcomers to the U.S. each year—and those people tend to be younger and to have larger families than the U.S. norm, thereby influencing the ethnic mix of the nation.

As the population grows you will feel more and more closed in, unless you live in states such as Alaska, Montana, Wyoming and a handful of other states with low population density. By 2010, our population density will be 85 people per square mile, a 32 percent increase from 1980. But in actuality, we live in much more densely packed areas: More than 70 percent of the population lives on just 5 percent of the country's landmass, underscoring our metropolitan nature. Ample evidence of this is found in the sprawling metropolis known as the Northeast. There are many more people packed into the Northeast than anywhere else in the U.S.—with more than 320 people per square mile, that region has nearly 10 times as many people per square mile as the West! But density varies dramatically, from our densest state (New Jersey, with more than 1,100 folks per square mile) to our sparsest (Alaska at one person per square mile and Wyoming at five per square mile). Virtually every state will experience an increase in density in the coming decade, but the effects will differ.[5]

You might be interested to learn that even as big as our population is, we are just a drop in the global bucket. The world's population at the start of the new century was about 6.1 billion. That makes the U.S. population—the third largest in the world—less than 5 percent of the total! Clearly, our influence in world affairs far exceeds that due a nation of our relative population weight. Keep in mind that the world's population is growing much faster than ours. Since 1980, the U.S. population grew by 21 percent while the world population expanded by 37 percent—almost double the rate of growth we experienced![6] If this pattern is likely to continue, our share of the global population will slowly erode.

If more elbow room is your dream, escaping to another country may be your best solution—or your worst nightmare. The least densely populated nations include Russia, Kazakstan, Libya, Mongolia, Niger and Saudi Arabia. Each of those has fewer than 25 people per square mile—less than one-third our national average. On the other hand, several nations—South Korea, Netherlands, Singapore and Taiwan—have average density levels that exceed New Jersey's.[7]

Race and Ethnicity Move Center Stage

One of the most striking transitions in our population relates to the dominant source of numerical growth. No longer does America's population expansion rely upon whites having babies. The white population, while still the majority, reflects a declining share of the national citizenry: formerly comprising more than 80 percent of the nation's people, whites now con·stitute 72 percent of the population, will decline to about 68 percent by 2010 and will be barely half of the population by 2050!

During this decade the white population will be the slowest growing of the four major ethnic groups in America, the Asian population will be the fastest growing, and Hispanics will add the largest number of people to the population. The black population will grow, but not fast enough to keep up with the growth of the Hispanic group. By 2010, Hispanics will pass the size of the black population to become the second-largest ethnic group in the U.S. In 2010, one-third of the population will be nonwhite.

Ethnic growth is very regional in nature. Two-thirds of the increase in the number of both whites and blacks will occur in the South. More than half of the growth among Asians will be found in the western states—two-fifths of it in California alone! While the Hispanic expansion is more widely distributed, the bulk of that growth will be in the West, largely in California. In fact, California will add three times more Hispanic people than the state that increases by the second-highest number (Texas). The four states that will account for a majority of all Hispanic growth are California, Texas, Florida and New York.

ETHNIC DISTRIBUTION OF THE U.S. POPULATION

Ethnic Group	Number of People (In Millions)			Percent of Total Population		
	1990	2000	2010	1990	2000	2010
White (non-Hispanic)	185	197	204	76%	71%	68%
Hispanic	23	31	42	9%	11%	14%
Black	29	34	39	12%	12%	13%
Asian	7	11	15	3%	4%	5%
Other	2	2	2	*	*	*

(*indicates less than 1%)
Source: U.S. Census Bureau

By 2010 we are likely to have four states (plus the District of Columbia) that have nonwhite majorities and another four that are closing in on that status.

The Aging of America

America's population is not just getting more numerous, but it's also getting older. Just a few decades ago our median age was near 30; presently it is in the mid-30s and will continue to climb during this decade. The major reason is the growth in numbers of people 65 and older.

One out of every 8 people in our country is 65 or older, giving us the third largest population of senior citizens anywhere in the world. (Only China and India have more—and we will pass India within the next two decades even though their population is roughly four times ours.)[8] In fact, the fastest-growing segment of our population is among people 85 or older. While they are relatively limited in absolute numbers, by 2020 their numbers will double.[9] The states that will experience the fastest growth among the elderly are mostly in the West: Nevada, Arizona, Colorado, Georgia, Washington, Alaska, Utah and California. Each of these states will double its pool of seniors between 1993 and 2020.[10]

There are several reasons for this proliferation of older people, and most of those reasons relate to the advances in medicine and health care. People's health consciousness has improved (dieting, healthy eating, exercise, medical exams); immunization, disease detection and remedy have improved; there are fewer infant deaths and deaths during childbirth; there are fewer contagious diseases; and incredible medical procedures have been developed to address virtually every ailment imaginable. The outgrowth is that U.S. life expectancy has risen to 76—lower than in Australia, Canada, Hong Kong and most European nations but still substantially higher than the U.S. average of the past. Scientists predict that we will reach a life expectancy of 80 by the middle of this century.[11]

In fact, our average age in America would be even higher if it were not for the recent surge in the number of births each year combined with a declining number of abortions. The Baby Boom years (1946-1964) made history, because 4 million or more live births occurred for the first time in the country's history—and it happened for seven consecutive years (1955-1961). Then came the infamous Baby Bust, when births declined to previous levels. Since 1988, however, we have returned to Boom birth levels. Although the U.S. has a relatively small average family size, we have a large enough population that even the smaller birthrate produces about 4 million live births annually.

Once again, though, the American trend is at odds with the global trend. Most countries are undergoing a serious youth explosion. Thirty percent of the world's population is under 15, and that number is still climbing. In the U.S., only 21 percent are under 15, and even that number is dropping.[12]

Progress in the Classroom

Gone are the days when a high school diploma was a sufficient credential to make it in our economy. There will be plenty of jobs available to high school graduates in the years to come—the growth of service-based companies will ensure that—but to really get beyond a survival-oriented lifestyle will require a college degree.

Our emphasis on education, after a couple of decades of decline, continues to escalate. Consider these trends:

- In 1970, slightly more than one-third of all three- to five-year-olds were enrolled in a prekindergarten or kindergarten class. That has nearly doubled (65 percent).
- In 1975, 16 percent of students dropped out of school without graduating from high school. That figure has declined slightly to 13 percent.
- Half of all high school graduates in 1970 went on to enroll in college. Today, two-thirds of high school graduates enter college.
- Community colleges and associate degrees are more popular than ever before. The number of students completing a two-year program has almost tripled since 1970, while the number of bachelors degrees has increased by half, and advanced degrees (master's and doctorate) have doubled. One out of four adults has a college degree.[13]

While a huge majority of elementary and secondary students attend public schools, the trend is for more students to get educated through home schooling, private schools or religious schools. At the beginning of the new decade there are an estimated 47 million public school students, 5 million in private and religious schools and 1.5 million students being taught at home. Home schooling has been the fastest growing of these routes.

Charter schools represent another innovation on the horizon. These are public schools that implement innovative teaching methods designed to improve student performance. There are nearly 2,000 charter schools in the U.S. as of this writing, educating about 350,000 students—a relative drop in the bucket. The early success of these schools makes it likely that charter schools will grow in popularity and enrollment during the present decade.

Another alternative is the public school choice program. Initiated in the late 1980s, this approach is an educational reform strategy that enables parents and students to select from various schools in the area (sometimes restricted to within a school district, sometimes including schools outside the district). Within some choice programs are magnet schools, yet another variation, which are truly niche schools—offering programs for certain types of students or a particular style of education. The school choice process has been widely embraced in the West and Midwest, but has been resisted in the Northeast.

Options, options, options. Like the rest of society, parents have demanded that there be an ever-broader range of educational alternatives to choose from. These variants of the traditional schooling process are helping to handle the sheer volume of children attending school. In terms of numbers of students, expect the number of elementary and secondary students to rise slowly during the decade, peaking in 2009 before starting a gradual descent.

The dynamics of college education are changing, too. A majority of the bachelor's degrees awarded, as well as associate's and master's degrees, are given to women. Part of the reason for this is that more and more young men leave college without a degree in order to take a job and begin their career—especially those who have computer skills and are attracted to the tempting starting salaries offered by businesses needing tech workers. A growing number of people 35 and older are also enrolling in college, some to finish a degree they abandoned when young, others to gain new skills and knowledge required to successfully compete in today's marketplace. This year, almost 3 million adults 35 or older are attending college classes.[14]

College is a different experience for today's students than it was for their parents. Campuses are more racially integrated than ever: the proportion of students who are nonwhite has more than doubled since 1970. The cost of a college education has also exploded, tripling during the last three decades. The average annual cost of tuition, fees, room and board at a four-year private college is just over $25,000, and about half as much at public colleges. To handle the cost, a large majority of students depend on loans and grants (more than $40 billion worth are given each year), work part-time or full-time while enrolled (81 percent), and stretch their degree program over a longer period of time. The average college graduate now takes nearly six years to complete what used to be known as a four-year degree.[15]

Distance learning has become a common experience, too. Because of hectic schedules, the costs of classroom education and the mobility of people, colleges have been putting technology to use. Half of the nation's colleges and universities presently offer courses or even entire degree programs by non-traditional means (audio, video or on-line resources). More than a million students are taking college courses for credit via distance learning programs—that's almost 1 out every 10 active students. Even at institutions where students attend classes in a traditional setting, half of all college classes incorporate e-mail in their coursework, and more than one-fourth use websites to transmit course materials and resources. Distance learning is even becoming a regular feature in elementary and secondary schools: more than 2 million students are taking courses via distance learning programs.[16]

In fact, computer skills are increasingly necessary for students at all levels of education. Nine out of 10 public schools had Internet and e-mail access for their students in 1999. Every year, tens of thousands of computers are incorporated into schools, with millions of young people bringing their own notebook, palmtop and laptop computers to and from home each day. Several studies have pointed out that the biggest barrier to more effective use of computers in our classrooms is that teachers have too little familiarity and training with computers. Even though some amazing educational software is available, more than 6 out of 10 elementary and secondary school teachers feel inadequately prepared to know of and utilize such tools.[17]

Education still pays off in the long run. The government's most recent data shows that the median income for adults:

- without a high school diploma was $16,124;
- without a college degree, $22,895;
- with a college degree, $40,478;
- with an advanced degree, $63,229.

If you estimate that these individuals would have a 40-year career, the differences add up. The gap between a college grad and someone without a high school diploma would be roughly a million dollars; the gap between the college grad and a high school grad would be almost three-quarters of a million dollars.[18]

Poverty, Wealth and the Rest of Us

The economic boom of the late '90s enabled Americans to achieve record-breaking household income levels while reducing the number of citizens living in poverty. From a global perspective, we're rich and getting richer.

One of the great perplexities of the early triple-zero decade has been the success of the network TV show, "Who Wants to Be a Millionaire?" The point of confusion is not why people enjoyed the trivia-based show but that in this age of megawealth, the prospect of somebody gaining a mere million dollars could still attract a crowd. After all, within six months of the start of the new millennium more than a dozen major news and pop-culture magazines featured cover stories of the new superrich, a class of young adults whose technological savvy and dot com success brought them incredible fortunes virtually overnight. Bill Gates, Steve Case, Larry Ellison, Paul Allen, Steve Jobs and a phone book full of other poster boys of the new aristocracy led the wealth parade based on their mastery of the digital economy.

But the success of "Millionaire" does, indeed, underscore an important point: While a relative handful of geeky risk takers were striking it big in Silicon Valley, most Americans could only lust after such affluence. Although the U.S. experienced a strong national economy during the '90s, the majority has little to show for it. In the past three decades household income levels have risen, but when inflation is accounted for, the rise has been negligible. For instance, married-couple families showed only a 20 percent rise in income (constant dollars) since 1970, almost all of that attributable to having a wife working in addition to her husband. (In family units where the husband worked but the wife did not, there was no change in household income in 30 years!) In single-parent families with a father as household head, there was actually a small decline in income, while single-parent female-headed families experienced a marginal increase—but only to a level still within sight of the poverty line.[19]

Saving for the future is as popular as the flu. Only half of all adults save money on a regular basis for purposes other than retirement, while one-fifth admit that they never even try to save for a rainy day. In fact, less than half of all Americans have as little as $3,000 in savings.[20] At the same time, debt has skyrocketed as people bet on the future and refuse to deny themselves the good life. The big weights are mortgage-based debt held by homeowners (more than 5 trillion dollars borrowed) and credit card debt (add another 1.5 trillion). By the time you add these with the other forms of debt people carry, the total hovers in the neighborhood of 7 trillion dollars.[21] That helps to explain why more than a million people every year file for bankruptcy.

Our distorted sense of wealth and reckless spending habits leave many people disappointed or frustrated regarding their financial standing. But for many people, the issue is not simply the inability to buy more luxury goods or retire early. Poverty is an irrefutable reality in our country.[22] The good news is that the U.S. has a smaller percentage of its population living in poverty now than at any time since the 1970s (about 13 percent). This is partially associated with the dramatic decline in poverty among the elderly: fewer than 1 in 10 senior citizens live in poverty, down from almost one-third just a few decades ago.

The bad news is that the 13 percent figure can seem deceptively low. While only 1 out of every 8 people live below the government-set standard, that represents 35 million destitute Americans. That's more people than live in the entire state of California (or in Australia, Canada or Holland). While whites form the smallest percentage of those in poverty (8 percent), they constitute the largest ethnic group of impoverished citizens (16 million). The poverty rates among Hispanics (26 percent) and blacks (26 percent) are much higher, with the rate among Asians (13 percent) in between.[23]

Children, in particular, represent a tragic story. Roughly 1 out of every 5 children in this country lives in poverty. The chances of escaping poverty if the child under six years of age lives in a single-parent, female-headed household are grim: 55 percent of these children live below the poverty threshold! That's 10 times higher than the norm for children under six living in a married couple household.[24] Studies have shown that because poor children have less opportunity to grow intellectually, emotionally, spiritually and physically during their key formative years, an unusually high percentage of them will struggle economically throughout their lives.

Among the most striking research we have conducted relates to Americans' response to domestic poverty. In brief, we found that Americans are indifferent to the plight of the poor. When asked specifically about poverty, 2 out of 3 adults said it is a serious national problem, and 4 out of 5 said that helping the poor is a good investment. Seven out of 10 adults asserted that they, personally, have a moral obligation to help the poor, and the same proportion assert that our country has a responsibility to address poverty. Few (just one in seven) believe that we have made serious inroads into alleviating poverty in the recent past.[25]

Our selfishness is evident in our hard-heartedness toward those who have little.

Unfortunately, that perspective has done little to motivate people to change that reality. We asked adults to identify the top problems facing America today, and poverty didn't make the top 20. Few churches have a serious ministry to the poor. A majority of Americans excuse themselves from involvement by noting that "one person really can't do much to help." Half of all adults did nothing at all in the past year to help a poor person, and just one out of every five donated time and money toward this issue.[26] If anything demonstrates the selfishness of our society, it may be our hard-heartedness toward those who live in our midst and have so little.

Why does this matter? First, as Christians we have a responsibility to help those in need. Second, things are likely to get worse in the future as we transition to a service-based and entertainment-based economy—two economic routes that create many new jobs, but most of them paying less-than-robust wages. Third, as the global economy defines itself, America's share in the pie is likely to diminish. In other words, we need to form good habits and solutions for addressing poverty today, before the real tough times hit—and chances are good that during this decade we will encounter one or two periods of economic turbulence.

Family in the New Decade

You can build a strong case for the resilience and nationwide acceptance of marriage. More than 2 million marriages occur every year. More than 4 out of 5 married adults say they have a happy marriage, three-quarters say that if they could start over in life they would marry the same person again, and 4 out of 5 adults who have never been married say they would like to get married. Although the lifestyle choices of many high-profile celebrities have made cohabitation particularly noticeable in recent years, the incidence of cohabitation (about 4 percent of all adults) pales against the incidence of marriage—and in most cases the cohabiters are simply trying out their relationship to ensure that they are marriage compatible.[27] (Currently, people are 10 times more likely to be married than they are to be cohabiting.)

Marriage is not dead, but it is losing ground. Americans' infamous independence and individuality, combined with our revised values and the deterioration of key interpersonal skills (e.g., communication, conflict resolution) have contributed mightily to the decline in marriage among adults, from 70 percent in 1960 to just 54 percent today. Divorce has undergone the opposite experience, rising from 2 percent in 1960 to today's level of 10 percent. (That excludes the 4 percent who are presently legally separated from their spouse—the waiting zone for future divorces.) About one-fourth of adults have never been married (26 percent) and 6 percent are widowed.[28] One out of 4 adults who have ever been married has also experienced a divorce—and, amazingly, the incidence of divorce is slightly higher among born-again Christians than among others.[29]

One-third of all households contain at least one child under the age of 18 and it is those children who struggle the most in the midst of the new family formats. One out of every 3 children under the age of 18 is living with a single parent; four-fifths of those are living with their mother. These single-parent families are not always the result of divorce: 4 out of 10 are single-parent mothers who have never been married. While that trend is most pronounced in the black community (one-third of all black children live in a home in which the mother had never been married, and almost two-thirds of the black children born this year will be born to unmarried mothers), the trend is no less noteworthy among whites and Hispanics. Between 1980 and 2000, the incidence of births to unwed mothers increased about 400 percent among white women and by more than 200 percent among Hispanic women.

Where Are We Headed?

Demographic trends are powerful indicators of some of the challenges lying in wait. Depending upon how we respond, these changes will either be great opportunities or terrifying obstacles.

As the decade progresses, you will marvel at all the new construction that will house millions of new people and tens of thousands of new businesses. And you'll also start to feel as if you're losing your personal space and that the natural environment is being unnecessarily decimated. You'll be right; the question is what you will do about it.

Here are some transitions you ought to prepare for:

- Rapid ethnic growth represents more than just more bodies—it reflects huge cultural changes to be appreciated and absorbed. Expect continued confrontations over language, customs, religious choice, educational focus, crime control and lifestyles.
- Blacks and Hispanics are likely to experience very public and hostile friction this decade. Violence and minor riots will probably take place as these two cultures jockey for jobs, government resources, political power, image and social position.

- Racism will grow more intense this decade as whites resist the gains being made by Hispanics and blacks. The catalyst for the animosity will be the heightened loss of control and familiarity within their lives. The foundation of the conflict, though, will be the inability of each group to understand what makes the other group tick.[30]
- In effect, the U.S. will start developing into ethnic colonies. Maryland and the District of Columbia will become a focal point for the black community; Texas, New Mexico, Arizona and Southern California will arise as a Hispanic colony; California will also emerge as an Asian capital. Images, leadership, and new lifestyles will emanate from these colonies to influence the ever-changing American popular culture.
- Political maneuvering will abound as the locus of power continues to shift away from the Northeast and Midwest to the South and West. The stuff will hit the fan when it comes time to budget for infrastructure maintenance and upgrades, since the two older regions will have neither the political clout nor the tax base to pay for the needed facelift.
- Current debates over gun control and school violence are only the tip of the iceberg. As the decade progresses, the crime rate will rise, attributable to the increased number of 16-to 24-year-olds (the highest crime cohort), the surge of moral anarchy (see chapter 9) and the tendency of Hispanics and blacks to use weapons to settle scores.[31] Future political leadership will therefore emerge from among those public officials on the city, state and regional levels who have shown their ability to minimize crime and violence.
- The quality of education will improve during this decade in response to the intense competition generated by school choice, vouchers, charter schools, home schooling and public outcry. Literacy levels, test scores and teacher quality will all improve, and the number of college graduates will also increase.
- Home schooling will maintain a steady but less pronounced growth curve during this decade.
- Larger sums of money will be allocated to teacher training in the area of technology, and greater and greater levels of school spend-

ing will be devoted to technology—especially for software, satellite broadcasting and other electronic resources.

- Women will assume a larger number of significant management roles as corporations discover that not only are they better educated, better communicators, superior resolvers of conflict and intuitively superior to men, but they also handle ambiguity better. In this, an age filled with contradictions, paradoxes, uncertainty and discontinuity, the profit motive will force many corporations to elevate women to key management and leadership roles. The income gap between men and women will further close—but probably will not reach parity.

- Economic bifurcation—the division of the population into two economic classes, with an ever-widening gap between them—will intensify. On the one hand, millions of the nouveau riche and the pretentiously rich will buy second homes, exotic cars and take expensive overseas vacations. On the other hand, poverty will increase, causing multigenerational families to increase, straining the revenues and volunteer efforts of nonprofit organizations and challenging churches to demonstrate love in action.

- Household financial turbulence will reign, a consequence of the core values we have embraced that preclude us from saving money, reducing credit card use, budgeting or sacrificing personal comforts in order to serve others or live responsibly. The resulting chaos will undermine millions of marriages, facilitate continued havoc in the job market and accelerate the numbers of business and personal bankruptcies.

- Families will become more diversified. Traditional marriages will continue, but a growing percentage of those unions will be second, third and fourth marriages. The number of gay marriages will more than double during the decade. Divorce will be common and cohabitation expected. Births outside of marriage will reach record levels.

- Aging will become an inescapable topic of heated political contention. Elder care, euthanasia, access to affordable health insurance and medical cost containment, in particular, will be major issues.

Obviously, it's anything but business as usual on the demographic front. The confluence of these transitions means that the social, relational and economic fabric of the nation is being completely rewoven. There are many more land mines strewn along the cultural pathway today than our predecessors ever had to encounter. Taken in context with the myriad of other transformations occurring, each of us is challenged to rethink what it means to be a Christian in twenty-first-century America.

What Can You Do?

Remember your first love: Jesus Christ. Why? Because in His words we find the keys to handling the challenges, the stresses and the opportunities that are about to befall us. Here are some specific challenges that might prepare you for the turbulence ahead.

- Plan to initiate relationships with the new neighbors you are bound to have in the coming years. As we remain a mobile society, with one out of six households moving each year, view those new tenants as your mission field. Engage them in conversation about meaning, purpose and faith; invite them to share your church experience; offer to pray for them when difficulties arise.
- In the ethnic and racial cauldron in which we find ourselves, strive to be a champion of peace and love by studying the other cultures living in your midst and understanding what makes them tick. By doing so, you will be able to appreciate people from different backgrounds, rather than having to compete with them for supremacy and resources.
- Pray, pray and pray some more. Pray for racial harmony. Pray for marital fidelity in our nation and for stable, loving, nurturing families. Pray for financial wisdom for adults. Pray for the teachers who will shape our children's minds and hearts. Pray for intergenerational understanding and cooperation. Pray, pray and pray some more.

- Study your circle of close friends and associates and see how many of them are of different racial or ethnic backgrounds. If there aren't any, figure out why.
- Consider how you will physically protect your family in the face of a more violent society. Don't permit yourself to harbor any knee-jerk reactions regarding solutions such as guns or fleeing to the safety of suburban or rural locations. Test your thinking against Scripture and be sure your decisions represent reasoning you would be comfortable defending to God.
- Specify the outcomes you want from your children's education experiences. Then consider how adequately involved and invested you are in their entire education—academic, moral, spiritual, emotional and physical. How do you measure the value and acceptability of what they experience in school and at church?
- Save money. Budget. Set financial goals and work tirelessly toward satisfying them. Don't sell out to money, but don't ruin your witness to the world and your family by mismanaging or ignoring your finances. If you need help planning your financial world, get professional advice.
- Work on strengthening your marriage, no matter how good it is. Keys to a strong and healthy marriage include constant communication, regular and enjoyable sex, engaging in prayer and spiritual growth together, addressing points of conflict when they arise, working in tandem on the training of your children and sharing experiences of mutual interest. Satan loves to destroy families; don't help him by neglecting your marriage.
- Prepare today for the possibility of health problems with relatives for whom you might become responsible. Make sure they have current and valid wills or estate plans in place. Work out a care plan that everyone agrees on. Don't wait until the crisis hits.
- Have a Bible-centered perspective on success and fulfillment. You'll be surrounded by tales of fast money, sexual promiscuity and legislated immorality. Know what you believe, why you believe and what difference those beliefs will make each day as you encounter new challenges to your perspectives and lifestyle.

• Get ready to endure faster change and widespread discontinuity. To handle it, develop moral and spiritual foundations that will serve as your source of stability, continuity and sanity. The better you handle discontinuity, the more chances you will have to influence the many people you know who are clueless as to how to deal with discontinuity and instability. The chaos we create on Earth can be used by God to bring truth into people's lives.

In the midst of incredible change, the natural tendency is to go with the flow and make the best of your conditions. Jesus, however, showed us an entirely different way. His approach was to understand those conditions, remain fixated on Kingdom principles and live in such a way as to bring glory to God—even if it meant fighting the flow of the culture. We are called to live in the world but not to become seduced and influenced by it. You have the power of God to influence that world if you are willing.

Notes

1. U.S. Department of Commerce, Bureau of the Census, "Methodology and Assumptions for the Population Projections of the U.S.: 1999-2100," *Population Division Working Paper #38*, Frederick Hollmann, Tammany Mulder and Jeffrey Kallan (Washington, DC, January 13, 2000).

2. Ibid.

3. U.S. Department of Commerce, Bureau of the Census, *Population Projections for States by Age, Sex, Race, and Hispanic Origin*, Bureau of the Census (Washington, DC, February 1996), P25-110.

4. U.S. Department of Commerce, Bureau of the Census, Population Division, *Population Projections for States by Age, Sex, Race, and Hispanic Origin: 1995-2025*, Paul Campbell (Washington, DC, October 1996), PPL-47.

5. U.S. Department of Commerce, Bureau of the Census, *Statistical Abstract of the U.S.: 2000*, Bureau of the Census (Washington, DC, 2000), table 27.

6. Ibid., tables 1331, 1334.

7. Ibid., table 1334.

8. U.S. Department of Commerce, Bureau of the Census, "Census Bureau Predicts 65+ Population to Double in Eight States by 2020," Census Bureau news release (Washington, DC, May 20, 1996).

9. Ibid.

10. Ibid.

11. Ibid.

12. *Statistical Abstract of the U.S.: 2000*, table 1336.

13. Ibid., tables 301-334; U.S. Department of Commerce, Bureau of the Census, *Educational Attainment in the U.S.: March 1998 (Update)*, Jennifer Day and Andrea Curry (Atlanta, GA, n.d.), PPL-99.

14. Ibid.

15. *Statistical Abstract of the U.S.: 2000*, tables 307-334; *Money Matters*, American Council on Education (Washington, DC, 1999).

16. Data taken from statistics on the *National Center for Education* website. http://www.nces.gov (accessed August 2000).

17. Research by Market Retrieval Data, report in *Research Alert Yearbook 2000* (New York: EPM Communications, 2000), p. 66; statistics on the *National Center for Education* website. http://www.nces.gov (accessed August 2000).

18. U.S. Department of Commerce, Bureau of the Census, *Higher Education Means More Money, Census Bureau Says*, Jennifer Day (Washington, DC, December 10, 1998).

19. *Statistical Abstract of the U.S.: 2000*, table 824.

20. *Saving Money* (Minneapolis, MN: Lutheran Brotherhood, 1999).

21. *Statistical Abstract of the U.S.: 2000*, tables 820, 824.

22. In this section we are addressing only economic poverty, as measured by income. The federal government classification on poverty is for a family of four to make less than roughly $17,000 per year or about $13,000 for a family of three.

23. U.S. Department of Commerce, Bureau of the Census, *Household Income at Record High; Poverty Declines in 1998, Census Bureau Reports*, Bureau of the Census (Washington, DC, September 30, 1999).

24. Ibid.

25. These statistics are from a national survey we conducted for World Vision, a Christian ministry located in Seattle that addresses poverty throughout the world. The survey involved interviews with 1,002 adults, conducted in July 1999.

26. Ibid.

27. The sadness, apart from moral considerations, is that statistical evidence shows that people who cohabit prior to marriage have an 81 percent greater likelihood of getting divorced than those individuals who do not cohabit. In this sense, then, cohabitation does not so much protect cohabiters from divorce as facilitates it.

28. U.S. Department of Commerce, Bureau of the Census, *Marital Status and Living Arrangements: March 1998 Update*, Terry Lugaila (Washington, DC, October 29, 1998); U.S. Department of Commerce, Bureau of the Census, *Household and Family Characteristics: March 1998 Update*, Lynne Casper and Ken Bryson Washington, DC, 1998); *Statistical Abstract of the U.S.: 2000*, tables 62-87, 1419.

29. The statistic has been quite consistent since the mid-'90s. Based on nationwide surveys among adults 18 and over, the percentages of people who have been married and have experienced at least one divorce are 27 percent among born-again Christians and 24 percent among non-Christians, for a national average of 25 percent. For more information on this, see George Barna, "Christians Are More Likely to Experience Divorce Than Are Non-Christians," *Barna Research Group*. http://www.barna.org (accessed August 2000).

30. The differences among the races are much more significant than many people believe. To understand some of the gap between whites and blacks, see George Barna, *African-Americans and Their Faith* (Ventura, CA: Barna Research Group, 1999).

A forthcoming book by George Barna on understanding the differences among the races will provide a broader examination of the distinctions among the four major racial groups.

31. The firearm-related death rate for black males in the 15-24 age group is five times that among white males of similar age. Likewise, the homicide rate for Hispanic males 15-24 is almost seven times the rate among their white peers. These, and similar statistics, come from the most recent *Health Status Highlights* report from the Department of Health and Human Services.

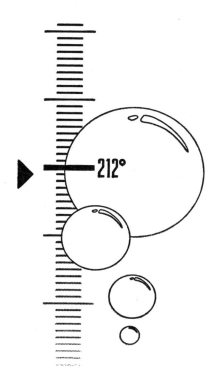

CHAPTER THREE

FIVE GENERATIONS, FOUR DISPARATE NATIONS

Future Glimpse

Jill had no idea how long she had been sitting at her desk at work, staring at the form she had been assigned to complete to report the details of a guest relations problem. Her boss wanted her to just write down the facts, plain and simple, so that they could get to the bottom of the issue, figure out who was to blame and take the appropriate action. But her interviews with the young front desk clerks had proven to be anything but plain and simple.

All they could focus on were their feelings and how they felt that they should have a chance to deliver their side of the story verbally rather than have it recorded on paper by an interloper. In their minds, there was no right or wrong response in the situation, and they certainly had no intention of being reprimanded by a bunch of stuffed shirts with fancy corporate titles. "If they don't like the way we handle their guests, let them come and do it," was their response.

Recently Jill had become acutely aware of how the young, the middle-aged and the old seemed to live in different worlds. Her bosses, mostly older men, wanted memos—follow the company format, submit documentation in a timely and orderly fashion. Her staff, all younger adults, wanted meetings so that they could express themselves fully and help her figure out what the appropriate steps should be. Her direct boss was interested in efficiency and productivity so that he could climb the corporate ladder. Her younger charges had no plans of sticking it out at the hotel—or even in the hospitality industry—for any prolonged length of time. They were more interested in making their workplace a comfortable environment and being treated like team members, not rule-bound slaves. Jill always felt caught in the middle.

It was the same at home. Jill would field a call from her parents and, despite promising herself that she'd behave, no matter how provoking her mother was, the end result was inevitably an argument over Jill's lifestyle, her parenting philosophy, her indecipherable religious views, you name it. When she would ask the kids to do something, even the simplest request inevitably precipitated an argument. Young people seemed incapable of accepting a simple, reasonable request without a discussion. Even the decision-making styles differed so overtly. Jill wanted the facts, so she could logically think through the options and optimize her choices. Jackson, Allie and Brittany put things together in a whole different manner—in ways Jill could barely comprehend.

Sometimes these tensions drove her absolutely crazy. So much of it seemed to be age-based—maybe it was the old "generation gap" coming back to haunt her. Right now she just wanted to bury her head in her hands and cry. *We all live in the same world, experience the same reality*, she thought. *Why can't we just agree on a few simple concepts and approaches and get on with life?*

She looked at the black and white form resting calmly on her desk while she churned inside. Suddenly she snatched the paper, crinkled it into a ball and tossed it into the wastebasket next to her desk. *If corporate wants to resolve the issue, let them come and do it,* she thought. *There are better things to do in life than try to bridge the gap between the old guard and the anarchists.* She wasn't paid to fight *that* battle.

Each Generation Is Unique

In the 1960s, Playtex was the nation's leading manufacturer of intimate wear for women. Toward the end of the decade, sales of one of their core products—girdles—were falling to unhealthy levels. Their fundamentals were in good shape: The product was well-made, the price represented a good value for the money, the promotional approach featured a well-crafted message going to an appropriate target market, and the distribution channels were numerous and well-trafficked by shoppers. Everything about the product and the process that had enabled Playtex to become the industry leader seemed to be in place. The experts were stymied.

After researching the problem more carefully and creatively, Playtex discovered the problem: There was a new generation of women who were not willing to wear uncomfortable, confining clothing that made them look and feel old-fashioned. The Baby Boom generation was changing the course of our culture by altering the fundamental assumptions of behavior, based on a wholesale shift in attitudes, values and beliefs. Marketers slowly awoke to the reality that the past is the best predictor of the future—until a new generation comes of age. At that point all bets are off and the process of discovering what drives the new group takes center stage. Playtex rebounded by developing new styles of intimate wear for the "liberated woman" of the new era.

Fifteen years later a similar episode occurred. Music companies had traditionally sold records by getting their music broadcast on key radio stations across the country. When a new record that had sales potential was released, the music companies made sure that the recording artist was on the road, doing concerts to promote the new product and to generate word-of-mouth support. If people liked the music, they'd run to record stores to purchase the tunes they liked and the industry would tally the sales and identify the bestsellers. The reporting of what was hot, communicated through Top 40 lists to consumers, and heavy rotation lists for radio stations, would then trigger the cycle of success begetting success. For more than 50 years, even before the emergence of rock and roll, that formula had worked.

But suddenly, in the mid-'80s, the sales formula changed and caught many artists and record companies napping. The culture had become much more visually stimulated, driven by the rapid household adoption of VCRs and cable television. Giving the public access to both a greater quantity of video-driven messages and greater personalization of those messages changed the way people began experiencing and thinking about reality. For young people, whose choices of preferred music drove the success or failure of the record industry for more than half a century, radio was no longer the pivotal medium of exposure. In an age of computer-generated graphics, new video editing techniques and an abundance of niche-oriented television channels delivered via cable systems, the low-fidelity sound and visually unstimulating presentation of radio simply was no longer compelling. Seemingly overnight, music sales were dependent on having a music video in heavy rotation on the new marketing vehicle of choice: MTV.

Watching a band or two lip-synch their current hit song on "American Bandstand," on a prime-time variety show or on a daytime talk show would no longer cut it. The culture had shifted, especially for young people, and the music industry needed to catch up. Finally, it did. When MTV launched in the early '80s it filled the gap caused by the erosion of radio audiences, the death of disco music and the need of the Buster generation for something unique to define itself. The music video channel, which was fresh, hip and provocative, was just the thing. Songs that weren't even getting radio airplay were suddenly moving up the sales charts. Bands that had never headlined concerts were now hot acts on the road, having built a knowledgeable following before ever having played live in a given town. The identity-starved Buster generation had found a vehicle it could call its own—and, in the process, that generation changed the nation's culture in irrevocable ways. And record executives had to retool their artist development and marketing plans to accommodate a new world.

The Power of Generations

These stories show the power of generations: population segments that share common formative experiences that result in habits, values and life skills that are unique to that group of people but influence the entire nation. In recent years it has been common to market products and services on the basis of generational idiosyncrasies. Baby Busters drove the emergence of the hypercasual clothing industry, the alternative music scene, cause-related marketing, and life lived through technology. Baby Boomers have fueled fast food restaurants, designer coffee and clothing, the rush to buy SUVs and luxury cars and 401K retirement plans. Builders are buying second homes and taking expensive and exotic vacations in record numbers.

A generation has traditionally been thought of as a time period—perhaps 30 years or so—between which the birth of a parent and the birth of his/her children typically occurs. Culturally speaking, a generation is a two- to three-decade slice of time marked by some defining event or characteristics. Practically speaking, the very concept of generations, just like everything else in our world these days, is being compressed. Consequently, the Baby Boom generation is widely accepted to be the post-WW2 explosion of babies that lasted for 19 years (1946 through 1964); the Baby Bust is comprised of the individuals born during the comparatively lean birthing years of 1965 through 1984; and the Mosaics, who will be born through the middle of this decade (1985 through 2004), are their successors.

The significance of generations is that they tend to think and act in unison on many matters. Just as the Boomers radically reshaped our culture—the Playtex example is one minor instance out of dozens of changes they introduced to our society—so does each generation have a character and lifestyle of its own. By understanding what has shaped each generation, you can better anticipate the future, understand the present and appreciate the influence of the past.[1]

You undoubtedly know that part of the significance (and power) of the Boomers is that they have been the largest generation in America's history. Something to keep your eye on is the impact that the Mosaics will have since they are likely to surpass the number of Boomers and become both the most wired and most prolific generation ever. An anomaly in the statistics of the generations, by the way, is that there are sometimes more people in the generational cohort than were actually born during the birthing years of that cohort (e.g., 69 million Busters were born from 1965 to 1984, but there are 75 million Busters today.) That condition exists because the number of immigrants who entered the country and fit within that cohort more than compensates for the number of people from that generation who have passed away.

THE SIZE OF OUR FIVE GENERATIONS[2]

Generation	Birth Cohort	Number Born	Number Alive in 2000
Mosaics	1985-2004	59 Million	58 Million
Baby Bust	1965-1984	69 Million	75 Million
Baby Boom	1946-1964	76 Million	79 Million
Builders	1927-1945	52 Million	42 Million
Seniors	-1926		21 Million

Life Stages Have Impact

Generational influence should be differentiated from life stages. A life stage is a period that we all go through, usually during a certain age range or family cycle, that dictates how we think or act. For instance, parenting is a life stage, usually occurring in the 21 to 54 age bracket, that causes us to buy different products (e.g., diapers, children's clothing, toys), associate with different organizations (e.g., schools, churches) and focus on different ideas and issues (e.g., child safety, quality of schools). Comprehending these life stage influences is also very critical to addressing life in a timely and intelligent fashion but should not be confused with generational impetus. There are numerous life stages, such as adolescence, the teenage years, single and searching, newly married, young parent, midlife, empty nesting, retirement, post-divorce, widowed and so forth. Consider the following life stages based on age.

People in their 20s tend to be single or newly married, may just be entering parenthood, are typically shifting from formal education into a career, have a changing network of friends, are strutting their sexuality and independence, and relate to their age group as their dominant reference group.

In their 30s people often are married and have young children and adolescents; are settling into a career path; make friends in relation to their job and family; are focused on career achievement, family nurture and security; and seek societal acceptance and recognition. Returning to the church for the sake of the children is a common thread during this stage.

Once people reach their 40s things get much more complicated. The children are getting older (and more complex), marriage often dissolves (or becomes more complex), and the career either becomes a source of renewed energy or fosters a transition due to feeling plateaued. Boredom and maintenance become preoccupations, adventure and meaning assume great importance, and well-established relational networks are a source of stability.

Adults in their 50s are usually faced with the kids leaving the home; prestige and responsibility in the workplace; and more time to devote to hobbies, relationships and special interests. The life focus starts to transition to retirement and handling economic well-being. People become more politically attuned and self-confident.

In their 60s and beyond, adults tend to focus on being grandparents and are often widowed. These people are winding down their careers and reducing their work schedules, and peer group activities become more important. Health issues are more relevant, as are religious beliefs. Establishing economic security, personal independence and life fulfillment rise to the top of the list as concerns.

As you can see, understanding life stages can help us predict a lot of attitudinal and behavioral transitions that will affect society. But within each life stage, the individual's choices are substantially influenced by his/her generational cues. Will the new parent, in his/her mid-20s, choose to get involved in a religious community to help shape his/her parenting style and his/her child's values? How will the unhappily married guy in his early 40s handle the possibility of a divorce? How will the 70-year-old widow craft her estate plan to distribute her wealth after she dies? The events, icons, experiences and tools of one's generation impact these decisions.

Generational Distinctions

In the '60s the term "generation gap" was coined to explain the culture-shaping divisions between older and younger people. While national awareness of

the generation gap has receded, that gap has remained firm and significant. Our research over the years has identified a number of unique perspectives and behaviors that differentiate these generations. These attributes and ways of life will continue to shape how each group handles the future—and therefore, how the force of their choices will impact your life.

The generation gap has remained firm and significant.

Let's explore how three adult generations handle a variety of life components. (In this overview we will combine the Builder and Seniors generations since they have so much in common. To simplify the identification process, we will refer to this combined group as the Elders.)

Attitudes, Values and Perceptions

So much of our existence is driven by the ways we define success. Elders generally think of economic security and strong family relationships and experiences as the outcomes that constitute success. Boomers changed the nation with their focus on emotional and psychological happiness and the acquisition of wealth as the marks of success. Busters reacted to that definition by embracing social influence and clear meaning in life as their indicators of success. Each succeeding generation has reacted in a negative way to the success view of their parents' generation. The result has been considerable tension over lifestyles, values and the focus of our energy.

A related issue is the primary needs of each generation. The driving force for Elders has been continuity. They worked hard to construct a stable, powerful and world-respected country; the strength of the nation and its institutions is a legacy of which they are proud. Boomers have chosen to take that a step farther and to personalize what their parents did. While Elders were nationalistic, Boomers have been very individualistic. Their defining felt need has been for dominance. Whether that is the result of upbringing, the massive numbers of their generation or a natural extension of what their parents pursued, Boomers have consistently committed themselves to owning, leading, mastering and dictating everything they touch. The response of Busters has been predictable and significant. Their major felt need is for respect. They believe that few people care what they think or feel, listen to what they say or appreciate their contributions to society.

Not surprisingly, the major fears of these groups are a reflection of their driving needs. Elders fear futility; they pray that their earnest efforts at building family unity, social infrastructure and national pride will not be forgotten, devalued or dismantled by those who follow them. Boomers fear powerlessness. The corporate ego of the generation causes most Boomers to believe that what they have to offer is the most significant and appropriate input possible. The notion of not being in charge or not having control terrifies most people in their late 30s and 40s. Busters fear abandonment. While their parents were off building their empires, Busters grew up feeling that nobody cared for them or invested in them. The fear of continued abandonment colors many of the perceptions and responses of this group even as it matures into midlife.

A related consideration is the primary life concern of the group. Elders worry about the fragmentation of our society and how that absence of unity and cohesion is undermining the character qualities that Elders worked so hard to create. They sense that people are losing direction and purpose as a society due to the extreme emphasis on self. Boomers are a perfect reflection of that concern. The "me generation" is concerned about its own comfort and power—two attributes that Boomers feel they can never get enough of. Meanwhile, Busters have struck a balance between the concerns of the two preceding generations, raising up quality of life issues as their worry. The quality elements that most trouble Busters have to do with the viability of relationships, having a meaningful purpose in life, living in comfort and protecting the natural environment.

How the generations weigh and address these issues is also quite unique. For instance, Elders immediately consider the underlying purpose of something. As bottom-line individuals, Boomers are more interested in the product or outcome than the purity of something's purpose. Busters have shown a great disinterest in the product, preferring to focus on the process of getting wherever that they wind up. Their process orientation is a reflection of their desire to receive respect. They believe that if you treat them with care, concern and integrity, the most important outcome has already been achieved.

One consequence of these perspectives relates to how the generations think about and respond to change. Elders, being interested in continuity and purpose, are the least excited about change. This antipathy goes well beyond the life stage resistance to the unknown and the unfamiliar. Boomers, given their inclination to rule the world, accept change as a tool to facilitate the reality they desire. Change does not come easily to Boomers, but they are open to transformation if it promotes their ultimate goals. Busters drive both of the older generations crazy with their penchant for change. Having grown up in a culture that experienced increasingly rapid and fundamental transitions, Busters know little else besides change. The absence of constant change often causes them discomfort: There is a lack of excitement, a fear about stagnation and a questioning of leadership competence if noticeable changes are not part of the regular regimen. To Elders, change is scary; to Boomers, a necessary building block; to Busters, the essence of life and a sign of health.

These views raise an interesting response to contradictions in one's own thinking or reactions. Increasingly, life is a daily confrontation with contradictions and paradoxes. We suffer from overstimulation but willingly increase our media intake. We seek spiritual wholeness but demote deity to human status. We elevate the importance of our image but let ourselves become overweight. We extol the virtue of tolerance of different viewpoints but demonstrate heightened intolerance of conservative Christianity. Mothers want to spend time with their children, but they believe they have to work to maintain a particular lifestyle. Brand awareness is up, yet brand loyalty is down. More messages are sent, but fewer are received.

Elders deal with the contradictions by pretending they don't exist. Their creed is "If I ignore it, it will go away." Boomers, ever the controllers and power brokers, feel as if they have to solve every contradiction. Logical thinkers to the hilt, they see every contradiction as a problem awaiting their attention. Busters are generally oblivious to contradictions and paradoxes; when they are aware of their existence, their typical reaction is to exclaim "cool." What a linear thinker (such as most Boomers and Elders) interprets as a paradox may simply seem like a creative combination to a mosaic-style thinker (such as most Busters).

Behaviors and Lifestyles

Given the distinctive ideas and assumptions held by these groups, it's not surprising to see that they have unique activity patterns as well. Take, for instance, their routes to successful living. To Elders, the path is filled with hard work, commitment and diligence. "Nothing good comes easy," is the hallmark of this group. Boomers believe that getting a solid education and developing clever strategy is what drives success. "If you can imagine it, you can do it." To Busters, success is about relationships. Dialogue, give and take, and networking are what make a person a success: "It's not what you do or who you know but what you do with who you know that counts."

Technology, the inescapable fascination of the '90s and beyond, has elicited divergent responses from these generations. Elders tend to view electronic technologies—VCRs, computers, CDs, cell phones, pay-per-view, GPS, the Internet—as a nuisance. Their greatest dream is to die before having to learn how to operate all this stuff. Boomers don't particularly understand how the technology works, but they sure comprehend the value of these innovations toward achieving world domination. Deep down inside, they don't especially like electronic technology, but because they recognize its power as a means toward their ends, Boomers are dedicated to controlling ownership of it. To Busters, technology is their trump card in a deck stacked against them. They created the technological revolution, and they plan to ride it for all it's worth (and for some young technology entrepreneurs, it has proven to be worth a lot). They see technology, not simply as a way to riches, but more as a means to achieving a better quality of life.

Employment issues are also handled differently. Elders were of the one-company-for-life mentality. Because their values included loyalty and long-term outcome development, they were willing to stay with an organization that exploited them if there was a sense of incremental progress and personal meaning derived from the work. For Elders, career was a means to an end: security for their family. They demonstrated a world-class work ethic because it was their responsibility to their employer and to their country. That ethic reflected their character. Boomers didn't buy into any of that. Loyalty went out the window the first time that a better offer came down the pike. A job is central to the self-image and public image of Boomers. Nothing is more embarrassing or more frightening than being unemployed. Boomers define their success by their job title, the size and location of their office, their access to the throne of corporate power, the size of their paycheck and the magnitude of their perks. Busters laugh at that approach. To them, there is no such thing as a career. Life is a series of jobs strung together to subsist. Their self-image emanates from their relationships and influence; a job is something to endure more than a banner to wave. Each new job provides a new relational network to tap and new experiences to try out.

Views on family further display the competing notions of what is right. Elders held family as a sacred union to be cherished, nurtured and appreciated. (It has only been recently that divorce has become an accepted outcome among this group—largely because their children made it so easy and so fashionable.) Boomers like the concept of family, and it has its fulfilling moments; but for many of them it is simply in the way of being able to experience all the best that is available to an independent, open-minded person. Consequently, marriage is a great institution—and Boomers are intent upon experiencing it often, or at least until they get it right. Busters, the people who suffered the consequences of Boomer self-indulgence, are more committed to entering marriage cautiously and trying to resist divorce. Cohabitation is one response to taking marriage and family seriously. (Oddly, so is the explosion in the number of women bearing children without a husband.)

Responses to authority clarify many of the issues facing our nation today. Elders accept authority figures and their declarations as necessary for the orderly operation of life. Obeying authority is the mark of a good citizen. Boomers disagree: to them, obeying authority is the mark of a brain-dead citizen. They prefer to control the levers of power and authority, calling their own shots and making sure everyone falls in line with their own ideas and plans. Busters differ again: *What authority?* they ask. They are more prone to simply ignore authority than to consent to it. As free spirits who feel abandoned by their elders, they feel no social or moral obligation to obey authority figures who represent goals and values they reject. Theirs is a type of nonviolent resistance without an underlying cause (beyond integrity to their own ideals).

One of the most important cross-generational gaps is in regard to relationships. On this component, the two older generations significantly diverge. Seniors have always viewed people as the point of life. Builders saw people as the reason for working hard and building a great country but never really invested themselves in personal relationships; theirs were always functional, productive relationships. Boomers have a utilitarian approach to people: They love people as long as they can use them to achieve their goals. They took the Builder approach to an extreme. Busters have returned to the Seniors' way of looking at people: Individuals are important and valuable by their mere existence, not on the basis of their economic potential or productive capacity. Success is intimately tied to one's friendships and the depth of those relationships. Boomers work the Rolodex to exploit people's skills and knowledge for gain. Busters work the Rolodex to maintain a heart connection that brings meaning and focus to their life.

All of this relates to whom each generation sees as its primary reference. Elders look to family as the group that contributes the greatest meaning to their life. Boomers identify with their coworkers, since their common struggle is to accomplish their goals. Friends constitute the dominant reference group of Busters, since it is on the basis of one's relational network that you do or die. In their eyes, you can get by if you lose your job or your treasured possessions; but if you lose your friends, you are already dead.

Faith and Spirituality

Faith matters to all three groups. To Elders, faith is the foundation of your life. It builds your character and provides perspective. It puts you in touch with your family, your community, your friends and God. Elders, therefore, appreciate religious institutions as vehicles for facilitating the value derived from faith. Boomers appreciate faith because it provides security. The traditions and structures may not work for Boomers, but the content of faith makes some sense; Boomers seek to absorb the "right information" and apply it to their daily battle for progress and supremacy. They'll accept religious institutions as long as they produce more benefit than cost. Busters see faith as a framework for discovering important insights and developing lasting relationships. The institutions are irrelevant to them since their personal interest is in people, not trappings. For them, faith is a macrovalue, not an entire, independent dimension of life.

The faith of choice is Christianity for Elders, albeit a version of Christianity influenced by their work ethic, their trust in the mass media and its interpretation of reality, their family pursuits and their concerns about continuity, legacy and fragmentation. Boomers have faith, but it is largely in themselves. As the self-declared masters of their world, they have taken a syncretistic approach to faith: A little of this faith system plus a little of that religious system and before you know it, you have a faith that feels good, fits good and fosters good. They call it Christianity, but most Boomers have recast the faith of Jesus, Paul and Peter almost beyond recognition. Busters have taken it a step further, elevating existentialism as their core faith system. They are less prone to playing religious games, because they resent pretension and mindless routine. They are more likely to find spiritual meaning and growth in a wide-ranging, intense discussion with friends around a candlelit table at a restaurant than they would be to experience God in a megachurch sanctuary that has all the latest technology and topical preaching.

You probably cannot make sense of the faith world of these groups until you comprehend their views on moral truth. (The next chapter will dive into this topic in greater depth.) Elders were not certain, but they had a sneaking suspicion that there probably were some absolute moral truths that God had ordained. Boomers took the mystery out of the process and determined that there are no absolutes—unless they determine them—and therefore all moral truth is relative to the individual and to his/her circumstances. This is one of the few areas on which Boomers and Busters agree. Where they diverge is on how to apply this view to a meaningful and defensible lifestyle.

Personal Development

Part of the challenge related to interacting with each generation is that they grow differently. Take the thinking styles of these groups. Elders and

Boomers are generally linear thinkers. Many Busters are mosaic, non-linear thinkers. The way we communicate, solve problems, motivate and evaluate must be different because the thinking styles of these groups vary so fundamentally. What we sometimes pass off as ADD behavior in young adults is probably just their mode of processing information: They do not possess the same basic assumptions about how information must be related and interpreted. They are not illogical but merely processing data on the basis of different rules.

The way that these groups approach learning is distinctive. Elders like to know the ultimate outcome and then build plans that they stick with in order to achieve efficiency and order. They tend to be incessantly incremental; they do not give up, and they make slow and steady progress. If you want to influence them or help them grow, they are comfortable with traditional procedures and formats.

Boomers don't want somebody else's plan; they want the facts and then they will attack the challenge with their own ideas and formulas. They grow best through presentations of possibilities and the promise of impact. They are comfortable with high-gloss, professional presentations; they have an immediate suspicion about the value of anything that does not smack of being excellent and "cutting edge."

Busters grow entirely differently. They want neither a predetermined plan nor a set of imposed facts. They want to inhabit the discovery process, so questions and dialogue are the keys for them. (Remember, outcomes are less meaningful than process to this group.) They want to know about personal experiences; stories sell ideas to them. Informal dialogue is a key to motivating them to act.

Leadership is a critical aspect to getting things done in life—and, as you probably expected, each of these groups respond to a different style of leadership. Elders want the authoritative but democratic (i.e., consensual) leader to reign. That person must speak to the issue of building continuity from the past to the present before Elders will take seriously anything proposed for the future. Boomers love a driver—as long as that person's goals and vision coincides with their own. They will follow someone who seems to know clearly where he/she is going, why he/she is going there and how he/she will take everyone else along with efficiency, unity and appreciation for individual efforts. To lead Busters, though, you have to involve them in every step of the process. Team leadership is crucial to getting buy-in from this segment. They are wary of the high-energy, smooth talking, big vision leaders. Busters want a life that is authentic and genuine—and they want leaders whose style and objectives reflect those same qualities.

Introducing the Mosaics

As if you didn't have enough on your hands making sense of those four generations, realize that there is a fifth waiting impatiently in the wings: the Mosaics. Analysts have conjured up various names for the group—Millennials, Generation Y, Postmoderns. By the time you read this, there will probably be a dozen more new terms used to describe the group born after 1984, the successors to the Baby Busters. We have named them the Mosaics because it is an apt description of their thinking style, their relational approach and their lifestyle in general.

Frankly, it is too early to know much about this group since millions of them have not even been born yet! However, if the early signs emerging from the oldest of the Mosaics—who are currently teenagers—are any indication, there are a few qualities about them that we may want to watch for and ruminate upon as the years progress. Here are a few tidbits of insight for you to ponder.

Compared to Busters, Mosaics appear to be a tougher breed. They are less emotionally sensitive, more self-confident and less likely to buckle under stress. Mosaics seem less cynical about the present and less pessimistic about the future. This is partially because they have adjusted better to divorce and blended families, and partially because many of them are embracing a different set of ideals than did Busters.

Mosaics appear to place greater emphasis on many Boomer ideals, such as educational achievement, economic ascendancy and self-reliance.

If Boomers are the quintessential networkers and Busters have become the prototypical community builders, Mosaics will be known for their emphasis upon relational tribes. Already we can see that they have prioritized personal relationships and the value of team decision making and group experience. They are limiting their relational network in size, however, to facilitate a more intensive group-level determination of their daily choices and future character.

If Elders resist technology, Boomers exploit it and Busters appreciate it, Mosaics may best be described as relying upon it without much notice of it. They have grown up entirely in the age of technological innovation that shocks the rest of us; to them, a major technological innovation per day is to be expected. Mosaics have taken the next step beyond adopting technology as a useful tool; they have actually internalized it as part of who they are.

They are unusually comfortable with variety. They like many styles of music. They mix with peers from different racial and ethnic backgrounds. They root for a combination of teams, not just the hometown team. Given their exposure to so many disparate options and the cultural view that all are of equal value, they feel no compulsion to choose one over another.

Like Busters, the emerging generation is very comfortable with contradictions and paradoxes. As mosaic-style, non-linear thinkers, they do not even interpret many of the contradictions identified by Boomers and Elders to be contradictory or paradoxical. They rather enjoy the tension of competing realities and appreciate the diversity reflected by such mutually exclusive elements coexisting.

Absolute truth is a foreign concept to most Mosaics. They are the first truly postmodern generation. As such, they generally adopt an odd mixture of democratic capitalism, nihilism and pantheism.

Mosaics are less likely to attend a Christian church after they graduate from high school than were any prior generation. They have a less pronounced interest in religion and no interest in religious institutions (e.g., denominations). They currently attend churches in record numbers but mostly because it's a place where their friendships can continue to develop. For Mosaics, even more than for the Busters, faith is more about relationships than beliefs and rituals.

Perhaps your reaction to this profile is similar to that of one parent who recently read the Barna Research report on teenagers and was moved to ask: "Is there anything we can do to speed up the return of the Lord?"[3]

Bridging the Gap

Can you see now why we have so much chaos, misunderstanding and animosity in our culture today? Maybe next time you have a lunch conversation about the state of reality, you'll have a bit more compassion for the elected leaders and pastors who are supposed to keep us happy, healthy and moving forward in this age of dissension, discontinuity and disparity.

What we have is a culture in which we no longer define ourselves according to our similarities but according to our differences. We are proud of our unique qualities and want everyone else to appreciate those traits, too. In fact, we often describe ourselves in terms of what we are not—not a Republican, not a liberal, not a religious zealot, not a feminist, not wealthy, not a political person—to make sure that people from disparate backgrounds cannot overlook our distinctiveness.

To further stamp our differences into everyone's consciousness, generations even develop their own cultural currency. Each generation creates its own language. Each has its own music. Each raises up its own core beliefs. Each identifies with a unique set of heroes and leaders. The message is clear: There is not a one-size-fits-all approach that will work anywhere, in any dimension of life—not in worship styles, not in dress styles, not in political campaigning, not in marketing communications. We have devalued commonality in favor of radical uniqueness.

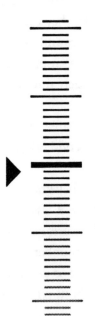

We are more interested in freedom of expression than in commitment to unity. We would rather experience intra-generational intimacy than cross-generation pollination.

We now define ourselves according to our differences.

The way to make progress, of course, is not to choose one generation's approach and ram it down the throats of the other generations but to absorb each group's telltale attributes and figure out ways to bridge the gaps. This calls for very nimble leadership, but it also requires each generation to recognize the magnitude of the demands it is placing on leaders and institutions and to be a bit more forgiving than might otherwise be the inclination. It means withholding our rush to judgment in favor of a more circumspect attitude.

Certainly the best news of all is that we serve a God who is big enough to handle all this confusing and contradictory repositioning. He provided us with a guidebook that allows for enough methodological flexibility to encompass such demanding and disparate groups of people without losing the purity and power of the heart of the Christian faith. Just as He has given us the freedom to develop in this way, and He loves us in spite of our quirks and idiosyncrasies, so should we seek to remain fixated on the basic principles He has provided and to discover ways of focusing everyone on the common threads of our faith, no matter how far-flung our application of those principles might be.

Where Are We Headed?

As time passes, each generation continues to evolve, responding to new cultural imperatives and their own values and history. The days to come will be a study in conflict and camaraderie among generations. The tension that exists today will ebb and flow in uneven patterns of growth and deterioration. The probable outcomes we will see occur include the following:

- Boomers, Busters and Mosaics will continue to wrestle with family issues, especially those related to marriage and divorce. The penchant for dialogue that characterizes the younger generations will mean a continued need for counselors, although the distrust of high-priced professionals will increase young adults' reliance upon friends and acquaintances, and especially on-line relationships, as their source of direction.
- Millions of Busters will get over their generational identity crisis—being called Generation X didn't help—and will mold a generational persona that incorporates their technological expertise and contributions, their relational bent and their appreciation for multicultural experiences.

- Fewer people will return to churches for the sake of their children. As Busters and Mosaics dominate the ranks of parents, they will seek a spiritual dimension for their children; but lacking positive experiences with churches and an appreciation for the substance of Christianity, they will feel less tied to the traditional approaches of religious training.

- Generational friction will grow over who is responsible to take care of aging parents. Boomers would rather pay the bill than have to deal with their parents, much to the chagrin of their parents. Busters would rather not pay the bill and will resent the expectation of having to care for parents from whom they are emotionally disconnected. Some Busters, however, will see the vulnerability of their parents as the window of opportunity they have been seeking through which a real bond can be forged between them.

- Work habits will raise the ire of each group. Builders will resent the increasingly common and overt efforts of Boomers to move them out of the picture. Boomers will resent the salary demands and perceived lack of commitment to building the business demonstrated by Busters. Mosaics will irritate Busters by following the Boomer work style and leapfrogging over Busters, gaining promotions in the corporate hierarchy.

- The Buster and Mosaic emphasis upon group interaction will affect the entire nation. Individualism will persist but will be tempered in some novel ways. Boomers will invest themselves in repairing their damaged relations with their parents and, to a lesser extent, with their children. Busters will continue to focus on affinity groups while keeping an eye out for opportunities to patch things up with their estranged parents. Mosaics will foster their tribal relationships, regularly redefining tribal membership as they mature and their life goes through transitions.

- Elders, overwhelmed by the pace and magnitude of change, will disengage with the mainstream of society in favor of exploiting the numerous leisure opportunities they have at their disposal. Many of them will also help out in Builder-owned businesses on a part-time basis, just to keep their minds alert.

- Discontented with the existing business environment, the corporate world will be reshaped by a rush of alliances, home-based businesses, and individuals for hire as specialists. Rigid corporate structures and practices will be softened as organizations strive to retain the talent they need to keep the whole business growing.
- Technology will cause further tension between generations. Boomers will remain relatively content with '90s technologies while Busters and Mosaics will demand the newest innovations. Technology manufacturers will be challenged with supporting the old technologies for the affluent and numerous Boomers while simultaneously catering to the more leading-edge needs of the younger base.
- Mosaics and Busters will find their love for and reliance upon technology as their common bond. Boomers and Mosaics will bond on the basis of shared economic objectives and a shared value placed upon knowledge acquisition. Busters and Seniors will bond on the basis of a common emphasis upon relationships, emotional sensitivity and the importance of life purpose. Millions of Builders will turn bitter, feeling largely ignored and disconnected.
- Expect to see local churches fragmented into unique congregations, each intent upon having a customized expression of its faith irrespective of what the other congregations within the same denomination are doing. Music, language, rituals, dress, traditions, scheduling, substance, giving, networking and leadership will be designed to satisfy the needs, style and expectations of the age group that is driving the development.
- Busters and Mosaics will periodically return to reflecting upon the nature of truth as they strive to resolve the enduring frustration that they experience with life.
- The emphasis of Busters and Mosaics upon relationships will bring about an increase in time spent communicating with other people. The emphasis on the personal value of individual viewpoints, combined with the widespread absence of conflict resolution skills, will establish an undercurrent of dissatisfaction with

the expanding stream of communications and network of relationships.

- The most effective organizations will be team led and will incorporate representatives of each generation into its core leadership team. The mistrust that individuals have for leaders of other generations, combined with the unique communication styles of each generation, will require such a diversity and blending of leadership talent.

What Can You Do?

As Christians, our religious faith should influence how we see and respond to generational distinctives. It is important to recall that the notion of a generation is eternally meaningless; it is a sociological concept that helps us to make sense of our experience, but it has no basis in God's eternal order. Rather than focus on how to maintain the distinctives of our five generations, our challenge is to take the principles found in the Bible and creatively and strategically apply them to the tensions and opportunities resident within the generational battles that rage around us.

- Take some time to think about the differences that your age and the shaping events of your generation have made in the development of your values, relationships, goals and perspectives. Would the ideas provided below help you to become an agent of reconciliation among generations, rather than a soldier of separation?
- Are there any threads of misunderstanding, dissension or even hostility within your extended family that can be traced back to taking cues from the culture rather than the Bible? If so, resolve those issues on the basis of God's principles and truths. The world is fascinated by conflict, but it is crying out for acceptance and understanding. Model it for them.
- Use your understanding of generations to help you comprehend the world, but avoid the temptation of rigidly generalizing. Some Busters are identical in their thinking and behavior to the proto-

typical Boomer. Some Mosaics are indistinguishable from Builders. Millions of Boomers act more like Busters than they conform to the patterns of their own generation. Generational analysis is not an inevitable and unalterable truth. Treat every person as the significant and unique individual that God made him/her to be—regardless of his or her age or life stage.

- If you have influence in the leadership of your church, don't allow the church to wait until wayward parents choose to return because of the desire to have religious training for their children. Aggressively seek to build relationships with those families, to provide ministries that will affect them in practical and life-changing ways.

- Evaluate your networks—the people who are part of your intimate circles of work associates, church contacts and personal friends. If they are comprised exclusively of people from your own generation, reconsider how to expand your networks to incorporate people from different generations. We will not destroy illegitimate age-based barriers through isolation, nor will we better understand or appreciate other age groups if we do not interact with them.

- Get used to seeing leaders who are significantly younger and older than you. Judge them by their leadership capabilities, not by their age. You will be better off for it.

Notes

1. J. Walker Smith and Ann Clurman, *Rocking the Ages* (New York: Harper Business, 1997) is an excellent resource regarding generations and the events that have influenced the four oldest generations.
2. This information is drawn from various reports produced by the U.S. Census Bureau.
3. Our latest research on teenagers is contained in George Barna, *Third Millennium Teens* (Ventura, CA: Regal Books, forthcoming).

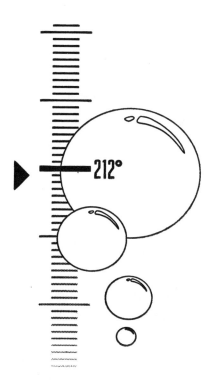

Chapter Four

America's Evolving Values

Future Glimpse

The front door opened and Jackson sauntered into the house. Within a couple of seconds he entered the kitchen and was suddenly confronted with his mother, who was calmly sitting at the kitchen table, staring at him, expressionless. Despite her placid exterior, she was seething inside.

"Where were you?," she asked quietly. Jackson knew what the soft voice and narrow, piercing eyes meant: he was in for it.

"Whaddya mean?" he asked, stalling to size up the situation.

"I waited for you for over an hour at that store. You promised me you'd be there at four o'clock. I left work early to be sure I'd be there on time, so you wouldn't be inconvenienced. And I guess you weren't. Only I was."

"Gimme a break, Mom. It's no big deal. I just couldn't make it."

His decision to minimize the situation infuriated her. Her voice got a touch softer and her brow furrowed as she cocked her head slightly, making no effort to hide her disbelief. "Excuse me? I go out of my way for you and waste an hour of my time and it's no big deal? Do you know what I gave up to help you today, and you didn't even have the common courtesy to call me on that damn cell phone I pay for you to carry around?"

Jackson broke her gaze and stared into his glass of milk. "Aw, get over it, Mom. I didn't have any choice; other stuff came up. You gotta be more flexible. Things happen."

"Oh, really? Do you know how it makes me feel to stand around a store for a full hour, not knowing if something terrible happened to you, if I was at the wrong store or if you just plain didn't respect me enough to honor your commitment? Do you know how it made me look, being stood up by my own son when I'm there to buy him things he asked for, but didn't care enough to show up?"

"Come on, Mom, you're over the edge on this. You'll never see those people again. Your image is intact."

Who the hell raised this kid to be such a sarcastic, uncaring twit? she thought to herself. *Two decades of sweat and energy to create this thankless, self-absorbed, unfeeling monster?* She stood up and put her face within inches of her son's, intent upon staring him down. "How would you like it if I did something like this to you?"

Jackson laughed. "Are you kidding me? You do it all the time! Sure, you call me on the cell phone at the last minute with your lame excuses, but it's the same thing—it's not convenient for you, something better came along, you don't feel like you're in control. Whatever." He placed his half-empty glass on the table and walked out of the room, leaving his mother's eyes to burn holes in the back of his head.

So that's it, she thought. *You matter more than I do. What's good for you is all that matters. Understand your needs and forget about anyone else's. That's what the world is coming to, isn't it?* Jill sat down again and stared at the floor. How could life go on in a society where the only thing that mattered was taking care of yourself—no matter what it did to other people?

Not All Values Are Equal

As Christians, we accept the Bible's teaching that all things were created by God, and thus we reject the popular idea that the world evolved without God's hand in the process. But there is an aspect of evolution that Christians ought to acknowledge: the evolution of America's values. Although we are God's creatures and are called to reflect His character and values, America has morphed into a nation of people who consistently reject His values for those that result from our mindless love affair with pop culture.

Values are the concepts we embrace that define what is right, worthwhile or desirable in life—in other words, the principles and standards that we choose to live by. Traditionally, societies have stayed true to their values for prolonged periods of time. But these days everything is up for grabs; everything is susceptible to change. The age of unquestioned, predictable and enduring core values is history. Driven by our ongoing search for meaning and fulfillment without having to rely upon God, our core values have been changing with unusual rapidity in the last few decades.

As it turns out, all values are not created equal. There are primary values and secondary values. For instance, generosity, humor and risk taking are secondary values: we appreciate them and, all things being equal, would rather experience and exhibit them than not, but we could get by without them. On the other hand, independence, experience, belonging and happiness are "must have" values; they describe what is most important to us in life. We will compromise, if need be, on integrating our secondary values into our life situations; but we typically will go to the mat to defend or incorporate our core values into every last fiber of our life.

The Cornerstone Value

There is one more level of values of importance to this discussion: the cornerstone value. Just as the Christian faith has a cornerstone belief (i.e., we exist to know, love and serve God with all our heart, mind, soul and strength), or professional sports are based on a cornerstone goal (i.e., winning or being the best), so do Americans develop their lives around a cornerstone value. That is a value on which most of our other values hinge; it is the nucleus that spawns other operational values within us. Perhaps the most fundamental value that drives our lifestyles and decision making is whether or not we believe that absolute moral truth exists. Few perspectives in life have a more significant impact on who we are, how we live and what we believe than our personal conviction about moral truth.

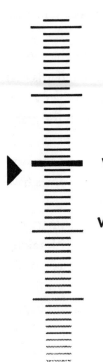

The constant retooling of our core values can be largely traced to a seminal shift in our thinking regarding our perspective on truth. In short, most Americans have chosen to reject absolute moral truth in favor of relativism. That single change has opened the door to a wholesale revision of our entire set of values—and the resulting behaviors.

> ## We have opened the door to a wholesale revision of our values.

This transformation has done more to undermine the health and stability of American society—and, perhaps, of the world—than anything else. It is not a change that happened overnight. The confluence of "new thinking" that swept America in the late '60s and early '70s became a staple of pop culture. The result has been a wholesale revision in people's thought patterns and behaviors based on the notion that a person is the center of his/her universe and is, therefore, responsible for determining what is right and wrong, appropriate and inappropriate, useful and useless, significant and insignificant. In this system, without any grander vision of truth, meaning and value, each person thereby dictates the standards and principles that will rule his/her world, regardless of anyone else's standards and principles.

At the start of the third millennium, America is a nation in which only one-fourth of all adults and just 1 out of every 10 teenagers believes that there is absolute moral truth. The majority of America, therefore, either believes or yields to the belief that all moral truth is relative to the individual and his/her circumstances.

Interestingly, Americans have chosen relativism without much enthusiasm or conviction for that position. Our research shows that even though one's stand on this matter is one of the most important choices an individual will make in his/her life, very few adults and teens ponder the existence and nature of truth. Most of those who do think about it don't make much headway: a majority of them remain confused, frustrated or undecided as to what they think. Consequently, most people revert to the default position of the prevailing culture: moral truth is relative. We found that even a majority of those who contend that moral truth is absolute are somewhat confused about their belief and are likely to contradict themselves when questions about truth are posed from different angles.

The Route to Relativism—and Beyond

Born-again Christians, who ought to be the most verbal and convincing defenders of absolute moral truth, are more likely than nonbelievers to support the absolute stand with certainty; but the "absolutists" represent less than half of all born-again adults. While the Christians who back the absolutist view outnumber those who promote the relativist view by almost a 5 to 1 ratio, we also discovered that when Christians were asked about truth in different ways, their confusion and lack of conviction was overt. The reason you don't hear many believers discoursing on the principle of truth is probably because so few of them, regardless of their leanings, have a well-researched, clearly articulate and compelling perspective on the matter.

What happened? How did Christians, the very people to whom God entrusted the substance of truth and morality, arrive at this vapid posture? As best we can untangle it, the route was circuitous. The teaching that people receive from their churches—the place where, hopefully, the truths asserted by God are clearly, consistently and convincingly expounded—has generally been ineffective at helping them comprehend moral truth. Our studies show that few churches use their teaching times—sermons, Sunday school, VBS, small groups, membership classes—to intentionally and relentlessly communicate a coherent and cohesive worldview in a systematic fashion. Church-based teaching is generally founded on Bible content, but that teaching also tends to be random in its context and delivery. In addition, the role models who impact Christians have fared poorly at portraying absolute moral truth through their words and actions.

AMERICANS ARE CONFUSED ABOUT MORAL TRUTH

	All Adults	Born-Again Christians	Not Born Again
Moral truth is absolute—very certain of it	28%	44%	17%
Moral truth is absolute—probably	5%	5%	6%
Moral truth is relative—absolutely certain of it	10%	8%	12%
Moral truth is relative—probably	9%	5%	11%
Not sure what to think about moral truth	48%	38%	54%

Source: Barna Research Group, Ltd.; OmniPoll 1-00, January 2000, N=1002.

Certainly, if the public were willing, it could discern the contours of a truth-based worldview from Scripture. However, most people's experience with God's Word is irregular and superficial, at best. Few Americans read the Bible often enough, broadly enough and sufficiently circumspectly to enable them to develop a truth-based worldview. Add to that the fact that they are immersed in a culture that promotes relativism and that the Church rarely holds its adherents accountable for their values and beliefs, and the consequence is that moral truth is essentially rejected. The practical result is obvious: without a solid moral foundation, churches and church people are affected by the culture more than they are affecting the culture's views and behavior.

Truth and Our Worldview

Whether you realize it or not, your view of moral truth is at the core of your worldview. (In this text we are speaking of a worldview as a way of interpreting all aspects of reality.) Chuck Colson has argued that the dominant American worldview of young adults can be summed up in one word: "whatever." Without the clarity and consistency of absolute moral truth, we are reduced to doing what seems right, what feels good, what produces the least resistance and what provides the greatest personal fulfillment.

Naturally, our unconscious dismissal of absolute morality and ethics has produced a plethora of attitudinal and behavioral changes, including the reforming of our values.

But if you thought the move toward moral relativism is alarming, realize that tens of millions of Americans have taken the next logical step beyond moral relativism. Cultural analysts argue that there are really three dominant strains of thought in America today. There is the traditional or pre-modern view that says absolute moral truth exists, it is knowable and it has consequences for people's lives. The modern view maintains that all truth is relative to the person's perspective. The newest iteration, which is increasingly popular, is known as postmodernism. This philosophy asserts that there is no truth at all: Efforts to discover absolutes, much less to live them, are fruitless. Postmodernism is based on existentialism, which claims there is no meaning or purpose to life; personal experience is all that a person can know and appreciate.

Did you ever wonder how so many people can own Bibles, perhaps even read the Bible, and yet so completely miss the mark in their attitudes, values and lifestyles? It is largely because of the worldview disconnect. To the postmodern person, the Bible is simply a collection of time-honored stories that amount to another self-help volume. It is to be read just like any other self-help book: with some skepticism and for personal gain. Postmoderns outright reject the idea of the Bible being an accurate guidebook for life, much less the literal Word of a holy, omnipotent and omniscient God. They do not memorize or apply Scripture because, in their worldview, the Bible has no greater power, virtue or value than books by Stephen King, Jerry Seinfeld or Dr. Seuss.

In fact, postmodernism renders Jesus' entire death and resurrection little more than an interesting but obscure story of one individual's compassion, heroic effort and ultimate demise. Postmodern people view it as a story that offers insight into one person's challenges and responses, but not as a standard by which our lives are to be shaped or judged. The life of Jesus, in other words, is just another story among the billions of human histories that we might reflect upon and is no more or less meaningful than the stories of James Cassidy, Sheilah Brown, Jose Rodriguez or Choi En Liu—whoever they are.

Your Worldview Matters

Can you understand, then, why the Church is struggling for significance in this age? For two millennia, the Christian Church has stood for God's truth. More and more, Americans are embracing the idea that there is no truth, or at best, that it is defined by each individual, from moment to moment. Consider the practical effects of our abandonment of absolute moral truth:

- divorce, homosexuality and abortion are no longer moral issues to be decided on the basis of God's Law but on the basis of personal preference; we even call those who support abortion "pro choice," as if God has granted us the platform to make such a determination;
- pornography is generally protected as "free speech," but prayer at public schools and the posting of the Ten Commandments in courthouses is outlawed;
- widespread and public use of foul language is accepted as a right of personal expression; mass media broadcast such language without fear of reprisal;
- lying and cheating are described as inappropriate behaviors, but most people believe that the problem is not the act of lying or cheating but being caught lying or cheating;
- personal bankruptcy filings have increased every year for the last seven years, based on the popular notion that people have no moral obligation to pay their debts;
- the prison population is larger than ever and continues to grow, thanks partially to more diligent law enforcement efforts, but even more so to a population that equates lawlessness with freedom and personal rights;
- suicide among young people continues at alarmingly high rates, fueled by the postmodern perspective that life has no real meaning;
- racism, carefully masked, festers just beneath the surface of our society because we believe that we are better than others—all people are not equal in the eyes of most Americans;

- computer hackers have become a subgroup of their own, spawning an entire industry of software developers and law enforcement specialists who focus on protecting people's computers from viruses and other forms of malicious hacking;
- the number of lawyers in the U.S. has nearly tripled since 1970; we have more lawyers than doctors, and the growth of the legal profession is eclipsing that of the medical profession.

The impact of this shift cannot be overstated. It affects every decision and every behavior. It influences our relationships. Our adoption of relativism has served as the catalyst for a movement toward, and the foundation facilitating, a culture that is accepting of moral anarchy—a society in which every person is the law unto him- or herself and there is widespread chaos and confusion regarding what is appropriate and inappropriate conduct.

Relativism and Ministry

America's love affair with relativism even influences how we think about and engage in ministry. Consider some of the implications of the rejection of absolute truth for traditional Christian activity.

Evangelism

The Great Commission clearly commands Christians to share the good news about Jesus' life, death and atoning resurrection with the world. But in a relativistic society, such a challenge is less inspiring and meaningful. In fact, for many people, including tens of millions of devoted Christians, evangelism is dismissed because it is both countercultural and optional. In a culture in which there is no absolute moral truth, the Bible is not a definitive source of guidance for behavior. Its exhortations to strategically share the Christian faith with nonbelievers are seen as well-intentioned but unmotivating demands.

Follow the logic behind the worldview-based abandonment of Christian evangelism. If, as most Americans (including a large majority of born-again

Christians) believe, there is no such thing as absolute moral truth, then there is no such thing as an absolute notion of what is right or wrong. Without that, there can be no agreement on what is sin, leading to the conclusion that there is either no such thing as sin or that sin is a personal matter determined by one's feelings, needs and circumstances. Consequently, without absolute moral truth as the standard, the common conclusion is that the greatest end in life is comfortable survival, which, therefore, means you have to do whatever is right for you at the moment. Sin, therefore, is an antiquated or at least irrelevant concept for people. In the absence of sin, there is no possibility of ultimate spiritual judgment and no possibility of eternal spiritual condemnation, since there would be no offenses for which a person would be condemned. Without condemnation, there is no need to be saved. Without a need for salvation, evangelism is a meaningless task.

Discipleship

The Great Commission exhorts us to not only share information about our faith with the hope of leading others to Christ, but we are told to "make disciples" (see Matt. 28:19). Much of the New Testament is a practical and impassioned call to all believers to continually grow in their faith. The growth process, commonly called discipleship, is evidence that we are becoming transformed people, not simply individuals who took out eternal fire insurance and then went on living high-risk lifestyles. If you can tell a Christian by the fruit of his or her life, then it is personal involvement in discipleship that bears such fruit.

> **The Great Commission exhorts us to share the good news.**

As you might imagine, relativism undermines the need for discipleship. After all, if there is no absolute moral truth, then the Bible is not the source of moral truth; and God is, therefore, not the ultimate authority. Without an ultimate authority, there are no universally accepted standards and no reliable principles that lead to righteousness. In fact, without absolute morality, there is no standard of righteousness. If our goal is not to achieve a level of righteousness, then we have no need to change who we are, which then negates the very act of discipleship—a conscious imitation of Christ with the intent of becoming more Christlike. In a postmodern society, becoming more Christlike is no more desirable than becoming more Hitlerlike.

Worship

God's greatest joy may well be receiving the praises and worship of His people. Scripture instructs us to worship God in truth and in Spirit, and that our lifestyle should be an act of continual worship to God.

Once again, the postmodern perspective intrudes in our efforts to commune regularly with God in ways that honor and glorify Him. If all moral truth is relative, then there is neither a source of truth nor an ultimate deity, since deity has absolutely pure nature and is omnipotent. Without the existence of a deity, worship makes no sense; indeed, there is nothing worthy of worship.

The Values We Embrace

Relativism (or the absence of any form of truth) has become our dominant value. As such, that choice has led to the adoption of a raft of other values that are consistent with the vacuum of moral absolutes.

But defining the values of Americans is not as simple as ticking off a list of highly regarded attributes. It seems that there are three levels of values that we might examine to better understand what moves Americans. There are the core values—the elements that describe what we deem to be compellingly appropriate, valuable or fulfilling. Next there are the secondary values—elements to which we typically give intellectual or verbal support but which we inconsistently or selectively carry out in practice. A third level entails the former core values that have been rejected in favor of new alternatives. This third level—former core values—is helpful to examine because it enables us to more clearly see the progression in our values choices.

The accompanying chart shows some of the key values that fit each of these categories. Notice that our core values have shifted to facilitate a more fluid and upscale quality of life. These values drive us to seek greater control over the decisions and rules that influence our lives and to exact a greater degree of self-determination through the choices we make from a plethora of alternatives. Our core values emphasize the importance of the pace at which we live—it must be variable but allow for speed—and show that people desire immersion in life rather than being an innocent bystander or a victim of the system.

Our secondary values are also intriguing because they point out those elements that we lean toward—or away from—but have not completely embraced. In some cases you can see that these values call for sacrificial caring of others or a willingness to participate in give-and-take relationships. These values also suggest that we are lukewarm about making total commitments. Our secondary values underscore the tensions with which we live. For instance, there is the psychological approval of helping those in need but the counterbalancing refusal to sacrifice what we possess in order to supply such help. There is the widespread assent to supporting causes, groups and individuals who are important in our lives, but not at the expense of surrendering our flexibility or limiting our options. These kinds of tensions have always existed in people's lives; what's new are the competing forces that are pulling us in opposite directions and are defining our priorities, our lifestyles and our culture in the process.

The list of abandoned values constitutes a history lesson. As you read through that group of values you will note that we have given up on absolutes—in any dimension of life—as well as the very idea of accepting standards of performance or behavior against which we will be judged. We have lost our interest in accepting responsibility for much of our lives: what we think, what we say, how we act, what we pursue. Civility is one of the casualties of our changing values, along with dependability. To determine whether America is better off or worse off because of the rejection of these values depends upon the values you possess. But it is probably fair to say that from a traditional Christian point of view, American society is less consistent with biblical values today than it was in the recent past.

VALUES IN AMERICA

Core Values	Secondary Values	Abandoned Values
convenience	simplicity	discernment
options for expression	compassion	fiscal responsibility
time maximization	teamwork	absolute morality
belonging	integrity	loyalty
comfort	youth care	conformity
experiences	family cohesion	consensus
happiness	humor tolerance	tradition
independence	volunteerism	continuity
flexibility	reciprocity	respect
authenticity	generosity	submission to authority
education options	networking	accountability
entertainment	spiritual depth	discipline purity
diversity	risk taking	good citizenship
customization	change	thrift
participation	wealth	sacrifice
gender equality	physical health	patriotism
technology	achievement	career
instant gratification		idealism
meaning		predictability
skepticism		
image		
control		
relevance		
impact/influence		
personal empowerment		
relationships		
self-image		

Christians and Their Values

Keep in mind that talking about America's values is somewhat misleading. Such a portrait relies upon a discussion of averages, which means that there are millions of people who possess very different values than those that typify the population at large. While these generalizations are helpful in giving us the big picture, they may distort our understanding of reality by ignoring or minimizing the existence of divergent realities.

Since the Christian faith is so intimately related to leading a values-driven life, you would expect the values of committed Christians to conflict with the overall national preferences in values. The Christian faith is not merely about intellectual assent to worthy ideas but about faith-based principles that lead to significant life transformation. You might, therefore, expect believers to possess a very different values profile than the norm.

Unfortunately, that expectation is not met. While the values system of the typical Christian is not identical to that of the typical nonbeliever, there is more similarity than distinctiveness between the two. All too often, the values of the Christian Body bear little resemblance to the biblical principles those individuals have been taught.

The core values of the Church are a mixture of the world's values and a series of spiritually oriented preferences. The worldly elements lean toward material well-being and satisfaction as well as gaining the approval of the world. The religious component of our values structure encompasses the elevation of our individuality as believers, the ability to determine our own direction and a general sense of purpose as a body of believers.

If you were to make a list of the core, secondary and abandoned values of born-again Christians and compare it to a list prepared in relation to nonbelievers, you would be shocked at the overlap. The primary difference is that the Christians' list would be more extensive because of the inclusion of their spiritual values in addition to their operational values.

You might discover that the spiritually oriented core values that get appended to the Christian list would include the significance of children (a secondary value to nonbelievers), spiritual mission, spiritual growth and joy and celebration. Most believers hold a higher view of their parental responsibility and the significance of their children—perhaps not really the family values content that the mass media assign to born-againers, but recognition of family responsibility and worth. Most believers also prioritize a sense of their spiritual purpose, the importance of growing in their faith and the privilege of experiencing and appreciating the uniqueness of their life in Christ.

The big gap is between the secondary values of believers and nonbelievers. It is in this category that most of the spiritual values of believers reside. They are the kind of values that get more lip service than practice and that tension causes considerable stress and frustration within millions of believers. That tension is little more than a reflection of an internal battle between the world's ways and Christ's ways. Among the values that would appear on the Christians' list, but not that of the nonbelievers, would be tradition, moral absolutes, respect, humility, forgiveness, servanthood, community service, regular prayer, unconditional love, fiscal responsibility and worship of God alone. Two items on the nonbelievers' secondary list—wealth and risk taking—would not be likely to appear on the believers' list.

The abandoned values lists are where the greatest differentiation would occur. Notice that the values forfeited by Christians are those that had given a true spiritual edge to their lives—components like radical obedience to God, stewardship of all dimensions of their life, voluntary submission to spiritual peers and a commitment to theological purity. Instead of an intense focus on their core attributes as believers, most Christians have settled for a second-class faith commitment, mouthing the words and doing some of the overt acts of obeisance, but partitioning their heart into religious and nonreligious chambers. Like a cancer, the nonreligious chamber continues to eat away at the religious, reducing the magnitude and significance of the religious side.

VALUES ABANDONED BY CHRISTIANS

radical obedience	biblical knowledge
holistic stewardship	theological purity
church loyalty	salvation by grace alone
submission to authority	elder care
accountability	family spirituality
diversity	holiness
discipline	patience
persecution	confession of sins

Imposing the World on the Church

Take a moment to consider how our core values influence how we pursue and experience our faith.

Our desire for convenience has changed how we select and engage with our church. Rather than starting with a theological perspective and picking a church that will foster spiritual growth that is consistent with our biblical convictions, most of us select a church that is close to our home and that offers worship services at times that fit our schedule. If a worthy activity occurs at the church that conflicts with other preferences in our life, the chances are good that we will reject the church activity because it is not convenient—which, in this case, means it is not a priority.

Our longing for stimulating experiences means that we will attend a church that is in vogue, and our first order of business is to take advantage of the satisfying events it has to offer. It becomes vitally important for us to feel good about our church choice and church experiences. If we attend the worship services and begin to feel that they are stagnant or that we are not having a good enough experience, we blame the church leaders for losing the focus or allowing the quality to diminish. It rarely crosses people's minds that they bring something to the table, and maybe the problem is personal, not external.

Because we value happiness so highly, we applaud the preacher who delivers sermons that are upbeat and encouraging, and subconsciously communicate our displeasure with messages that are critical or too challenging. Most of us have unknowingly slipped into the mind-set that God wants us to be happy, so any pain or hardships that we experience are certainly not God's plan for us—especially if the suffering is in any way caused or facilitated by the church. We ignore Bible verses that warn us that the Christian life will bring suffering and difficulty, and we seek out the feel-good verses.

Because we value independence, we are less inclined to become a church member or to remain loyal to one church over the long haul. At the first hint of struggle, many believers start their search for a new church. We have become a people of low commitment, wanting to keep our options open. Classes that teach the Bible over a five-year period have lost favor because it's too much of a commitment. Small groups that have an open-ended commitment have proven to be less popular than those that require a limited duration obligation (i.e., anywhere from six weeks to nine months).

You get the drift. If you really want to drive the point home sometime, take a couple of days to read books from some of the renowned church leaders of the sixteenth, seventeenth and eighteenth centuries, such as John Wesley, Martin Luther, John Calvin and Jonathan Edwards. The centrality of God's principles in their lives and how those principles shaped their decision making is so foreign to our viewpoint these days. Granted, we live in a completely different era and have very disparate pressures and options facing us, but the ways in which those individuals would handle the challenges of the modern day would likely be quite different from the ways that most of us approach our daily battle.

Perhaps the most significant revelation emerging from an examination of our values is to realize how extensively we have shaped our worldview and values around the indices of worldly success and acceptance. Rather than following Jesus' exhortation to be in the world but not of it, we seem to thirst for the opposite reality: to be inseparable from the world we are in, while retaining the aura of a devout follower of Christ. If one of the fundamental purposes of the Church is to influence the world to understand Christ through our imitation of His life, many of our current values—or, at least, how we apply them in daily situations—prevent us from exposing the world to an authentic glimpse of the nature and behavior of the Son of God.

And perhaps the critical issue is not confusion over the nature of our values or the substance of values that correspond to biblical wisdom, but a gnawing sense that if we truly pursue those ways of life, then we will forfeit our prospects of worldly success. For instance, most Christians espouse the importance of living with integrity; but incredible numbers of us lie, cheat and steal along with the rest of society, without much sense of remorse. We are likely to shrug off those failures as a natural part of life in a fast-paced, morally ambivalent, hard-to-get-ahead world. Another example relates to compassion and service, a pair of ideals that most believers accept as central to biblical Christianity. Unless circumstances facilitate convenient and relatively costless acts of service, surprisingly few Christians put themselves out for their neighbors in need.

Even a cursory reading of the list of values abandoned by Christians in the past three decades reveals the shallowness of our spirituality. Many of the values that once made Christians proud to call themselves by the name, and that fueled their ability to persevere in the face of persecution, have taken a place on the Endangered Values list. Most of America's Christians retreat from religious persecution in favor of cultural acceptance. Our theological confusion has redefined salvation almost to the point of universalism. The idea of striving for holiness is not even on the radar screen of most Christians, partly attributable to the absence of clear standards, serious spiritual relationships and consistent accountability. Believers are more likely to church hop in search of the latest hot church than to model loyalty and commitment at a less prestigious place of worship.

These are hard words to hear and to absorb. Our tendency is to identify exceptions to criticisms and cite them as proof that all is well with the Church in spite of a few glitches here and there. Indisputably, there are many exceptions to the description provided above, and millions of followers of Christ *are* on the right track. But an objective, overall depiction of the values of Christians is not flattering—and it certainly does not do justice to the One who gave His life for those who seek His love and forgiveness.

Where Are We Headed?

It would be heartwarming to suggest that things have become so uncomfortable for us that people are ready for a major change—i.e., a shift back to more biblically defensible values and ways of life. That is not completely out of the question, but several things would have to happen for such a transformation to occur. First, people would have to recognize that there is a major problem. Second, they would have to reflect on the problem to understand its nature and the possibilities for change. Third, they would have to identify alternatives to the existing ways. Fourth, they must commit to significant change, with an ideal in mind of what they wish to become. Fifth, they would need to adopt a detailed plan of action to bring about the change. Sixth, they would have to implement the plan. Seventh, they would need some standards by which to judge the progress of their efforts and perhaps even invite certain people to hold them accountable to reach those mileposts.

This process is very possible, but not very likely. Why? Because key players do not even recognize that we play a major role in instigating such change. For instance, our research shows that most pastors claim that they are doing a great job of providing congregants what they need to think biblically and to have a Christian worldview. One of our studies even showed that a majority of pastors argue that most of their regular attenders have a biblical worldview in place. And we cannot count on congregants rising up to demand that they get the kind of teaching and accountability required to facilitate a seminal shift in our values. Much like an uneducated man dying of some internal sickness he cannot diagnose, most churched adults don't know even the basic contours of what they are lacking and, thus, cannot request help to get what they need.

Further, Americans have not reached a point of such pain that they are willing to examine their own culpability in our moral morass. Yes, recent public opinion surveys show that moral decay now rates as one of our top-rated national problems. But those surveys also show that fewer than one out of every five adults rate moral deterioration to be of such importance. In fact, we have seen that most Americans who acknowledge that our country has moral and spiritual problems point the finger at others—the problem is caused by other people not toeing the mark. Few adults currently accept personal responsibility for any degree of the moral dilemma of the United States.

So, here is what we are likely to face during this decade:

- Postmodernism will spread like a computer virus, insinuating itself into every corner and crevice of our culture, with people barely aware that such a sweeping philosophical change has overtaken us.
- Two catalysts—the emergence of the Mosaics and the implications of moral relativism and postmodernism—will facilitate continued experimentation with and shifting of our values. Mosaics will carry out the time-honored tradition of an emerging generation rejecting the values of the generation that preceded them.

Meanwhile, the reality of relativism and existentialism will mean that there is no fundamentally solid value on which to build a set of values, leaving Americans adrift in their own vague search for meaning and truth.

- Expect the gap between our verbalized values (what we say) and our practiced values (what we do) to grow wider and wider.
- Frustration will build as people become increasingly bothered by—and, eventually, intolerant of—the inconvenience and disgust resulting from the absence of a moral consensus. The do-your-own-thing mentality will eventually create constant conflict and dissension as people, used to getting their own way and believing that it's their right to have what they want, encounter constant resistance from others who are simultaneously seeking their own way.
- Around mid-decade we expect to see a nascent grassroots movement from within the Christian community to reintroduce people to the idea of living in accordance with a biblical worldview and discovering how to get there. If that effort can establish credibility through successful outcomes, then it may become a groundswell that influences millions of people—even many outside the church—well into the next decade. In other words, it may be our self-wrought pain and frustration that initiates a return to saner values and lifestyles.

What Can You Do?

Because your values determine who you are—your character, your relationships, your career choices, your lifestyle, your morals—this is a matter of huge importance. The time that you invest in clarifying your values and ensuring that they are God-honoring, scripturally defensible and consistent with each other will be well worth your effort. Consider carrying out the actions described below.

- Identify your core values. You cannot get very far until you know where you stand today. To figure that out, write down the values that are most important to you—the ones that you believe are critical to being who God wants you to be, that are consistent with biblical principles and that you cannot afford to compromise. Then read through the Bible to identify the values that characterized the people that pleased God or the values that God specified for us to embrace.[1] Compare your list with the list drawn from the Bible. Note the gaps and create a plan for making the changes that will enhance your values.

- Get serious about your understanding of and commitment to God's truth principles. Can you identify the essential elements of moral truth? Can you articulate how those aspects of truth could be manifested in your daily behavior? Can you point out ways in which God's views on truth conflict with yours or with those that are common in our society? If you were to be a living example of God's truth in action, what would your life look like—and what would it take for you to get there? Essentially, we're talking about developing a clear and comprehensive worldview based on God's truths. That worldview will change everything about the way you live because it will become the filter through which you see the world and make your decisions.[2]
- Engage others in your family and church in discussions about values and worldviews. Such discussions will enlighten you as well as increase your accountability for your convictions about truth and values. Teaching others is often the best way to truly learn something for yourself, so exploiting opportunities to mentor others in these matters would also enhance your own development.

Until the Church reflects the different type of thinking and behavior that God intends for His people to possess, the Church cannot hope to influence the world for God's purposes or to enjoy the benefits of His ways. The process of revolutionizing the Church through a biblical approach to morality, truth and worldview happens one changed person at a time. Are you willing to start that process today?

Notes

1. You might reflect on values such as those provided in Matthew 5—7, 1 Timothy 3:1-14, Galatians 5:22-24, Exodus 20 and the entire book of Proverbs. The Bible is packed with information about values; all you have to do is look for those insights.

2. To think through how to create a worldview, read about the nature and process of developing a worldview—and then do it! Some useful guidebooks might include *The Making of a Christian Mind*, ed. Arthur Holmes (Downers Grove, IL: InterVarsity Press, 1985); D. Bruce Lockerbie, *Thinking and Acting Like a Christian* (Portland, OR: Multnomah Press, 1989); Os Guinness, *Fit Bodies, Fat Minds* (Grand Rapids, MI, Baker Books, 1994); Charles Colson and Nancy Pearcey, *How Now Shall We Live?* (Wheaton, IL: Tyndale House Publishers, 1999); and George Barna, *The Second Coming of the Church* (Nashville, TN: Word Books, 1998), chap. 11.

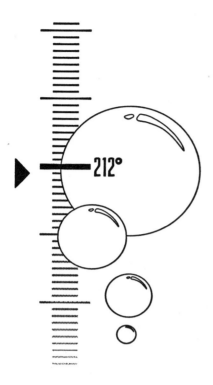

212°

CHAPTER FIVE

THE WAY WE LIVE

Future Glimpse

Jill was trying to calm down. She had just stormed out of the hotel pool area, after a heated exchange with a hotel guest whose teenage son's boom box was blasting rap music that filled the pool room with deafening noise. The rules, clearly posted on the wall, stated that no music was allowed in the pool area except through headphones. Jill had politely asked the parent to have the kid turn off the music and obey the rules.

"But there's nobody else here. He's not bothering anyone," was the reply.

Jill explained that nobody else would dare use the pool given the noise level. "Look, we're on vacation, and this is what makes my kid happy. If someone else comes in, we'll turn it down." The man went back to reading his newspaper, as if she had disappeared.

One last time Jill appealed to the man's responsibility to comply with the rules of the hotel. "Lady, rules are made to be broken. Especially stupid ones, like this." Again, he reopened his newspaper and focused on the business section.

Jill went back to her desk. What could she do? Call the cops? Bad for business. Whine to her boss? That'd make her look weak. Turn the kid's machine off? She'd probably get arrested for something or other. It was a no-win situation.

Jill thought about a term she'd heard on the radio that morning, some social analyst describing America as struggling with "moral anarchy." She'd never heard the term before, and it didn't make much sense to her then; but all of a sudden it was crystal clear! She started considering other instances of moral anarchy. People ripping off their employers, taking pens home, making personal calls, using company time on the Internet to buy and sell stocks. Jackson's school making kids walk through metal detectors at the front doors to prevent students from entering with guns and knives. Gun-toting cops walking the aisles at professional sporting events. People hogging the fast lane on the freeways, refusing to move to their right when they clearly were holding up long lines of cars that wanted to move faster. Plagiarism among authors and journalists. Clergy who made up illustrations to drive home a point in their sermons and made it seem like the stories were true. The more she thought about it, the more depressed she became; the list of abuses seemed endless.

As she shook her head in dismay, she allowed herself one tiny consolation. If the boom-box kid got hurt in the pool, nobody would ever hear his screams for help over the din of his music. *That'd serve him right*, she thought. *Fair play after all?*

Trade-Offs

Pity the person whose job it is to make sense of American lifestyles these days. Perhaps the most succinct description offered recently comes from comedian and social critic George Carlin.

The paradox of our time in history is that we have taller buildings, but shorter tempers; wider freeways, but narrower viewpoints. We spend more, but have less; we buy more, but enjoy it less. We have bigger houses and smaller families; more conveniences, but less time; we have more degrees, but less sense; more knowledge, but less judgment; more experts, but more problems; more medicine, but less wellness. We drink too much, smoke too much, spend too recklessly, laugh too little, drive too fast, get too angry too quickly, stay up too late, get up too tired, read too seldom, watch TV too much, and pray too seldom.

We have multiplied our possessions, but reduced our values. We talk too much, love too seldom, and hate too often. We've learned how to make a living, but not a life; we've added years to life, not life to years.

We've been all the way to the moon and back, but have trouble crossing the street to meet the new neighbor. We've conquered outer space, but not inner space. We've done larger things, but not better things. We've cleaned up the air, but polluted the soul. We've split the atom, but not our prejudice.

We write more, but learn less. We plan more, but accomplish less. We've learned to rush, but not to wait. We build more computers to hold more information to produce more copies than ever, but have less communication.

These are the times of fast foods and slow digestion; tall men and short character; steep profits and shallow relationships. These are the times of world peace, but domestic warfare; more leisure, but less fun; more kinds of food, but less nutrition. These are days of two incomes, but more divorce; of fancier houses, but broken homes. These are days of quick trips, disposable diapers, throw-away morality, one-night stands, overweight bodies, and pills that do everything from cheer to quiet to kill.

It is a time when there is much in the show window and nothing in the stockroom.[1]

How do you make sense out of lifestyles that are inherently senseless? The very act of seeking to analyze peoples' lives assumes that there is some logic to the choices and behaviors that we will observe under our social microscope, but perhaps our fundamental assumption is unwarranted. Americans are more often than not mindless reactors, not introspective synthesizers or innovators. It may be asking too much to try to find the threads of intelligence, wisdom, strategy and purpose in the lifestyles of people whose idea of wry intellectual depth is a Doonesbury cartoon or whose nominee for poet laureate is Garth Brooks.

Listen to how your friends describe their lives, or how your family members recount their daily travails. Our research shows that we are doing the best we can to get by from day to day but finding it immensely difficult to achieve the quality of life we desire.

Two-thirds of all adults admit that they like to be in control. Much to their chagrin, a large majority, however, feel as if their lives are moving too quickly and are beyond their control.

Six out of 10 Americans say they are skeptical. Such an attitude has become one of the defenses we use to protect ourselves from being ripped off, manipulated and exploited. Unfortunately, that inability to trust others or to see the best in a situation often robs us of the joy of living.

Half of all adults concur that they are just too busy. This is the result of working more hours (a larger share of our population works, and the average work year has risen by a cumulative four weeks per year over the last two decades) while trying to satisfy our seemingly insatiable thirst for excitement and newness.[2] Three-quarters of us recognize that we like to try new experiences, which of course contributes to our exhaustion and inability to ease up. The pressure of juggling so many activities and responsibilities, combined with the stress of fulfilling ever-increasing productivity expectations, wears us out. One study shows that Americans don't even sleep the minimum number of hours required for the human body to renew itself. Most people feel as if they are falling farther behind—and are more fatigued than ever.

Half of us acknowledge that we are still seeking just a few good friends. The demands of the day make it hard to carve out enough time and energy to invest in deep, meaningful friendships. Most people have numerous acquaintances and professional relationships—perhaps more than ever—but still feel emotionally unfulfilled and strangely disconnected.

One of the most confounding and bothersome stresses we face relates to the purpose of our lives. Less than 1 out of every 20 people can identify what they believe is God's unique vision for their life. Half of us say that we are still trying to figure out the ultimate meaning or purpose of our lives. Two-thirds say that it is to enjoy life as much as possible, yet there seems to be a subconscious sense that there has to be more to life than mere pleasure seeking.

One-third of us contend that we are stressed-out. But that's as an overall description of who we are; more than four out of five people indicate that they are dealing with significant stress in various dimensions of their life. Some of the stress is caused by our insistence on being self-sufficient (92 percent)—that is, self-reliant, self-directed and personally responsible for all that we experience. Things have gotten so stressful that the average employee now takes off 15 nonvacation days each year from work—and only four of those are due to illness! The other two weeks' worth of time off is to facilitate the handling of other stresses in their lives.[3]

Surprisingly few of us know how to deal appropriately with conflict. Our most common tendency, relied upon by 7 out of every 10 adults, is to avoid the situations and people with whom we are experiencing conflict. That may explain why half of all employees say they regularly experience anger at work and why unresolved conflict is one of the primary causes of divorce and family strife.

Financial problems plague millions of Americans. Four out of 10 describe themselves as being in debt, while the nation's consumer debt load has risen to $1.5 trillion. Like a carrot dangling tantalizingly on a stick in front of us, we tend to feel that if we just made an extra $10,000 to $20,000 per year we would be "financially comfortable," but when we reach that amount the true comfort level always seems to be another $10,000 to $20,000 beyond our grasp.

Although dieting and nutritional books regularly fill the best-seller lists, and most adults claim they are exercising, government studies are showing that we are eating ourselves into the grave. The U.S. Department of Agriculture estimates that less than one-eighth of us eats a healthy diet. The result, according to the American Heart Association, is that more than half of all Americans are overweight and 1 out of every 5 is obese.

Sex remains a preoccupation with most people, but we struggle to find true love. A national survey by Maritz Marketing Research reported that not even a majority of adults are satisfied with their love life. People were more likely to say it is "merely okay," terrible or nonexistent than to say their love life is in good shape.[4]

The driving life goal for most of us is to achieve happiness. Sadly, few reach that goal. Since 1950, a wide variety of studies shows that there has been no increase in people's sense of happiness despite the fact that real income has doubled and that quality of life measurements show that our external circumstances have improved greatly. Happiness has proven to be elusive for more than four decades: It is our summary description of what we most desire in life, but it is so elusive that most adults cannot even provide researchers with a preconceived notion of what it is. Perhaps, as people tell us, we will know it when we achieve it.

You get the idea. We roll out of bed, muster the courage to face another grueling day, put on our happy face and hope for the best. More often than not, we climb back under the covers at night feeling successful for having endured another day, but disappointed that we did not get closer to our ultimate objectives. We tend to harbor these feelings as secrets, unwilling to admit publicly that we're not pleased with the way life is going. We don't want to be whiners, but somehow life just isn't working out the way we thought it was supposed to.

Maybe It's Our Goals

A large share of our frustration surely results from the goals that we have set for our lives. More than two-thirds of adults have set the following six objectives as major goals for their life.[5] We're falling short of the mark on all of them.

91 Percent Want "Good Physical Health"

As noted above, in spite of exercise regimens and special diets, we generally fail to reach our health objectives. Stress contributes to our shortcoming, along with an intake of food that our bodies cannot handle. Look at how much of each category of food the average adult consumes in a typical year:

282 pounds of dairy product	278 pounds of vegetables
25 pounds of candy	138 pounds of potatoes
30 gallons of beer	229 pounds of meat, fish and poultry
52 gallons of soft drink	185 pounds of grains
14 gallons of bottled water	31 pounds of eggs
3 gallons of wine	22 pounds of salty snack foods[6]

It's hard to believe we can ingest all of that (plus goodies contained within a few other categories we did not list) in just 365 days! No wonder more than 58 million Americans suffer from one or more types of cardiovascular disease. A recently discovered problem: we are less willing than ever to sacrifice good taste for healthy food content.

81 Percent Want to "Live with a High Degree of Integrity"

This has risen in importance to people during the last decade. At the same time, though, our self-reported incidents of lying, stealing and cheating have increased. Depending upon your moral convictions, you could add use of pornography, indulgence in adultery, gossip and breaking personal promises on top of that to get a more accurate assessment of our true nature. Two-thirds of all adults defend such misdirected behaviors as "necessary" to get by in life these days. Such justifications add to the personal anxiety and dissatisfaction we feel with life.

79 Percent Want to Have "One Marriage Partner for Life"

One-quarter of the population has already missed the boat on this goal. Divorce rates are continuing to climb, adultery remains rampant, and cohabitation simply skirts the issue. The sentiment is laudable, however; if only we could tame the rest of our desires and focus our skills on developing better communication and shared experiences with our spouses, we'd have a better shot at reaching this goal.

75 Percent Want "Close Personal Friendships"

Many people have at least one such friendship in place, but most adults say that they feel isolated, alone, misunderstood and disconnected. With technology, busy schedules, fear of crime and loss of privacy, and minimal communications skills all contributing to the difficulty of developing lasting and meaningful friendships, this ideal, as much as any other, causes intense frustration and a sense of failure among people.

75 Percent Want to Have "a Clear Purpose for Living"

How muddled life becomes when you don't know where you're going! That's the confusion of most adults and teenagers: what is the meaning and purpose of this life, anyway? While it is ironic that 6 out of 10 of us say we are spiritual and almost 9 out of 10 say our religious faith is very important in our lives—and yet we are stymied as to purpose and meaning—the bottom line is that we are aimlessly wandering the planet in search of true value. This goal is absolutely on target; it is our approach to unpacking and then meeting the goal that leaves much to be desired.

70 Percent Want to Have "a Close, Personal Relationship with God"

If we were serious about that goal, what a difference it would make! God has told us that if we are serious, all we need to do is draw near to Him and He will gladly respond in kind (see Jas. 4:8). Perhaps the confusion here is thinking that simply attending church services or owning a Bible or occasionally offering a prayer in desperate circumstances will suffice. Once again, this is a goal that is worthy of pursuit, but it demands much more effort than we are giving it.

We are sentenced to a life of disillusionment if we define success in terms of accomplishments, self-image and material possessions. Until we get the foundations of successful living in place, the probability of achieving even modest levels of meaning and joy is unlikely. We have been created for a single purpose: to know, love and serve our Creator God with all of our heart, mind, soul and strength. The daily activities in which we engage are merely designed to be ways of fulfilling that calling, not ways of gaining fulfillment in themselves. We can only hope to find meaning and purpose and value in this life when we focus on the next through striving for radical obedience to Christ. When Solomon, reputedly the richest and wisest man ever to live, devoted himself to answering the very same questions we ponder today—regarding purpose, meaning, value, success—he concluded his investigation this way:

"'Meaningless! Meaningless! ... Everything is meaningless!' Here is the conclusion of the matter: Fear God and keep his commandments, for this is the whole duty of man" (Eccles. 12:8,13).

The Daily Distractions and Diversions

One of the interesting solutions people have developed is to overcome their lack of fulfillment by cramming their days with activity. Perhaps the underlying idea is that if we have a sufficient variety and quantity of experiences we will stumble onto the magic elixir of life satisfaction—kind of like the chances of winning the lottery, but you know how many people play that, despite the odds!

So, how do we spend our time? What kind of lifestyle patterns have we developed? Sadly (for the authors, at least) our society is no longer characterized by a handful of simple lifestyle patterns—the working dad, stay-at-home mom, two kids in school who do their homework and play in the backyard afterwards, share a family meal at dinnertime, then congregate in the family room to watch TV and talk during the commercials. If such simple schedules ever existed, they haven't been seen for a long time. The best you can do these days is identify the common activities of people and imagine the endless combinations through which people engage in these activities.

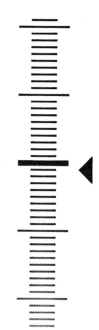

> To overcome their lack of fulfillment, many people cram their days with activity.

Even a list of our common activities gets pretty lengthy. But you will probably recognize most of these items as staples in your personal calendar.

Using the Mass Media for Information, Entertainment or Company

We have become media addicts. In an average day each adult spends more than four hours watching TV; three hours tuned to the radio; about three-quarters of an hour listening to recorded music (CDs, tapes); a half hour reading the newspaper; and another hour with other forms of media (e.g., videos, books, magazines). Add it up: that's more than nine hours each day that we allow ourselves to be bombarded with mass media input. Naturally, we are not always focused exclusively on the medium of the moment. (Television is a great example: most women, for instance, say that they are usually doing something else while the TV is on, using their multitasking capabilities to accomplish as much as possible while still absorbing the benefits of whatever TV has to offer.) Nevertheless, nine-plus hours of external programming per day explains a lot regarding our values, goals, behaviors and choices.

Working

Almost 9 out of 10 men under 65 and 2 out of 3 women under 65 have a part-time or full-time paid job. In spite of the promise of expanded leisure with the integration of technology into our lives, our work hours have actually expanded, and income in real dollars has declined. It has become fashionable to dismiss work or career pursuits as the locus of our self-image and sense of purpose in life. However, in the vacuum of alternatives, work still represents the single most significant activity toward defining who we are in our own minds.

Driving the Car

Whether it is sitting in traffic, shuttling kids from soccer to music lessons to the movies or home from school, the front seat of the car is the third most common place for you to find the typical adult (behind home and work). That's especially true for women with school-aged children, who drive an average of 70 minutes each day, making about five unique trips, although that covers only 30 miles.[7] Although most of our auto trips are confined to local environs (our daily commute to work averages 22 minutes to cover the dozen miles to work), the average household puts some 15,000 miles on its cars each year.[8] Even if you do all of your driving at very fast speeds on unpatrolled highways, that's a lot of hours spent behind the wheel. By the way, our cars eat up our schedule even when we're not driving them. Sixty-five percent of Americans actually consider their car to be part of their family, and the typical car owner devotes more than six hours each month to maintaining the car.

Shopping

This has become much more than a maintenance activity for most Americans. Research reveals that women, in particular, use shopping as a major remedy for stress. The data also shows that we get impulsive when turned loose in stores. Last Christmas, alone, 6 out of 10 consumers got swept up in the buying spirit and lavished an average of $118 of unplanned spending on themselves—they just couldn't resist all that stuff that was calling out their names![9] Shopping absorbs more time than ever, partly because of the plethora of choices we must make to buy even the most mundane of products. Branding has become the hot topic in marketing circles precisely because people are so overwhelmed with the blizzard of product choices; purchasing products with recognizable and trusted brand names simplifies an otherwise daunting task. We have varied our approaches to shopping— in store, through the mail, on-line, by telephone—but the net result is that we spend more than $3 trillion every year—that's roughly $38,000 per household. For some people, shopping has literally become a full-time job.

Going On-Line

As of the writing of this book, about half of the country goes on-line with some regularity. That proportion will continue to climb as technology becomes cheaper and easier to use, and as the technosavvy Busters and

Mosaics represent a growing share of the population. While few on-line sites are "sticky" (i.e., cause people to stay on them for a prolonged period of time), the average total time spent using on-line services for e-mail, chat rooms, digital commerce and all other forms of web use and Net surfing was about an hour per day (as of late 2000). That figure varies wildly, though, depending on the population segment being examined. The facility and comfort of young people with the Internet, combined with having grown up with it as part of their natural activity, suggests that millions more hours will be devoted to on-line experiences each year.

Completing Tasks Around the House

These include such mundane endeavors as personal hygiene duties, house cleaning responsibilities, gardening and yard maintenance and paying the bills. For the most part, we deem these tasks drudgery, but they have to get done. All told, they consume up to an hour a day.

Exercising

Not everyone engages in physical exercise, of course, and those who do often wish they could shortcut their routine. Even so, just over 50 million adults (about one-fifth of our population of people six years of age or older) are frequent exercisers. The number of participants has stagnated in the last decade, but a large majority of adults say they intend to initiate or step up their fitness regimen in the coming year. We'll see.

Eating at Restaurants

The home chef is a fondly remembered artifact of the slow life from yesteryear. In spite of the recent surge in home gourmet cooking, we still invest more time and money in eating out than ever before. More than three-quarters of all adults eat out each month, and the sum of our out-of-home meal buying was $250 billion. On a per person basis we spent an average of nearly $2,500 per household last year. That's a lot of burgers and fries.

Maintaining Our Relationships with Family and Friends

Although one-quarter of U.S. adults are introverts, almost everyone makes time to keep up with family and friends. Three-quarters of all Americans say they went somewhere to visit with friends or extended family, and three-quarters also spent time entertaining friends or extended family in their own home during the past week. This is one of the few lifestyle categories that people are likely to say gets shortchanged in their weekly schedule.

There are, of course, dozens of other activities that fill people's lives on a regular basis. Those listed above, however, constitute the actions that consume the lion's share of our week—an average of 15 or 16 hours per day. Add to that the seven hours of sleep we typically get, an hour or so for other miscellaneous activities and—well, it's time to start the cycle all over again.

We live in the age of creative lifestyles. Rather than wrap our activity patterns around a set of values, we are more prone to chase the opportunities that promise the greatest fulfillment and pleasure. This flaunting of our freedom to innovate in every dimension of life fuels our endless flirtation with moral anarchy. Just as we have taken the liberty of radically revising our values system over the last decade, by the end of the current decade you can expect Americans to again reinvent themselves, reformulating their most fundamental values, goals and daily behaviors in an inexorable search for purpose, meaning, significance and acceptance.

Moral Anarchy Redux

Now step back and look at the big picture. Recall that our lifestyle choices are the product of our values and that the most significant reality pertaining to our values is our rejection of absolute moral truth. That determination has enabled us to continually tinker with a variety of activities and attitudes in our quest for fulfillment. It was suggested in the preceding chapter that the most profound outgrowth of our rejection of moral absolutes has been the onset of moral anarchy in American society.

Through our study of lifestyle preferences, we can begin to understand how moral anarchy has become so prevalent. What may seem like a series of unfortunate but disconnected acts are really a malignant array of interwoven repudiations of the old moral order.

Take, for example, the person who hugs the fast lane and moves slower than any other car on the road. He is not simply ignorant or unaware, but unabashedly selfish and defiant—a prime example of someone whose worldview elevates self to the exclusion and detriment of the existence and rights of others. The public outcry over school shootings has consistently overlooked the reasons why so many adolescents and teenagers bring guns and knives to school or join gangs. Those discussions have camped on preventative medicine rather than identifying the disease itself: the devaluing of human life and the elevation of personal preferences.

More than just a few people and organizations advance the cause of economic decadence. There is no other way to characterize paying $40,000 for a pair of Wilt Chamberlain's sneakers, spending $40 million to build a 50-room private residence, shelling out $2.2 million to air a 30-second commercial during the Super Bowl. It becomes economically immoral when you realize that tonight literally hundreds of millions of people will go to sleep hungry, naked and dying with curable diseases. How many attorneys make a fabulous living by knowingly filing frivolous lawsuits? Does something strike you as out of whack when the recording industry celebrates the drop in inventory shrinkage (i.e., shoplifting, employee theft, vendor fraud) to only $200 million annually?

Our commitment to decadence transcends the lust for financial gain. Dozens of organizations further the cause of sexual decadence through websites, magazines and movies that feature unspeakable pornographic acts, promoted as acts of free speech.

What passes as simple rudeness or carelessness is not what it seems. Common acts such as discarding cigarette butts on the ground, passengers boarding their airplane before their row number is called and the trashing of public restrooms are symptoms of the deterioration of fundamental values.

When people consciously drive no more than eight or nine miles an hour over the speed limit because they figure they won't get pulled over for such a minor instance of law breaking, that is a moral issue—not because of the speed of their vehicle but because of their willful disobedience of the law. When a taxpayer fudges a few numbers on his income tax forms to shave a few dollars off his tax bill, assuming that such indiscretions will not trigger an audit, an issue much bigger than federal revenues is at stake.

How else, other than moral anarchy, could you describe the efforts of people, who would otherwise be described as technological experts or even geniuses, who use their know-how to send harmful viruses through the worldwide network of computers using the Internet? Is there any way to morally justify the television networks freely giving prime-time coverage to negative role models like boxing champion Mike Tyson, who earnestly tells millions of viewers how he enjoys hurting people?

One of the authors had lunch with the president of one of the largest seminaries in the U.S. and was told that he'd recently been forced to install a high-tech security system in the campus bookstore when the losses from shoplifting hit $1 million per year. On a different but no less significant scale, what kinds of problems exist when fast-food restaurants cannot put napkins in containers on the counter, because they get ripped off?

Is there a problem when preachers fabricate stories to prove the point of their sermon? What about students, businesspersons, journalists—virtually everyone—making illegal copies of pages from books, magazines, reports and other copyrighted materials? How many movie rentals on video are illegally copied by homeowners for the continued enjoyment of their children, justified by the notion that they rented the video from which they are making the illegal copy?

Do you doubt that we could go on listing instances that demonstrate the atrocious dissipation of our moral standards? And can you think of any individual, organization or movement other than the Christian Church that has

America might adopt forms of hypertolerance that would make the Sodomites blush.

a vested interest in overcoming the public impulse toward moral anarchy? Even if people or organizations do not like the onslaught of moral anarchy, they can twist it to their advantage without remorse or loss. But the very underpinnings of the Church are moral in nature, and its calling is to restore the moral purity of people so they may become more like the One who created them.

Restoring the moral commitment of Americans may be the biggest challenge on the horizon for the Church. Recognizing the nature and magnitude of that challenge is the first step toward solving the problem. The stakes are huge. If the Church fails to rise up and play the role of social reformer, America is likely to adopt forms of hypertolerance that would make the Sodomites blush. The patron saint of truth will be Pontius Pilate, whose immortal words of disdain, "What is truth?" (John 18:38) will reign as the creed of the masses. The postmodern bent toward rejecting the very existence of truth will serve as the basis for moral and ethical decision making.

Where Are We Headed?

Our current values (and the resulting behaviors) have increased our stress and anxiety levels substantially—and it is likely to get worse before it gets better. In the next 10 years you can count on a majority of Americans to buckle under these self-wrought pressures and to redesign their values and lifestyles accordingly. This will be a decade of both creation and reaction, a time of push and pull in which contradictions will reign supreme and the search for clarity and stability will emerge big-time.

Here Is What Awaits Us

Americans will verbally celebrate the creative genius of our species, yet crave a slower pace of life. Thus, we will encourage the development of new technologies and applications at the same time that we will reduce our willingness to buy the next big digital idea. People will spend more time and effort pursuing simplicity, maximizing the benefit of the tools and alternatives already accessible to them. We will welcome continued change but with a greater level of skepticism due to our realization that every change brings with it a parcel of changes we did not anticipate.

We will require change agents to link their new ways to the old structures and procedures. Continuity will be a higher value in the years to come as we grasp for some semblance of wholeness, predictability and stability. We will show less enthusiasm over grand benefits promised in the hope that such emotional and behavioral reserve will coerce the champions of change to provide persuasive evidence that their changes will foster a superior quality of life.

Our affection for infinite options from which to choose will finally numb us to the realization that there is such a possibility as too much of a good thing. Our response will be to seek a landscape with fewer but higher quality alternatives. In the '80s and '90s the pendulum swung in the direction of enlarging the playing field; the pendulum will now begin to swing back in the direction of quality rather than quantity.

At a subconscious level, millions of us are fearful about what life is becoming in the midst of the massive doses of change and moral anarchy that are engulfing us. While few Americans can put their finger on it, tens of millions harbor an uneasy feeling that the recent bubble of security and prosperity is going to burst at any moment, destroying our comforting illusion of power, control and limitless opportunities. The dominant defense against such a tragedy will be to develop a more meaningful web of personal relationships. People will turn to community as their primary solution to their emotional unrest. The adages "misery loves company" and the more optimistic "there is security in numbers" encapsulate our determination to make new friends and get connected to groups that will help us handle our problems. The Mosaic generation is instructive in this regard: their development of a new form of tribalism is a model of things to come.

We will probably continue to sedate ourselves with the opiate of entertainment. With an ever-growing field of entertainment options, thanks to technology and our shift to a service-based economy, we will continue to celebrate the exploits of athletes, actors, musicians and artists beyond rationale. Our household budgets will reflect the heightened priority of being distracted by mindless and meaningless leisure diversions.

To derive a semblance of control over our lives, people will seek to restrain public access to personal information, promoting privacy to major-issue status. Laws will be passed to protect people's right to privacy, consumer campaigns (and counter campaigns by the marketing industry) will be waged to prevent organizations from collecting and mining extensive data, and organizations will trumpet their policies and procedures designed to avoid personal intrusions. Several public officials will make a name for themselves by becoming the defenders of personal privacy.

Marketing manipulation will get out of control as marketers strive to overcome people's skepticism. Even in daily conversation you will notice that your friends will exhibit diminished trust in your statements of fact (don't take it personally) and will expect demonstrations of proof.

The hectic and harried lifestyles we lead will combine with our deflated sense of moral responsibility to cause people to be less reliable. Promises will be broken, appointments not kept, volunteers harder to enlist—all because we are just too busy to juggle all of our commitments. Rather than scale back our promises, we will instead simply fail to follow through—and will think nothing of it.

You may hear the triple-zero decade referred to as the "Lowest Common Denominator (LCD) decade" since people will attempt to handle life by rising up to the lowest possible standard for getting by. Meaning and purpose will be demoted to the level of achieving comfortable survival. Money will gain even more credence as the symbol of success. Faith will mean knowing the name of a church, recalling a few Bible stories and owning a Bible.

Living the good life will be irresistible for millions of people who will never be able to afford that life. Home foreclosures, repossessed cars and canceled credit cards will be increasingly common as people figure that everyone else is living off "free money" so they might as well, too.

If you think Americans are overweight now, hold on to your silverware. The growing stress levels, diminishing capacity to deny ourselves the things we like, rising levels of marital conflict (and divorce) and financial pressures will move us back to the kitchen table for another helping of calorie-saturated comfort.

This will be the decade of "Clintonian integrity." (Okay, maybe that's not the label that will stick, but the concept will make waves.) Just as our former president showed how to wiggle out of telling the truth when it was inconvenient, people will follow the lead of our former leader and learn to mislead people by redefining terms, avoiding direct answers and shifting the focus of the conversation to less relevant matters. Americans will go through a change in their decision making, because they will soon realize that they can't trust many—if any—people to tell the truth. Intuition will become a prized asset.

Our work lives will change as more people work from home and increasing numbers piece together a living based on holding down multiple part-time jobs.

What Can You Do?

In a decade when everyone's lifestyle will be so uniquely representative of themselves that there will not be "lifestyle patterns" per se, Christians will nevertheless have continual opportunities to show what a difference their faith makes in coping with the omnipresent chaos. You will see lots of chances to integrate your faith and worldview into a situational solution that will stun your acquaintances. Here are some examples of possibilities that may emerge in your life.

America's hunt for simplicity will ironically involve the development of an entirely new industry to support that quest. You can outsmart the masses by eschewing the self-help books, the conferences and the courses on a lifestyle of simplicity by spending time studying how the master of simplicity—Jesus—managed to hang on to His focus and His agenda without capitulating to the world's demands and snares. His ways were effectively adopted by many of the Early Church fathers, too, so their stories and writings might be of assistance. Become a role model without getting trapped in the inevitable complexities of the simplicity movement.

Demonstrate your leadership skills by using a powerful leadership tool: In the midst of hardship or chaos, change the central question. While others ask How can I succeed in a world of chaos and confusion? you might ask What does success look like in the kingdom of God, and what can I do to achieve it? By rejecting the core assumptions and objectives of the multitudes, you automatically distance yourself from the failed strategies that they will propose as the paths to success. If you are truly living for Christ, success in the world is all about being obedient to Jesus, anyway.

As our society reverts to relationships as a means of dealing with cultural stress and change, be sure that your relational community is not one based on people who are accessible, nice and make you comfortable. Christian community is at its best when you are surrounded with people who share common spiritual goals and sincerity about growth, and who make you a bit uncomfortable by the maturity of their witness and the wisdom of the questions they raise. While the world is seeking relationships as an anesthetic to deaden pain, you should develop relationships that make you more alive and perhaps even heighten your sensitivity to the moral and spiritual inconsistencies in your life.

With the heat being turned up in our culture, people will shy away from standing out, preferring to simply get through another day without suffering. As a representative of Jesus, you will have many platforms on which to softly demonstrate the difference your faith makes. Two ways will be by delivering on every promise you make, and always speaking the truth. That kind of reliability and honesty will be so unique that your life will be a compelling reflection of what a life transformed by Christ is all about. Yes, they should know we are Christians by our love, but they should also recognize us by our unfailing integrity, too.

If you have invested money that you have saved in retirement funds or other accounts, watch your invested funds carefully. The 50,000 or so businesses that have been declaring bankruptcy each year over the last few years will seem like a drop in the bucket in the years to come as the global economy changes the rules of business success.

Notes

1. George Carlin, "The Paradox of Our Time." http://department.stthomas.edu/csla/reflections/paradox.htm (accessed November 22, 2000).
2. These figures are from the Families and Work Institute based on a national study they conducted among full-time workers.
3. "America@Work: An Overview of Employee Commitment in America" conducted by Aon Consulting, Chicago, IL, in 1999.
4. "Maritz Ameripoll #101: Love and Romance" conducted by Maritz Marketing Research, Fenton, MO, in 1999.
5. To read a summary of the goals we have in life, how born-again Christians differ from non-Christians on these goals and how our priorities have changed since the

early '90s, see George Barna, "Americans Identify What They Want Out of Life," the *Barna Research Group.* http://www.barna.org.

6. These volumes are drawn from research conducted by the U.S. Department of Agriculture.

7. "High Mileage Moms," *Surface Transportation Policy Project* (Washington, DC, 1999).

8. Department of Commerce, U.S. Census Bureau, *Statistical Abstract of the United States, 1999,* U.S. Census Bureau (Washington, DC, 1999), tables 71, 1027, 1370.

9. Maritz Marketing Research, *Research Alert Yearbook, 2000 Edition* (New York: EPM Communications, 2000), p. 49.

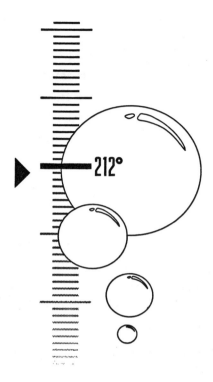

212°

CHAPTER SIX

TECHNOLOGY AND YOU

Future Glimpse

Jill loved technology. And Jill hated technology. Based on conversations with her girlfriends, she knew she was not alone in this state of suspended ambivalence over the true master of the universe: technology.

A commentator she heard on the news the other day described her state perfectly: technostress. On the one hand, her life was all about managing the technological devices that made her existence more efficient, exciting, fulfilling and economical. On the other hand, the unfathomable speed at which the world of technology changed made her feel like she was in the ocean, sinking quickly, with the waterline almost beyond her line of sight. If she didn't buy the latest digital stuff, she'd feel like a dinosaur—her tech-crazed husband and tech-natured kids would see to that. If she didn't take the time to learn the new applications, she'd feel like an imbecile and be left in the dust of society. But who had the time or inclination to become a walking encyclopedia of software applications? If she even heard the term "killer app" one more time, she'd scream!

In her calmer moments Jill could list the numerous benefits that technology had provided to her and her family in the past decade. Brittany had grown a new tooth where there was none before through the use of some new- fangled bone-growing process at the university dental school. Jackson, Procrastinator General, had become incredibly adept at throwing together impressive presentations for school by mushing together music, video clips, information and color photos into automated presentations that wowed his professors (and probably did nothing to fool his classmates). Jill and Carl saved hundreds of dollars on travel each year by gambling on-line, rather than at Las Vegas. (Of course, they more than made up for their travel savings through their losses sustained at the digital gaming tables.) The smart house, the GPS in her car, the global shopping options, the instantly accessible and customizable entertainment alternatives—all of it was wonderful. But it still left her in a state of cybershock.

She worried about what was coming: Holographic experiences so dynamic you couldn't tell if they were real or virtual. Pornographic experiences that simulated sex. Intelligent computers creating even more intelligent computers, without human intervention. On-line organizations that knew more about you than you knew about yourself—and invaded your privacy whenever they felt you'd appreciate the intrusion. Brain and body implants supposedly to help remedy disease and other infirmities. Who was in charge here, anyway? Anyone at all?

Even at work and in the retail shops, she just couldn't get used to the omnipresence of computers and digital reality. Hotel guests would stand in front of her at work and be talking—but to whom? The person connected to them through the wireless phone, with the microphone attached to their collar? To the chip in the headset they were wearing that was accumulating the data they'd need for their meeting in a few minutes? To her, live and in person? It all got too confusing sometimes.

If forced to choose, she'd probably opt to stay in this wacky new silicon-charged world. Maybe what she really needed was a new robot to manage her emotional and mental stress from her technology overdose. The irony of the idea didn't even phase her anymore.

The Ground Rush with Technology

If one of your parents or grandparents lived through most of the twentieth century, imagine what it must have been like for them. They would have seen and experienced things that *their* grandparents couldn't have dreamed up, even in their wildest fantasies. To move from the one-room schoolhouse, rural simplicities at the start of the century to the wired sophistication of urban America at the end of that era would bring on true culture shock. What an exciting, frightening, amazing and unique time to have been alive.

The grandfather of one of the authors came across the Oregon Trail in a covered wagon when he was two years old. He used to regale the family with stories of his parents' friend Buffalo Bill. He saw the development of the automobile, survived the first "war to end all wars," experienced the highs of the Roaring Twenties and the lows of the Great Depression.

He lived to see the second "war to end all wars," the birth of the cold war, Sputnik, the floundering of the American Dream after President Kennedy's short-lived "Camelot" administration and Americans landing on the moon. You only need to go back 100 years to predate antibiotics, military radar, powered airplanes, nuclear weapons and television. He lived to see the impact of the Rural Electrification Act, the enormous effort to build roads and the Interstate Highway System and the loss of China to Communism. He died just as personal computers were beginning to make their mark in the early '80s.

What a ride! But if you think Grandpa witnessed rapid development... hang on. The pace of development and change during the next 10 to 20 years will easily surpass the cumulative amount of technological change that occurred during the last 100 years. The rate of innovation and of innovation diffusion is accelerating.

How can that be? Rapid advances in computer technology, telephony, biotechnology and nanotechnology will redefine a world that many of us already struggle to recognize after the changes that have occurred in the past two decades.

Parachutists talk about not becoming transfixed by "ground rush"—that is, when the unfamiliar acceleration of the ground racing up to meet them temporarily mesmerizes the novice until it is too late. As Christians we must not get caught up in the excitement and rush of the moment. We must be disciplined enough to rely upon our spiritual training and to respond to the world on the basis of our faith-driven worldview. It is literally our job to be God's instrument of grace and restraint by making His views known and His ways implemented in this wildly changing environment.

> **Christians must work to preserve sensibility, character and restraint.**

Chaos loves a vacuum. In the middle of frantic upheaval, such as our culture is in today, many people seem transfixed with "ground rush." Their response to the changes afoot is to explore new and sometimes radically irreverent styles of living. It is precisely in these times of tumult that we, as God's salt on the earth, must preserve sensibility, character and restraint. The technological changes that are transforming our reality day by day are fueling the most amazing acceleration of innovation world history has ever seen. In turn, these innovations may be laying the groundwork for the most incredible global revival ever seen—or preparing humanity for its final act.

Distributing Innovation

To give us some perspective on how historic our present technological changes are, let's touch base with the seminal work on how innovations get distributed and integrated into a society. Almost four decades ago, in 1962, Dr. Everett Rogers published *Diffusion of Innovations*. In his groundbreaking book, Dr.

Rogers explained how innovations work. Among his conclusions was that it takes roughly 30 years for an innovation to be fully diffused into a culture. Ironically, his own innovative insights reigned, virtually uncontested, for about 30 years. But then, in what seemed like an overnight shift, his estimate regarding the rapidity with which change happens became ancient history.

Communications advancements over the last decade, along with bandwidth changes and the multiplying impact of network effects have altered the formula for change, ushering in an accelerated rate of innovation. Rogers was partially responsible for this state of affairs. After all, he was the first to identify the steps in the process of innovation diffusion, and it is the comprehension of those very steps that facilitated the rush of change that now defines our reality.

What this means for you is that the last 100 years of innovation proceeded at a glacial pace compared to what we will experience in the near future. Innovations like automobiles, electricity and airplanes will seem to have moved society forward at an agonizingly slow speed.

We need not speak in generalities. Let's check out some examples of rapid innovation diffusion that are on the horizon.

Viral Models Spread Innovation

Not long ago Hotmail, the free e-mail service, exemplified the changes happening in the world of innovation. At an industry conference held during their first year in business, Hotmail executives made a presentation to an incredulous crowd of computer industry luminaries. The Hotmail free e-mail service had already signed up 1 million members, and the company's executives were predicting that they would become the number two provider of e-mail services by the end of the year (trailing only America Online).

That claim was ludicrous on its face, with some serious competitors like AT&T, Microsoft and dozens of well-funded Internet service providers already in place and committed to crushing any competition, upstarts like Hotmail included. When the fledgling company's leaders were asked how they would make money, they did not seem to answer the question. All they could talk about was their growth rate, the number of (money losing) computer servers they were adding to support their incredible growth and the voluminous quantity of e-mail traffic they were facilitating. They didn't have a real business plan or a means of generating profits. Their first priority was to create a recognizable and likable brand. They planned to figure out how to make money later, after their brand and the resulting customer base were firmly established.

Many of the industry experts in attendance simply left the presentation at that point. Using a traditional model of business assessment, they were convinced that the absence of a revenue plan, combined with exponential growth and enormous costs, would bring Hotmail to a stinging (and costly) defeat. Boy, were they wrong! Not too long after that momentous presentation Microsoft decided that Hotmail's 10 million members were worth at least $40 each and bought them out. Hotmail was less than two years old.

Hotmail used what is known as a virus to generate its incredible growth. The virus was a simple text message offering free e-mail services that was included at the end of every e-mail sent by a Hotmail subscriber. The term virus has been adopted because this marketing process is much like a virus in the human body, spread multiple times from a single host creating a full-fledged epidemic. The objective of viral marketing is to exploit the nature of instant communications and the intrinsic value of an expanding network to achieve its goals. A message and call to action, advanced via viral methods, illustrates the potential of a fully networked world to adopt and diffuse innovations at astonishing speeds.

The Internet abounds with examples of the breakneck pace of innovation. Some very bright engineers in Israel replicated the viral marketing phenomenon with a product called ICQ Chat. America Online bought them for a reported $100 million plus, after a similar exponential growth pattern. Myfamily.com grew to 1 million members less than six months from its launch date by providing a platform for sharing family photographs and doing ancestor research on a sister site, Ancestry.com. One of the authors of this book is on the executive team of Ants.com, a viral community of freelance professionals that has relied on a viral referral and network marketing business model to grow more quickly than its rivals without the heavy brand-building expenses common to Internet start-ups. (As evidence of the power and feasibility of this concept, Ants.com experienced an average of about 4 percent growth per week while we researched and wrote this book.)

Moore's Law

These are real-world examples of runaway acceleration. Are they unique examples, or is there something more fundamental going on?

To arrive at an answer, it is helpful to review a well-known axiom in the digital world, known as Moore's Law. It states simply—but significantly—"computing power doubles every 18 months, while prices are halved." The namesake of the law, Gordon Moore, is no armchair theoretician. He cofounded Intel, the largest and most successful computer chip manufacturer in the world. He made this audacious proclamation over 30 years ago. Amazingly, he was right. Most technology futurists agree that this trend will continue for at least another 15 years.

We live in a linear world. When we think of change, we think in tangible, linear terms: double this, quadruple that. We've become numb to the massive changes that swirl around us. Moore's Law may sound like just another slick rule of thumb that has no special meaning to you. But it does have meaning for you, whether you own a computer or not.

We are used to marginal improvements in products sustained over long periods of time. In a linear world, twice as much effort rarely produces double the output. For instance, if you are a runner and are in that elite class of runners who have broken the four-minute mile, twice as much training is not going to get you to run a two-minute mile—ever.

But when we examine the world of computers and all that they affect, we operate on a different scale. The acceleration of processing power is not limited by linear increments of growth; it abides in the geometric world. A comparison of mathematical equations might clarify this. In a linear world, we would suggest that 2+2+2+2+2+2+2+2+2 = 18 or, if we get bold, 2 x 9 = 18. In the geometric world, however, $2^9 = 512$. Imagine how sustained geometric growth over time pulls away from the purely linear world at an ever-increasing rate. Using the example above, over the same nine increments of time, the geometric world experiences a 28-fold increase.

The world is changing at a geometric rate, which is what causes many of us to talk about the world "reinventing" itself on a regular basis. Two decades from now we are likely to witness the introduction of quantum computers. Those are an entirely new class of supercomputers that will make today's supercomputers look and feel like children's toys in comparison. In fact, the equivalent to today's supercomputers will be imbedded in children's toys by that time.

GEOMETRIC GROWTH

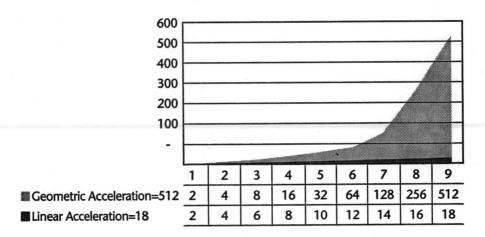

	1	2	3	4	5	6	7	8	9
▨ Geometric Acceleration=512	2	4	8	16	32	64	128	256	512
■ Linear Acceleration=18	2	4	6	8	10	12	14	16	18

Now think about some of the implications of this type of transformation. What would happen if the airline industry could reduce travel time at the same rate of improvement that the computer chip industry will achieve with microprocessor speed over the next 20 years? Instead of traveling at 600 miles an hour, as we do today, we would travel at 600,000 miles an hour in 2020. For those of us who fly coast to coast on a regular basis, the ordeal would no longer be so imposing; today's five-hour cross-country flight would take all of three seconds. We're not saying this will happen, of course; the laws of physics will preclude that possibility. But those laws will allow us to ramp up processing speeds immensely.

It can be difficult to fathom these rapid improvements. Let us put it into perspective: Sony's memory stick, used in many of Sony's consumer electronics devices today—simple audio and video components, for example—has more data capacity than the computer NASA used to manage the moon landing. Not bad for something smaller than your next stick of gum. Now that is a gigantic leap.

There is solid evidence that this level of innovation and acceleration in chip technology will continue for at least the next 20 years. For many years the ability to process one gigabyte of information per second has been the definition of a supercomputer (and, by the way, was deemed so powerful that the federal government classified such processing power as "munitions"). Apple Computers, however, recently crossed the one-gigabyte-per-second threshold with *personal* computers—the type that sit on the desk in dens across America. Ten years from now we will have 128-gigabyte computers at our disposal, and in two decades we will have 16,384-gigabyte computers.

Sometimes you probably feel like throwing your hands up in despair with all the talk about the computer revolution and the changes that faster and higher-capacity computers will bring into our lives. But we will continue down the path of heightened reliance upon computer technology. To date, Americans have purchased more than 1.6 billion consumer electronic products, at a cost of more than 400 billion dollars. (That does not include the hardware investments of American businesses and government agencies.) And the appetite for those products is rising, not falling. You may not have to understand the intricacies of how computers work or how much faster they will process information in the future; but one way or another, you should be prepared to go along for the ride.

The Bandwidth Revolution

Actually, our discussion about the increased processing speed and power related to computers was just to warm you up to an even more magnificent horizon of change—that related to bandwidth. While Moore's Law is about processing power, bandwidth concerns the speed with which we transmit information. If you think doubling computer-processing speed every 18 months is fast, then check this out.

At his annual Telecosm conference in the late '90s, technology guru George Gilder wowed his audience by describing the coming bandwidth explosion. The first speaker on the program talked about facilitating megabyte speed access to the Internet for consumers and businesses. He was followed by a company that presented gigabyte speeds as the soon-to-be norm, noting early in the presentation that megabit speeds were antiquated. Next came the terabyte company, then the teraflop company (1,000 terabytes) and finally the petabyte group (10 teraflops per second). That is 10,000,000,000,000,000 bytes of information per second.

It turns out that bandwidth—and, therefore, the speed at which we can send data—is doubling every 12 to 15 months, a rate even faster than that associated with processing power. The type of speed described at Gilder's conference is capable of transmitting the entire collection of the Smithsonian Institute in mere seconds. It is enough bandwidth to pump totally immersive, photo-realistic, stereoscopic, three-dimensional worlds right into your living room. You could call this "pseudopresence." This is virtual reality so compelling that you gain the sense of being in the same room with the person with whom you are conversing. Only the laws of physics that introduce a barely perceivable delay in communications over very long distances will slightly flaw this form of communication.

Increased bandwidth has been enabled by technological breakthroughs like Wave Division Multiplexing. This is a process whereby you take a single strand of optical cable and instead of sending a single laser light down its length you send multiple colors, allowing multiple streams of data to flow through communications lines that previously could handle only a single stream of data at a time. As a result, the telecommunications industry can now move 16 times more data via the same strand of fiber based on this innovation alone.

Metcalf's Law

And there's more. An engineer named Metcalf invented Ethernet, the protocol most networks use to move information from one computer to the next. He has been much quoted for his estimate that the real value of a network is a function of the square of the value of all those connected to the network. Therefore the value of four interconnected computers is 16 units (4^2), and the value of five connected computers is 25 units (5^2), six is 36 units (6^2), etc. Metcalf has underscored the significance of interconnectivity.

Perhaps you never thought about the significance of being networked. We hear about networks all the time, but do they really matter? To understand the impact of networks, consider the fax machine, potentially a very useful communications tool. Did you ever stop to realize that the value of a single fax machine is zero? If you owned the only existing fax machine, in spite of its enormous potential, even if you plug it in and attach it to a phone line, it will just sit there, absolutely futile and useless, until there is a second fax machine with which it can communicate. In other words, that tool only accrues real value when someone who has a fax machine needs a document from someone else who has a fax machine. Over time, when everyone has one, it becomes a standard and you cannot live without it. The fax machine has become a standard business tool these days, but it took a long time to achieve that status. In essence, we had to wait until there was a network of the machines in place for it to become an indispensable business tool.

Internet-connected computers have reached this status in the office and are rapidly becoming a must-have in the home. Generally this is a good thing; it improves communications, increases efficiency and enables people in new ways. It is not a panacea though.

But this relates to Hatch's corollary to Metcalf's Law: "The potential for value destruction equals Metcalf's Law minus the mitigating influence of God." Interconnectedness is a morally neutral phenomenon. It can, will and has been used for evil just as easily and as often as for good. In fact, without the mitigating influence of God, it would surely lead to the fueling of man's desire to sin.

In other words, there is nothing inherently beneficial about the connectivity achievable through the world's fastest-growing network, the Internet. The number of computers connected to the global Internet, already numbering in the millions, continues to accelerate. In addition, there are more than 100,000 registered networks using the Net.[1] Over the coming decade the explosion will continue, as every imaginable

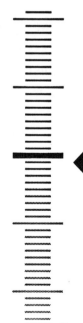

The Internet can and will be used for evil just as well as good.

product and resource will get connected. Your car, refrigerator, toaster, shoes, intestines, heart, dog and phone will be connected by the end of the decade, if you want them to be.

The World Wide Web through the Mosaic browser and then through Netscape has grown the Internet at a heretofore unheard-of pace. It rides the back of large infrastructure investments in telecommunications and personal computers. When first proposed as a major new channel for business, a new platform for conducting business and a potential for transforming the global economy, most of the political and industry power brokers yawned or laughed. Grandiose claims are a dime a dozen in our culture; performance is what counts. Today, few would minimize the astounding performance of the Internet and the World Wide Web. The Web has grown at a stunning pace and has become a platform for faster innovations still.

So Metcalf's law is driving much of the dot com value today. Though certainly overhyped during the short term, just as railroads were oversold at the start of the industrial revolution, real value is being created. As a report from Morgan Stanley pointed out, the creation of the Erie Canal (a completion of a network for the distribution of physical goods) caused an 87 percent decrease in the cost of distribution to the Midwest.[2] This type of value is being created today through the digital revolution.

Networks

There are numerous types of networks in the world today, computer, satellite, cellular, radio, cable and telephone. Combined they turbocharge global communications. These networks enable some of the most exciting, fascinating, profound, scary, innovative and evil of human activities. These networks, for better or worse, will enable the previously mentioned pseudo-presence machine.

While networks have fostered better access to current information for children doing their reports for school, or strategic analysis by companies in the marketplace, networks have also enabled moral decay to prosper in new ways. Credible statistics on exposure to pornography can be hard to find, but one recent survey revealed that 20 percent of adult males with Internet access at work had used that access to consume pornography.[3] Many analysts calculate the current revenues of the Internet pornography industry to be well in excess of $1 billion, making it one of the largest profitable Internet industry segments. A growing number of Internet search engines exclude sex-related key words in their list of the top searches because experience has shown that those searches dominate the engines and consume the capacity of those services. The penchant for private pornographic material delivered on-line, along with increasingly violent virtual games, is desensitizing enormous numbers of people to sin and debauchery.

The dirty underbelly of the Net is sex, but it is certainly not the only vice available on-line. Gambling has exploded. You can easily find gambling opportunities on-line, and they have moved offshore to get outside the reach of the federal government. It is still generally illegal to take and make bets on-line in the U.S., but such activity is not easy to track. We seem to be headed for a global implementation of the least common denominator rule. Something may be illegal in one country but not in another. In a fully networked world some countries may race to the bottom of the barrel to become the preferred safe haven for the most morally detestable "entertainment" imaginable.

The positive spin on the reach of networks, of course, is that global communication of religious, democratic and capitalistic ideologies are also unstoppable. Truly, we rapidly approach the day that the whole world will hear the good news of Jesus Christ. Will forward thinkers embrace these innovative networks for good purposes as ambitiously as those who have paved the road for evil?

Computers

All the talk about networks, bandwidth and processing power is frivolous, though, unless the basic tool—the computer—is accessible and useful. Although consumer computers were a science fiction fantasy just a couple of decades ago, home computer systems routinely outsell television sets in the U.S. The current generation of children will be known as the computer generation just like those born in the '50s and '60s were considered the television generation. These children cannot imagine life without a computer. It is normal to see a three-year-old working a mouse and playing simple games on a computer. The number of homes with multiple computers and even networks is exploding. Phone companies and cable companies are battling for control of the neighborhood network. Not only does a majority of all households have at least one computer, but an even greater number of people have access to them at work. Computers, of varying degrees of sophistication, are now found in cell phones, VCRs, pagers, handheld palm devices, calculators and under the hood of your car.

Computers have become so central to our lives that we often have no idea just how dependent we have become upon them. They manage stores, trade stocks, do taxes, help with worship on Sundays, automatically order inventory and even track and pay the performance licensing fee to the copyright holders of worship service songs sung during every church service each week. Computers are in your exercise equipment, musical instruments, lighting, heating, air-conditioning, sprinkler systems and power tools. A standard feature in many new-model cars is a GPS receiver and monitor.

Computers are not just in the environment around us. Some people are already wearing a dozen or more computer chips. Think about it: the combination of a digital watch, palm organizer, cell-phone and pager could easily require 10 computer chips.

What's next? Wearables? Implants? Yes. That is where we are headed. Nike is experimenting with chips in shoes. MIT is experimenting with sensors woven into the very fabric of a jacket, not to mention the sensors a person swallows or has implanted to track vital body functions.

Medical researchers have successfully started to explore control of a computer cursor through a direct connection to the brain. They coat small glass cones with a material that encourages neural growth, implant the cones in the brain and allow new neural pathways to develop around them. They then attach sensors to the glass cones and use software that detects and discerns neural activity. Simple cursor movement using this technique has been demonstrated.

In many metropolitan areas these days, you will see people wearing a headset for their phone. A few of them are connected to voice recognition systems like Wildfire that help to manage making, holding and responding to phone messages a hands-free exercise. If the person wearing that headset has a unified messaging system, they may be answering and sending e-mail through their phone while piloting their GPS-enhanced auto; listening to their digitally recorded, synthetically produced music and taking notes on their palm organizer. So who has time to drive? Is that why we have electronic cruise control, radar detectors and computer-controlled airbags, as well as General Motors' On-Star service that will detect that deployed airbag, call the ambulance and wire medical records to the nearest hospital? Oops, this isn't the future; you can buy these things today.

Nanotechnology

During the coming decade you will hear more and more about nanotechnology.

This is a manufacturing process whereby we build products from the molecular level up, constructing things smaller than 1-billionth of a meter. This capacity will lead to an entirely new form of manufacturing. Currently there are only a handful of ways to make something: you can cut, fasten, grow or cook things. Nanotechnology enables us to literally take one molecule at a time, place it on top of another molecule and create something. The interesting elements to this that have been explored at length in science-fiction writing, some cutting-edge magazines and the few institutions that are focused on the use of nanotechnology are in the areas of health care, manufacturing, military and environmental cleanup. A myriad of uses will develop over time; however, these are the most interesting uses being discussed today.

From the medical side, nanotechnology futurists imagine a day when we will inject a spoonful of nanotech machines into a person's body to enable those micromachines to literally insert themselves all over the body for a wide range of medicinal uses. They might be used to monitor bad developments (e.g., cancer), to clean out arteries, to assist in enabling organs to function better or even to insert themselves into the bony structure and create a carbon filament lattice structure that would significantly improve the strength of the bone tissue.

Pioneers even imagine a day when we might pour a five-gallon can of these onto a large oil spill and the nanomachines will process and clean up the spill. Some futurists envision nanotechnology in manufacturing, whereby these devices can replicate themselves and, with the assistance of remote artificial intelligence agents, be able to modify a manufacturing floor, move boxes around and do pretty much anything required.

The biggest problems that nanotechnology might create fall into two classes: first, the use of nanotechnology as a weapon; second, the use of uncontrollable nanotechnology manufacturing processes.

On the military side, imagine nanotechnology devices that had the exact imprint of particular persons, and these devices were released to search the world to assassinate the targeted individuals. These devices would be so small that there would be no way of stopping them. Such a device, at will and undetected, could crawl up a nasal passage, insert itself into the cranium and turn somebody's brain into soup.

The control dilemma is often described by futurists as the "gray goo problem," which is where a nanotechnology device has been given the ability to replicate and that replication process runs amok. Theoretically, the original device would continuously reproduce itself and, given how small these are and how difficult they may be to destroy, the world could literally have nanotechnology devices, similar to the killer bee problem in the Western Hemisphere, replicating themselves and spreading over an entire region. There may be no recourse to stop them. It all sounds like wild science fiction stuff, but who would have taken ideas such as the Internet, partial-birth abortions or a global positioning satellite system seriously just 50 years ago?

In spite of its emergence and the tantalizing possibilities (and dangers) it represents, the probability of nanotechnology having a significant impact on our lives within the next 10 years is fairly low. It will not be until beyond 2010—probably closer to 2020—that you will begin to see significant nanotechnology products released. However, now is the time to think through the implications of this development and to direct those developments in an intelligent and strategic manner for the good of our children's future.

Ubiquitous Computing

Something else on the horizon is ubiquitous computing. This describes an end state where there are computers and computer sensors everywhere, and they talk to each other. The cost of functioning computer chips will be minimal, perhaps as little as a dime apiece, and those chips will enable simple computations about the state of an object and then relate that information to cooperating chips. For many products, overall systems costs are lower if every item's location, description and current condition can be known on demand.

For the military this represents the nirvana of "total battlefield visibility." Until the latter half of the century, true battlefield knowledge was hard to come by. Generals set themselves up on vantage points that allowed them to physically observe the progress on the battlefield below, issuing orders, moving personnel, shoring up weak parts of the engagement from their perch. Communications were often dispatched via a human chain, one person to another person, until the message reached its ultimate destination on the field below. Obviously, much has changed. Today, field telemetry can inform us of the condition and status of individual pieces of equipment. In the foreseeable future it will work its way down to the individual.

Medical telemetry will be carried on the body of each soldier, with sensors and diagnostic routines woven into their clothing. Depending upon what the detection devices turn up, instant triage, assessment and deployment of rescue personnel can be triggered instantly. Just as important, there will be real-time inventory routing and adjustments. As material is lost (i.e., tanks are blown up) new material will get rerouted to where the needs are most acute on a real time dynamic basis. Total battlefield visibility could expand to include complete theater visibility and the amazing capability of fully dynamic resource allocations.

This same type of technology is coming to our lives and work. The fastest-growing market for cell-phone sales is teenagers. The fashion item of the '90s in the high school classroom was the pager. The law in California will soon require a chip in the phone that will enable emergency services to find you if you call them. Using these chips you will be able to know where your child's phone is at all times. Of course that means the phone company will be able to keep logs on everywhere you have ever been with your phone. Using simple statistical modeling, they will be able to predict where you are going with great accuracy.

You can order groceries via the Internet. Grocery shopping is one of the most despised activities in the home. So why go? The store will come to you at the click of a mouse. But why should you even need to click the mouse? IBM, Microsoft and a large group of other technology companies are working on a technology dubbed "bluetooth." This is a process designed to run on the smallest of chips that will enable appliances and other products with embedded computers to talk with one another. What does this mean? It means that your refrigerator will detect the newly acquired hot-dog buns, recognize that you intend to barbecue them, and let your supplier know that you need more mustard. Or if you ask, it will tell you that your children were into the cookie jar while you were out.

Sensors on automobiles will help you avoid accidents. Sensors in the automobile seat will detect a child seat and disable the air bag (already available in some cars). Roads will have sensors to detect traffic, damage and driving conditions. Augmented visual displays may help you drive more safely at night. Sensors in guns will keep them from firing. Sensors at a restaurant will detect when your glass is nearly empty and page your waitress with an increasingly urgent note that you need to be filled up. Golf courses today have sensors embedded in them to detect moisture and to only water where and when it is needed.

Once these ideas were the sole purview of science fiction, but now it's science fact. Everything will have a chip in it. A world of computerized sensors—what will that be like? Dr. Donald Brin, in his radically insightful and terrifying book, *The Transparent Society,* describes a world in which everything knowable is public knowledge. He paints a picture of the future where individuals wear computers and display devices that beam information directly onto the retina of the eye. While walking down the street you will access public databases and use face recognition technology, instant cell phone records and some simple probability software to tell you who that stranger is that just walked past. It could then tell you their police record, what their enemies think of them, their street address, probability-based income estimates, where they have been and where they are likely to be going. Dr. Brin argues that since this is inevitable and we may not be able to trust the government to treat this information safely, all of this information will likely become public knowledge. This brings a new depth to the concept of a global village. Literally everywhere you have been and are going—almost anything you have done and will likely do—can be known or predicted.

Did you go to church last Sunday? Are you a Democrat or a Republican? Are you for abortion or against it? What did you buy the last time you went to the store? Marketers certainly want to know what you picked up. Maybe your neighbor or your governor would like to know, too. If this feels like science fiction, here's a great little factoid. If you are in public anywhere in London today, the police can find your face in the crowd within 10 minutes.[4]

Recovering from Babel

Did you ever wonder what it was like at Babel? Did God simply introduce multiple languages or did He degrade language? Did He introduce misunderstanding, ambiguity and misperceptions? He probably did. There is evidence that the very structure of a language causes the brain to become wired in a certain way. For instance, Germans may be great engineers because the Germanic languages are more structured than other languages. If that is true, then attempts at translation may suffer because not only is the target language different, but the recipient of the translation also has a fundamentally different mental communication structure.

Since scientists postulate that the wiring of the brain is influenced greatly by the native language you speak, many of the differences that we see from one culture to another may be partially created from the unique characteristics associated with the languages spoken in those cultures. As such, we can hypothesize that God did not merely change the tongue but introduced multiple systems of thinking through the creation of multiple languages.

Most foreign language concepts can be re-created in another language, though specific nuances are likely to be lost in the process. Professional translators face this challenge all the time—particularly when a speaker chooses to use idiomatic expressions or humor.

In the days to come, these issues will be less troublesome. The future power of computer processing, combined with ubiquitous computers, lightning-fast bandwidth and the progress being made in speech recognition and language translation, will enable people all over the world to communicate as if they spoke the same language.

Everyone in the world will have the ability to talk directly to anyone else with the simple use of a real-time translation machine. We will create instant conference calls, using agent[5] technology, which will invite the world's most knowledgeable subject-matter experts into one another's presence to solve the most perplexing of problems. This will occur without language barriers or traditional search problems in finding experts.[6] Truly, a New World order will result, and it will be one that could lead to the twenty-second century equivalent of the Tower of Babel—where only the hand of God can stop man in his pursuits.

One of God's concerns about the efforts of those building the Tower of Babel was that people might work together to accomplish anything they agreed upon—and to do so without reliance upon God or giving the glory for their achievements to the God who enabled them (see Gen. 11:1-9). Recovering language capacity and connectedness within the human race is restoring power that leads to a terrifying possibility. As we know in Revelation, humanity will be saved from itself at the last moment. We have in our nature the desire and overpowering longing to sin. With instant natural language translation we overcome one of the barriers that God erected thousands of years ago to protect us from ourselves. Perhaps God will intervene again to save us from our own ego and evil intentions. Or, perhaps this time, He will allow the age of humanity to come to a close.

> **Perhaps God will intervene to save us from our own ego and evil intentions.**

Unintended Consequences

As you have undoubtedly noticed in the past few years, the rush of innovations and breakthroughs has been met with glee by millions of people throughout the world. But all is not as simple as it may seem. Just as a child may not think through what he is doing when he follows his parents' instructions and closes the locked door behind him, never thinking about how he will get back in the house since he does not possess a key, so do our techno-logical products generate conditions we may not have fully considered.

Unintended consequences come about through a lack of understand-ing of the full impact of a particular course of action.[7] Sometimes these are a direct result of actions we have taken, while other times there are more complex interactions at work. A recent example comes to mind. The FAA and some airlines have been pushing for child safety seats in airplanes for children under two who now fly for free on the laps of their parents. They estimate some fairly small increment in improved safety. The unintended consequence is that by moving the child off the free lap of a parent and into a paying seat, more families with small children will be financially forced to drive long distances instead, traversing over the interstate freeway system. Statistically, driving the freeways is far more dangerous than traveling by airplane. If the FAA and partnering airlines have their way, the unintended consequence of the new regulation will be that more lives will be lost. That certainly is not the intent of the FAA, but it will be a very real outcome, nonetheless.

Unintended consequences are one of the gravest threats emanating from our technological exploits. Aggressive bees were the intended conse-quence of simple cross-breeding experiments, but the infamous killer bees that have literally killed people are the unintended consequence of that experiment when the bees escaped. What else might escape the lab? Or how about Frankenstein-like, cross-species genetic manipulation? Ridiculous conjecture? Alarmist daydreaming? Take a moment sometime to check out those freeze-resistant tomatoes your children ate with their last "friendly" meal. You just might find freeze-resistant fish genes inside! What's next? How about "medgetables"—medicine delivered through nor-mal stuff we eat. Imagine, contraceptive corn on the cob, hepatitis-B fight-ing tomatoes and bananas that kill E. coli. These innovations are already in the works.[8]

Scientists used to need a million-dollar machine to create genetic strands to experiment with, but now they just log onto a well-known biotech website and custom order a sequence for overnight delivery. This firm uses patented inkjet technology to string together the strands requested via their website from around the world and then FedEx those strands the same day. Dr. Frankenstein needed Igor to go get body parts for him. Today he would surely be a geneticist ordering what he needed via the Web.

Think About This

Our recent research regarding the adoption of home technology by Christians shows an important pattern: Christians are every bit as likely to embrace a new technological innovation as are non-Christians. In studying the ownership levels of 10 types of consumer communications and entertainment technology, the penetration rates were identical for all 10 items between the two groups. On its face, that may not seem like a bad thing. As we have indicated, there are numerous positive applications of the innovations that are at or will be at our disposal.

There are challenging questions to wrestle with in regard to technology adoption. Simply because a new innovation is available does not necessarily mean that it is appropriate for us to integrate into our lives, as the notion of unintended consequences makes clear. But even from a theological point of view, we must look at technology and innovation in light of the scriptural challenge for Christians to be in the world but not of the world (see John 17:15-18). In owning and using technology, who controls whom: do we control the technology we consume, or does it control us as we consume it?

It is possible to argue persuasively that many Christians have been seduced by the power of the tools they have acquired. Born-again adults spend an average of seven times more hours each week watching television than they do participating in spiritual pursuits such as Bible reading, prayer and worship. They spend roughly twice as much money on entertainment as they donate to their church. Already, even though the Internet has just begun to spread its wings, believers spend more time surfing the Net than they do conversing with God in prayer.

There's nothing innately inappropriate about TV, cell phones, VCRs or computers. Each of these technologies has the capacity to help and the capacity to harm. However, it's easy to become paralyzed by the amount of information they produce, stressed out by the time demands they exert, burdened by the cost of these tools and morally compromised by the content that can be conveyed through these instruments. Ultimately these are issues of control and quality of life. These tools can produce great benefits, but they also challenge us to use our personal resources wisely. We have to regularly ask who is in control, and what kind of life do they produce.

Given the absence of a worldview that challenges the value or appropriateness of the rushing stream of innovations, the Church may be God's last wall of defense in protecting ourselves from our own creative brilliance and innovative genius. But are we too enamored by these tools to ask the tough questions and take the tough stands when necessary? Do we have the clarity of convictions to foresee the tragedies that might occur at the hands of these developments, and the courage to diverge from the world's preferences? Alternatively, are we willing to use our creative energies to innovate and use these new technological platforms for the spreading of God's good news and principles?

Prior to 1945, the prophecy expressed in Revelation—that we would have the power to destroy humanity—seemed to be in little danger of fulfillment. Things have changed at breakneck speed since then. Somehow, in spite of our own behavior, we survived the twentieth century. Will we be blessed with the opportunity to continue to serve Christ on Earth for yet another century or will we innovate ourselves to death?

Where Are We Headed?

We have spent most of this chapter describing what is heading our way technologically. Here are a few more tidbits for you to consider as we get comfortable with the third millennium.

- Your home will become a smart home, operated by computer-driven controls. Lighting, heating, air conditioning, security, yard maintenance, pest control, communications, food preparation—just about every function in your home will be able to run on the basis of your programmed instructions. (Of course, many people will prefer the old-fashioned ways—flipping on the light switch, manually programming the VCR, answering a telephone—but new homes will come with these capacities in place.)

- New energy sources will expand the range of possibilities open to us. Microturbines will run on natural gas, palm oil or even processed manure to run home generators (easing the burden on the regional power grid) or even cars. Since power spikes and blackouts will be more common (the nation's energy demands will be enormous), these kinds of back-up systems will become commonplace.

- Applying nanotechnology will become the domain of consumers, not just lab scientists. Already in development is a nanobox that would allow you to download matter and fabricate new products based on molecular-level design routines. These nanoboxes are not likely to be perfected by 2010, but you will be hearing plenty about them after the initial prototypes and testing find success before the end of the decade.

- The time-shifting allowed by technology—businesses running 24 hours a day, seven days a week—will invade most areas of our lives. (Think of stock markets that never close, lawyers and doctors always accessible, local retail shops that are open 'round the clock.) That means that there will be a fuzzy line between work, play and sleep; time will be under the control of your values and your global network. If you do business overseas, your work hours might place you on an entirely different track than those of your neighbors, who might work locally. The ways in which we consume entertainment—especially passive entertainment, such as television and videos—will also transition to accommodate our altered schedules.

- Music, videos and books will be available from millions of home-spun musicians, artists, producers and authors who will generate their new products from home. Musicians, for example, will compose and perform their music in their home studios, digitize it and sell it over the Internet without recording contracts, marketing budgets and the like. The democratization of the music world will facilitate new musical formats, radical changes in how music companies market their existing rosters of stars and a rewriting of copyright laws. Expect similar changes in relation to video and literature. Moreover, new software applications will make finding snatches of entertainment easier. If you want to get your hands on a song whose title you can't remember, hum a few bars into your computer's microphone and the software will analyze the tune, scan the Internet and tell you the name of the song, who has released it for public consumption and where you can get it at the best price.

- One of the hot new fields in the legal industry will be intellectual property law. The democratization of information and ideas that our new technologies foster will destroy the centuries-old rights that the creators of ideas, theories, stories, songs and other information vehicles have long held. The issues of free speech, freedom to conduct commerce, privacy and property ownership rights will continually clash as the laws are rewritten to accommodate the implications of our technological progress.

- Gordon Moore, of Moore's Law fame, warns us that the rapid developments in chip making will soon have computers whose intelligence is hard to differentiate from that of humans. To the dismay of some, our first clear contact with alien intelligence will be with computers that possess advanced artificial intelligence. One result is that incredible leaps forward will be made in science, engineering and medicine. Another is that simple robots will become more common by the end of the decade, and more complex versions will become integrated into our businesses and homes in each subsequent decade.

- Companies will adapt to new innovations rapidly—or risk failure. Organizational re-engineering will be a common practice as technology restructures job task as well as company products and systems.

- Permanent connection to the Internet will be a selling feature for a number of common household and personal products, as well as business processes. Manufacturers will promote products—such as eyeglasses, wallets, keys—with "Never Lost" labels.

- Family members and pets will be continually "traceable" via the Internet. If you enroll a child in a day care, you will be able to keep an eye on his/her activity by monitoring them on your PC screen or home TV screen (once it's hooked to DSL) via video-streaming technology.
- Sports records will be continually broken as technology facilitates the development of superior equipment and better training regimens. Equipment will even contain sensors that will enable you to keep score, to keep records and perhaps make suggestions about your performance and tactical choices.
- Computerized sensors embedded in roads, walls, bridges and other structures will inform engineers of when those entities need to be repaired or how they are handling stresses and strains of normal wear and tear. This will improve safety but also increase costs in the short-term.
- Don't worry about running out of gas. Gas stations will go mobile once the new cars include sensors and communications chips that will automatically alert roving gas trucks that your tank is nearly empty. You will actually become a gas "subscriber," choosing a favorite supplier whose trucks will be there before your engine sucks in the last drop of fuel.

What Can You Do?

The daunting reality is that the pace of technological change, and the complexity of the changes themselves, left most of us in the dust long ago. It is difficult, if not impossible, for most Americans to comprehend the nature and implications of each new breakthrough. Even so, we must do what we can to not only exploit the positive benefits of technological progress, but to also challenge the development of undesirable advances. Here are a few ideas to consider.

- Perhaps you are not a political animal, but as a citizen you have a responsibility to stay informed about developments in our culture and to communicate your concerns and desires to those whom you have elected to public office. Government regulation may not be our best bet for creating a sane future, but it is one means to placing at least minimal reasonable restrictions on what technologists do and how they do it.

- Christians should incorporate discussions and teaching about the implications of technology into the substance of the Church. We do not want to become obsessed with technology, but as believers we ought to be informed and responsible regarding how our faith and worldview affects advancing technology.

- Reasoned, articulate, nonhysterical opposition to digital pornography and gambling are minimum requirements for us to uphold. By alerting fellow believers to the rapid growth and destructive consequences of these vices we may help to control, if not alleviate, these lures that have become so readily accessible.

- Consider how we might create new, technology-enhanced platforms for ministry. Websites, streaming media, MP3 files, e-mail, webcasting and numerous other mechanisms can become effective ministry tools in the hands of innovative evangelists, teachers, disciplers and worship leaders. New technologies provide us with tremendous opportunities to impact the world for Christ if we take the time to understand other cultures and think through the application of these new technologies for ministry. Tribes and people groups that have never been reached will be accessible in new ways—if we are sensitive to the native customs and inclinations of those groups.

- Think about how you have integrated technology into your own life, and figure out who controls whom: do you really master the media, or does it exert a shaping influence on your thoughts, behavioral patterns and relationships? Technology is a tool that the craftsman must use; it is not a tool meant to enslave its creator.

As always, we must lean on the wisdom and guidance of God. Perhaps we have created the means for our own destruction, through technology that is disguised as helpful and promising. Only the Creator of all things can protect us from our own ultimate devastation.

Notes

1. Jill Rosenfeld, "Information as if Understanding Mattered," *Fast Company* (March 2000), p. 211.
2. Charles Phillips and Mary Meeker, "The B2B Internet Report," *Morgan Stanley Dean Witter* (April 2000), p. 11.
3. Andrew Quinn, "Does The Net Create Sex Addicts?" Reuters, March 1, 2000.
4. "Steve Mann has raised geek-freakiness to a high art. He was the original 'wearable computer' guy at the MIT Media Lab. I've seen Steve at several meetings. You can't miss him. He's the guy with the computer eyepiece duct-taped to his thick glasses, the bad haircut and the battery pack around his waist. . . .

   "In London, Steve says, the police net of surveillance cams and face recognition software can find any face in a public place in the city of London in 10 minutes." SMART Letter #40–June 15, 2000. Copyright 2000 by David S. Isenberg.
5. Agents are software code that specializes in searching the entire Internet for you. One of the first agent technologies deployed on the net was one created by Arthur Anderson's CSTAR (Center for Strategic Technology Assessment Research) division. One could specify what CD one wanted and it would search the web for the cheapest price on that particular CD.
6. There is a division of study in Economics called the economics of information systems. The study of information systems (not computers, but the how, why and what of communicating information in a community or system) rests primarily on transaction costs. It costs you a bunch of time (a proxy for money) to learn what the "best" stereo, computer or dishwasher would be for you. Industry faces this same problem when working on an innovation. We usually don't have the best information for the job at hand; we just have to make do. This will not always be true.
7. For a great book on "revenged effects," see Edward Tenner, *Why Things Bite Back: Technology and the Revenge of Unintended Consequences* (New York: Alfred A. Knopf, 1996).
8. Jessie Scanlon, Carolyn Rauch and David Jang, "Electronic Word 8.01," *Wired* (January 2000), p. 34.

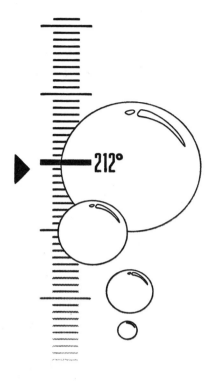

CHAPTER SEVEN

THE WILD WORLD OF TECHNOMED

Future Glimpse

Jill came bouncing into the bedroom in time to see Carl, sitting hunched over the side of the bed, clicking the remote to turn off the videophone. He looked ashen.

"Something wrong?" she asked innocently while thinking, *Maybe his boss is giving him a hard time again.* A sudden wave of panic struck her as she realized he may have been fired.

"That was Gail," he replied, referring to his older sister. "Mom just died." As he raised his head to meet her eyes, his body seemed to deflate.

Jill's heart sank. They both knew that his mother was seriously ill, but the finality of this outcome was hard to accept. Carla Moore was only in her early 70s. Just two months ago she had been diagnosed with a seemingly innocuous bronchial condition. The doctors prescribed a common antibiotic that, after a couple of weeks, had proven ineffective. The next three remedies proved to be equally useless. Testing eventually showed that the virus was not the benign strain they had been attempting to treat but another disease of recent discovery that seemed impervious to antibiotics. They all held out hope that a new experimental drug would destroy the intrusive virus. Now it had claimed yet another life. It was just one more member of the new class of diseases that seemed to be discovered each year.

What had happened to medical science, anyway? Wasn't this the age of wonder drugs and supercures? Jill went over to place her arms around Carl and console him. As she hugged him and gently rubbed his back, she realized that this was his third family member in three years to pass unexpectedly. His father had died in a car crash last year, when the car's computer system misdirected the steering mechanism and caused him to crash at high speed. The previous year his younger brother had succumbed to MacArthur's Disease, a debilitating brain dysfunction brought on by intelligence-enhancing stimulants that Jamie had been taking for some time. The family had attributed his increasingly cranky behavior to his mounting financial debt and work stress. As it turned out, his constant irritability, argumentativeness and odd tendency to shout pedantic statements to anyone within earshot were actually symptoms of the stimulants eating away at his brain cells. The pills had since been taken off the market—replaced by a new, enhanced version, but that couldn't bring Jamie back—or ease Carl's pain.

How ironic these untimely deaths seemed. Less than 24 hours earlier, Jill and Carl had been watching a documentary on their computer while eating dinner. The program described recent progress in genetics and how life extension was advancing—some people in Eastern Europe had apparently experienced significant gains in life span as a result of genetic manipulations that had been undertaken. All that stuff—genetics and superdrugs—gave her the willies. Then, again, she was already on the waiting list for an eardrum implant and a new bone in her big toe (it ached endlessly from an accident sustained in her youth and was never properly treated).

For now, it was time to take care of her depressed husband. Maybe a couple of Ziamedrican, the incredible antidepressant pills, would make him feel better. Even if science was not invincible, they might as well take advantage of the good innovations that had been developed.

The Marvel and Monsters of Medicine

The saving power of health care has been a metaphor of God's grace to us through His Son since Moses raised up the serpent in the desert to save the lives of all who would look on it. Jesus often used the healing of physical maladies as a platform for delivering His message of eternal spiritual healing. Medicine has been and will continue to be a wonderful vehicle for delivering God's grace to those in need.

These are unprecedented times. In all of human history, save for the last 50 years, acute diseases, chronic syndromes and terrifying diseases plagued the human experience. Except for the marginally successful sulfa drugs from the late nineteenth century, there were no known cures for common ailments such as strep throat, inner-ear infections, upper-respiratory infections, infections of wounds or childhood diseases like measles, mumps, chicken pox and even the flu. Until the dawn of the Industrial Age, the average life expectancy was 37. Humanity managed to push that marginally higher through the Industrial Revolution, but it wasn't until the advent of modern medicine, the development of widespread sanitation, along with the improvement in food and water supply, that life expectancy begin to significantly increase. A child born today can expect to live into his/her mid-70s.

LIFE EXPECTANCY BY COUNTRY GROUP

Country Group	Life expectancy at birth (yrs)	Infant mortality rate (per 1,000 live births)
Low income	56	58
(51 countries)	38-73	25-163
Lower Middle income	67	36
(40 countries)	57-77	14-71
Upper Middle income	69	36
	54-78	6-89
High income countries	77	7
Source: *Global Shift,* Peter Dicken, p. 446)	75-79	4-11

The most radical increase in life expectancy occurred after the discovery of penicillin, just prior to World War II. The development of antibiotics significantly increased average life spans, improved the quality of life and reduced the number of debilitating and deadly diseases. That is the good news.

The Impotence of Antibiotics

The bad news is that in April 2000 the first antibiotic in 25 years passed the FDA gauntlet and was approved for prescription by physicians. This is indicative of the fact that science has exhausted the most likely paths for discovery of new antibiotics. As a result, the pace of discovery in antibiotics has slowed to a near standstill. Why did the amazing rate of progress suddenly drop?

Many scientists posit that the catalyst for this condition is that over the last 40 years, doctors prescribed antibiotic medications at any hint of illness. The serious effects of this strategy cannot be overstated. In many ways, they have simply been responding to public pressure to come up with miracle cures and answers when perhaps none were really available. Our tendency to esteem physicians who do something, even if it is overprescribing medicines, has given them an inducement to do so. We intellectually understand and endorse the need for conservative treatments and the sparing use of antibiotics—as long as that tact is taken with someone else. We want our drugs, and we want them now. Life is too busy, we are too far in debt, and we treasure accomplishment and comfort too much to let illness slow us down.

Over time, of course, diseases mutate and become resistant to antibiotics. The powerful antibiotics that were introduced in the '70s, such as Keflex, have become commonplace prescriptions rather than a solution of last recourse. It is not uncommon to take an initial treatment of Amoxicillin or Ampicillin, and when that does not work, to immediately move to a more powerful class of drugs. There are now, unfortunately, superbacteria causing superinfections that resist even our most powerful antibiotics. So it was good news indeed in April of 2000 when a new antibiotic was released. The problem is that this step forward is not a panacea nor does it signal a new era of superprescriptions. It is likely that there will not be many discoveries for new antibiotics while an increasing number of the diseases that we face will prove themselves to be resistant to available antibiotics.

The Coming Dissatisfaction

Many medical analysts believe that we are approaching a time similar to that of the sulfa drug era, when drug treatments were only marginally effective. The diseases that humanity faces in the next 10 to 40 years may become so resistant to the existing drug regimes that we will, in essence, revert to where we were in the 1910s and 1920s. This is neither good nor expected news. In fact, it may surprise you, given that this is the age of radical, rapid and literally miraculous medical treatments. Yet, we must face reality: although we can do some of the most amazing surgeries and solve many medical calamities through exotic treatments and techniques, we may begin to lose the battle on the bacterial front.

We may be able to reattach a severed arm with the hope of full functionality while at the same time losing that patient to a simple staphylococci infection. Two things drive this reality. One, people tend to overmedicate. Two, we live in a global society, so that a drug-resistant strain of strep throat may emerge in some distant country and rapidly spread itself around the globe. In the spring of 2000, New York medical authorities began ramping up for a battle with a pathogen responsible for an outbreak of West Nile encephalitis. Authorities believe that it was introduced into the New York metropolitan area by a globe-trotting Nigerian who was infected with West Nile encephalitis and had been bitten by mosquitoes in New York. As it turned out, these mosquitoes were able to carry the pathogen and infect others. That example is likely to be repeated many times over the coming decade with a wide range of diseases and will be particularly alarming in light of the resistance of diseases and lack of new antibiotic solutions.

The development of new diseases represents a serious threat to national health. Although the cultural conditions are quite different, any country in the world is susceptible to the onset of a disease as significant as the AIDS virus that is devastating an entire generation in Africa. Negative population growth—that is, a net decline in population—is anticipated in some African countries because of this stunning epidemic. In Africa, AIDS is a problem for heterosexuals, not just homosexuals. The life expectancy in some African countries will drop below 30 years old—an incredible reversal of fortune in an age of prosperity and possibilities.[1]

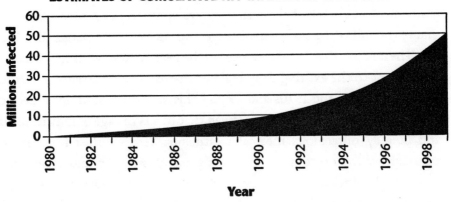

ESTIMATES OF CUMULATIVE HIV INFECTIONS WORLDWIDE

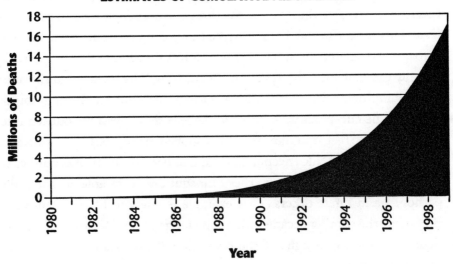

ESTIMATES OF CUMULATIVE AIDS DEATHS

Source: UNAIDS: *Vital Signs 2000*, p. 101

The AIDS pandemic is unlikely to be the last major health risk that modern medicine will have trouble managing—but emerging situations like that of Africa may present an opportunity for the global Church to get involved. For instance, the AIDS problem in Africa is not just a medical one but also a moral one. Understanding marriage to be a sacrosanct institution and the significance of sexual abstinence before marriage will severely curtail the spread of this terrible disease. Nations are on the brink of ruin for lack of a moral compass. You need only understand that the UN, UNICEF and other international institutions have deigned to save Africa with condoms—a solution proven to be ineffective—rather than to address the tough moral issues that underlie the real problem. It would not be out of line to suggest that perhaps only a spiritual revival can truly save Africa from itself.

In the long run, genetics may prove to be the silver bullet we are frantically searching for. Imagine, if you will, growing up 30 years ago and contracting a simple ear infection. Upon visiting your doctor, he identified the problem as *otitis media* (an inner ear infection) and injected a penicillin-based drug for that infection. The infection receded significantly in the ensuing 24 to 48 hours and you were cured. Now consider what happens to a child today who winds up in an identical situation. Upon being given the appropriate drugs, the chances are better than average that the first regime of medications will not work. The next step is to introduce, perhaps five days later, a new regime. Today, this tends to work. In the near future, however, it may not. The infection may continue and eventually cause devastating results from a rupturing of the eardrum to the infestation of other parts of the cranium, including sinus infection and potentially even a deadly form of encephalitis. This development has occurred in a short span of 40 to 60 years. Were it not for the potential for genetic treatments on the horizon, medical professionals would be more alarmed than they already are with the current progression of disease forms and their resistance to antibiotics.

Genetics—Silver Bullet or Nuclear Dawn?

On April 28, 2000, the *New York Times* published a front-page article announcing the successful first treatment of a disease with the utilization of genetic therapy.[2] Prior to that point, genetic therapies had been limited to fairly confined disease processes and had not been used to literally manipulate the genetic structure of the therapy recipient. With the April 2000 news announcement, however, medicine was opened.

Genetic therapies represent the most radical step forward in medical history. In time, genetic solutions will usher in a new era in mankind's health. The possibilities for genetics to improve the quality of life exceed those related to improvements in sanitation or even those gained from the development of antibiotics. So radical are these potential innovations that life as we know it may change significantly, introducing enormous potential for good—as well as evil—throughout the world.

Genetic manipulation will, in the near future, enable a couple to not only select the gender of their child, but also a wide range of physical, emotional and psychological characteristics. Do you want a child with blue eyes, brown eyes or green eyes? Maybe you'd prefer a child with one blue eye and one green eye. Do you want him or her to have a high IQ? Do you want him or her to be musically enabled? Would you prefer that he or she have Olympic-level stamina? Would you like him to look like an Adonis—or, for that matter, be Adonis? Or perhaps you just want all of the above? These kinds of choices will soon move from the realm of science fiction to the domain of parenting. This is medical history in the making.

Comedians have a field day poking fun at Los Angeles for being the plastic surgery capital of the world, a place where it's hard to find anything natural in an age when you can fabricate a superior alternative. But cosmetic surgery is child's play compared to what is about to unfold through genetic engineering. Parents will experience enormous pressure to select just the right combination of characteristics for their children, if only to make them competitive. After all, how will a child endowed only with the natural abilities and attributes given by God be able to compete with a child who has been genetically manipulated to be the smartest, most beautiful and physically strongest child possible? Imagine a centralized government deciding that it is politically expedient to win more Olympic gold medals than they ever have in the past and giving that state the tools to be able to literally create the strongest, the fastest, the most agile of athletes that humankind has ever seen. Today's heated debates regarding steroid use will be a laughable footnote in the history books. Imagine the joy, excitement and pride that a childless couple might feel upon learning that they have been selected by the government to bear and raise such a wonder child. Obviously, the moral and ethical dilemmas inherent in these choices and behaviors are many, but these are types of heavy challenges we will face in this new medical era. We are leapfrogging the notion of human breeding to take on the reality of genetic human engineering.

This leads to a closely related conundrum: cloning. The ability to successfully clone sophisticated organisms, like sheep and cows, has already been proven. Surely there is some great scientist out there who has already begun dreaming of going down in the history books as the first scientist to have cloned himself. Some people believe this has already happened but, for political reasons, has not been publicly revealed. Soon one will take the next logical step of using the cloning technologies to begin with a representation of himself and then insert into that child's genetic structure characteristics of strength, agility, brilliance and beauty.

Will we as a society be able to resist the opportunity to create a new Michelangelo using the base genetic material we can get from cloning ourselves? It is a temptation that will be difficult to resist. The darker side of cloning raises the possibility of intentionally creating an inferior class of people—literally, slaves—who will be less intelligent, less powerful, less beautiful, less human than ourselves—human beings designed with marginal mental capacity that equips them only to accomplish the most menial of tasks. Why take the trouble of creating incredibly expensive, difficult to manage and repair-prone robots when you can create a subhuman species to do all the things that you don't really want to do?

This genetic manipulation has the potential to spin completely out of control. A recent expose in the *Los Angeles Times* revealed that the annual revenues of the human body parts industry in the U.S. already exceed a billion dollars. The companies involved literally take bodies of the recently dead and run them through a medical reclamation process to extract bones and organs, repackage them into innumerable products and then sell them back to hospitals. The body parts of our loved ones can then be, unknown to us, inserted into other people who are in need of valve replacements, skin

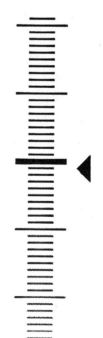

Revenues of the human body parts industry in the U.S. already exceed a billion dollars annually.

grafts, cosmetic surgery, you name it. This industry has sprung up in the last 15 years in spite of tremendous efforts to discourage this type of resale of human body parts. But the desire to live longer and more fully will almost inevitably overcome any legislative efforts to contain the proliferation of the sale of biological components that might enhance life. This ghastly industry goes on circumventing legislative intent through the culpable and cooperative assistance of those who refuse to address the moral issues of these endeavors.

How Far Will It Go?

Imagine the ability to genetically manipulate an entire class of subspecies that bears little resemblance to humankind, yet, in fact, is made up of components of humanity. Call it a cow, but it may have a human lung, human heart, human muscle, bone tissue, teeth, eyes and other organs that literally are exact replicas and genetically identical to those of your brother or sister. Or why not merely create a near mortal who has no brain function and is literally engineered to die so that we can harvest its body parts?

We face a future where great monetary awards await the country that exports these medical "products." To those who argue that this is incomprehensible, simply not possible, then they must explain the existence and growth of our own nation's billion-dollar human body parts industry. This is simply the latest in a long line of impossible developments that "society would never allow"—e.g., the Holocaust, slavery, partial-birth abortions. The lust for money, power and adulation often overwhelms the ethics and morals that limit evil impulses.

Scientists realize that the malevolent use of genetic engineering is well within the capabilities of modern medical science. Do we live far from the day where genetic terrorism is a reality? At what time will the world see genetics used for the purposes of grabbing global power? Even our own nation, ostensibly the most God-fearing country in the world, used nuclear weapons over a period of a few days to instantly kill some 225,000 Japanese civilians. The horror of that event did not repulse the world into agreeing to cease the production of such weapons but, rather, ignited a ferocious global race to create evermore viscous and outrageous weapons to promote the advancement of civilized life. How likely is it, then, that if genetic engineering holds the promise of control and power, societies will resist the temptation to develop it, full speed ahead?

How will we handle genetic power in the hands of a death squad intent upon annihilating an entire ethnic minority by creating a genocidal, genetic time bomb transmitted through the dispersion of something as simple as the common cold?

Geneticists will have ample opportunities to flex their creative muscles. Today's younger generations have made a social statement through tattoos, body piercing, hair coloring and cosmetics. But genetic manipulation in the future opens up entirely new options for creative expression. For instance, we will soon have the ability to literally manipulate the body and what grows on it. One futurist shocked a room full of senior strategists by describing the idea of genetic cosmetic enhancement—that's right, "cosmegenetics." He encouraged us to imagine a horn, tied to the limbic system, that someone might want to grow on his or her forehead. When the person became angry the horn would turn red; when the person became happy the horn would turn blue—or whenever the person had any type of emotion that created a detectable chemical response, the horn would change colors. The presenter was a highly respected, brilliant individual with a track record of accomplishment—Dr. Kao, M.D., Harvard M.B.A., jazz pianist, Tony-nominated playwright, author, and cofounder and board member of numerous biotech companies.

The process will unfold less dramatically, of course. After all, we are already the recipients of developments such as cross-species genetic manipulation used to improve the quality, durability and shelf life of fruits and vegetables. It's not much of a stretch to imagine such types of manipulation used, for "reasonable purposes," among humans. At first these innovations will seem minor, innocuous, even reasonable. People may be enabled to grow bumps, lumps, extensions, massive muscles, hair in unusual places, bony extrusions along the arms or even stronger facial features. Do you think people will be anxious to get that look they've always wanted, through the growth of a stronger jawline or higher cheekbones that are literally grown on top of the existing facial structure? What would prevent people from exploiting the chance to get stronger bones or better vision?

In due time, it will get weird—but that, of course, is the present-day perspective. Immersed in a world that will adapt to each new innovation, we will lose perspective on where we've come from and what we're doing and accept the marketing hype behind these alterations as reasonable and beneficial. Maybe you would prefer to have webbed fingers, if you want to be an Olympic swimmer. Would a career military professional like to have the brain power of a human along with the structural power and integrity of a large carnivorous animal like a bear, with massive musculature and dense bone structure?

It's not a large step to get from there to human machine integration. We've seen this already with implanted mechanical hearts and valve replacements, with the use of foreign materials that enhance ligature in knees and arms, or with steel and ceramic hip replacements. A logical step would be the use of smart parts that might understand what they are doing in the body, what function they are supposed to perform, and communicating that with the environment around them.

Doesn't this remind you of the cyborg of science fiction tales? Incredibly, we're headed in that very direction. At first you will see external devices attached to the body as mere augmentations to existing functions. In some ways, that's what cell phones, pagers and handheld computers represent. It is predicted that we will eventually merge with computers[3] and that computers will become so lifelike that many people will grant them human status.[4]

Is this too strange for you? We have already seen the first experiments of implanting chips and sensors in the body that enable one to be recognized in a specially designed environment that responds to those implants by opening doors, recognizing security levels and recording the whereabouts of the person with the implant.[5] Kevin Warwick, professor of cybernetics at the University of Reading in the U.K., has already taken this step and has been experimenting with this possibility since August of 1998.

Will ours become a world in which authorities know who you are, where you are, what you are doing, where you are going? Will it be a world where we are literally enhanced in multiple ways, whether it be a mechanical heart, stronger artificial joints, stronger ligaments, larger muscles, enhanced eyesight and computer-enhanced, cognitive processing? Welcome to a new world that humankind has never faced before. Bill Joy, cofounder of Sun Microsystems, a true genius who is highly respected in the computer industry, wonders whether humankind will be able to persist. He has opened a fruitful dialogue on technology and its implications for humanity among secular technologists, posing to the developers of this new world piercing questions related to many of the issues raised in this book. The Church has a rightful place in that discussion and must take its seat at the discussion table, although gaining access to a chair won't be easy, given the self-righteous disdain so many of the "digerati" have for us.

Science fiction is no longer just imaginative bedtime reading but truly a bizarre kind of aspirational expression or prophetic pronouncement. How should followers of Christ respond? It is one thing for people to grow a horn on their head, but something else to create a subspecies of slaves or murderous genetic weapons.

The Quest for Immortality

We were created to be immortal beings. In the beginning God created Adam and Eve to live with Him forever, giving us a heritage of longing to live forever in these bodies that were originally designed for immortality. After our fall through original sin, though, God cursed humankind with physical death but held out the promise of a bodily resurrection. Throughout human history, we have often rued the limitations of our bodies and our short life spans while maintaining the innate desire for immortality.

Interestingly, prior to the Flood, even with the curse of death, people lived for hundreds of years. Something happened after the Flood. No one knows exactly what, whether we were the unfortunate recipients of a gene pool that only has a life span of 110 to 120 years, or whether there was some massive environmental change as a result of the event that precipitated the Flood.

Think about how you would live if you expected to have a natural life span of 800 years. How risky does football, hockey, rugby or some of the more extreme sports look, in view of a potential life span that is unimaginable today? Would you drive a car at even the 55 mile an hour speed limit? Would you slow your life down to a pace that's more reasonable? Might you enjoy becoming truly world-class in the occupation that you've chosen, given the opportunity to practice that occupation for a few hundred years? Certainly life as we know it would be radically different if we had reasons to expect the longevity of the pre-Flood biblical people.

We have been able to extend normal human life significantly in the industrialized West over the last 100 years, and it's not unreasonable to assume that similar types of improvements and gains will be made in the next 100 years. What is unparalleled, though, is the recent discovery of what appears to be the equivalent of a genetic clock—or genetic time bomb—that literally monitors the reproductive capability of individual cells in the human body and clips the end of a genetic yardstick every time the cell reproduces. Eventually, as that process repeats itself over and over, there is nothing left to clip and the cell then dies a natural death. It appears that this is the instrument within our bodies that manages the life span of humans at the genetic level.

The gene that manages this life-span function in the human body is called the telomere. It facilitates cell reproduction for 26 to 52 cycles before the telomeres have been exhausted and the cell dies. Through the ongoing effort to understand and destroy cancerous cells and the enormous amounts of funding that the governments of the world have put into under-standing cancer and its causative agents, there has been a recent discovery that there is a genetic chemical closely related to telomeres called telom-erase. This chemical miraculously rebuilds a telomere from its current state back to its complete and original state. It does this whether the telomere has been snipped two or three times or whether it had been snipped down to a mere stub. Telomerase has the ability to take a cell that is about to die and reset its clock back to when it was first born. This is among the most mind-blowing of all genetic discoveries to date. Some geneticists contend that this discovery represents the mechanism for managing life expectancy. Perhaps Ponce de Leon was simply searching in the wrong place for the elusive foun-tain of youth.

We know that regardless of the medical developments and insights, humankind will not be able to reverse the curse of God and the penalty for sin (i.e., death). However, it is not outside the realm of Christian theology that we might be able to find and reverse the agent causing the reduction in life span from 800 years to the current 76.

Where Are We Going?

What do some of these astounding breakthroughs and possibilities mean for you? Here are some likely implications.

- Life spans will get longer. Already the average Baby Boomer can expect to live for 78 years. Unless a new class of diseases intrudes on our culture and halts our recent progress, life spans will increase. Children born this year will have an estimated life span of 85 years or more—and that's without harnessing telomerase.
- The emergence of new diseases is virtually inevitable. Expect those diseases to be transported from other parts of the world into the U.S.
- We thought that transmogrification was science fiction. They only got the implement wrong. It is not a machine. It is genetics. The human species faces the opportunity for the first time to choose to become something other than human. These options may not be in place by 2010, but consideration of the validity of these advances will be a hot topic of discussion.
- The Olympic Games will start testing athletes for genetic manipulations. Why mess with "blood packing" (working out at high altitude and then saving that higher oxygen-transporting blood for later transfusion just prior to a race) when you can alter your blood directly to carry more oxygen?
- Why implant a spike when you can grow one directly? Musicians will spearhead the experimentation of body-altering genetics treatments. Horns—unicorn-type horns, not trumpets and trombones!—will likely be the biggest rage.
- All things associated with health care will grow: nursing homes, day-care homes, in-house visits. Ever alert to new profit-produc-

ing alternatives, entirely new industries will develop that target the disposable income of retirees in relation to their medical well-being.

- Great debates and arguments about who should be allowed to work with the basic genetic structure of the human genome will explode. Professional codes of ethics and national and international laws will struggle to catch up to the rapid pace of exploration. You can count on at least one major genetic catastrophe before serious intervention will occur.

What Can You Do?

Have you conceived of any developments that require us to pray for wisdom and courage more than the forthcoming developments described above? Beyond such reliance upon the mind of God for direction, here are some things that believers should consider in response to these developments.

We must become engaged and involved. We bring to the party a biblical point of view about the sanctity of life; a holistic point of view of caring for the whole individual, including the spirituality of an individual; and a temperate view of innovation and change. The list of pending medical disasters and near disasters is fairly long, and without some careful oversight and patience, we run the risk of introducing new types of serious medical mistakes. Do you remember how asbestos was positioned as a miracle material that would protect us from fires and heat? Today, of course, we recognize the folly of those claims and know that it is an incredible carcinogen. Remember the fabulous medicinal benefits promised to pregnant mothers who used thalidomide? Thousands and thousands of massively deformed babies were born from that mess. Can Christians be a sane and steady voice of reason in a world that seems increasingly mesmerized by medical innovation?

Do you remember the early use of X rays to figure out what your shoe size was? And, of course, morphine, cocaine and barbiturates were considered nonaddictive in their earliest forms. Killer bees are known to most of the southwestern United States and Latin America. These terrifying bees are the responsibility of an early crossbreeding program to create a more productive bee by making it more aggressive. As it turns out, these bees are not more productive; they're just more aggressive and over the past 20 years have killed literally hundreds of people throughout the Western Hemisphere.

These examples have shown us that when a new medical marvel is on the doorstep, we don't know what questions to ask about its safety and other ramifications. When thalidomide was released, we didn't ask the right questions about the ultimate impact of that drug on the fetus. We asked plenty of questions about asbestos, but we never considered the potential impact of airborne asbestos particles. We must be engaged if we hope to avoid science's earlier failures to protect us.

Christians are an important constituency in the public and private dialog that must take place regarding the morals and ethics of pending possibilities. No matter how disdainful some people may be of our antiquated positions, we must take our rightful place at the table and engage proponents of change in an honest and knowledgeable discussion about the long-term implications of some of their work. We should certainly oppose some of the more radical elements of these innovations until we have a deeper understanding of their impact on society. Cosmetic-genetic enhancements will not necessarily improve the human condition. An individual's creative impulse to grow a new horn needs to be weighed against the long-term potential genetic degradation of the gene pool.

It is likely that a movement will develop in support of all innovations and all exciting future possibilities. Might the spirit of this movement infect our entire culture? Will we see the rise of a line of thinking that captures the imagination and foresees a technical utopia where all human suffering is mitigated through some application of superior science? This will ignore the reality of separation from God, the devastating impacts of sin, the inevitability of the Judgment Day and the accounting for all we've done. This reality must not be replaced with hope through technology, life through genetics and happiness through hedonistic self-expression. A conservative approach to the development of the more radical potentials of technology needs to be adopted.

We need to bear in mind that even though everything is changing, nothing in the human condition has changed. The eternal war between good and evil rages on, just as it has since the fall of Satan. We are principals in that battle. The final outcome has already been irrevocably determined, but the conflict continues to create casualties. Human nature, the fall of man, God's love, mercy and grace continue to be the major themes of history. Though technology used by the principals in the battle may change substantially over the next 10 years, the core theme will be about how the actors used these tools in relation to the broader historical purpose. The real story is not about technology but about our response to God. We must oppose attempts to replace God's hope and mercy with inferior technological substitutes.

Notes

1. Thomas H. Maugh II, *Los Angeles Times,* July 11, 2000, p. 1.
2. Gina Kolata, "In a First, Gene Therapy Saves the Lives of Infants," *New York Times,* April 28, 2000, front page.
3. Ray Kurzwell, *The Age of Spiritual Machines* (New York: Viking Press, 1999), p. 334.
4. Ibid, p. 224.
5. Kevin Warwick, "Cyborg 1.0," *Wired* (February 2000), p. 144.

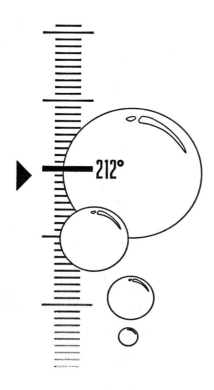

CHAPTER EIGHT

BUSINESS AND EMPLOYMENT

Future Glimpse

Jill found that the most challenging aspect of her job was not the customer relations (tough) or the financial complexities (tougher) but fostering a value-added, entertaining environment for hotel guests (impossible!). When she was a child, her parents' goal during family vacations was to find quiet, economical hotels in which to sleep. But that wasn't enough to attract guests these days. You had to provide them with a memorable experience or plan to have numerous vacant rooms.

In just the last year she had completely revamped the public spaces on the hotel grounds and how those spaces were used. She started by hiring entertainers for "children's hour" that happened every evening in the hotel lounge (musicians, jugglers, magicians—anyone who could capture and maintain the attention of kids for an hour). She had overseen the installation of a mammoth video wall in the pool area—an entire wall now contained a 40x60-foot screen to play videos while people swam. On weekends the hotel ran special trips to nearby nature and entertainment venues, packing buses with guests who bought the discounted packages. From 5 P.M. to 7 P.M. each evening there was a complimentary meal provided to guests in the hotel's restaurant, featuring a local chef providing a brief lesson on cooking the specialty of the evening. Every hotel provided amenities such as free DSL connections in guests' rooms and unlimited satellite television channels. There had to be something more memorable, more exciting, more—well, to Jill, it was just more work!

She had to admit, though—she had fallen prey to the same mind-set even when she was shopping. She patronized the retail stores that merely provided good prices less frequently these days. Instead, she often shopped at the new retail giants, those that gave her a break from the daily pressures and humdrum reality by entertaining or inspiring or somehow transporting her mind and emotions from the constant grind to another place—all this while she shopped. Like a growing number of people, she didn't even mind paying slightly higher prices for the experience. After all, she reasoned, she was buying more than the product; she was having her mind and heart massaged before returning to the avalanche of details and tensions of the real world.

Sometimes she wistfully recalled "the good old days" when shopping was about buying the best quality products for the lowest price. She'd have to store that memory to share with the grandkids someday.

The New Face of Business

When Peter Drucker coined the term "knowledge worker" a couple of decades ago, he hit the nail on the head! We have shifted from an economy dependent upon brawn to one reliant upon brains. Forty years ago a high school diploma, natural intelligence and a desire to make it in the business world qualified you to seek employment in most medium- or large-sized companies; you were likely to get hired and make a decent living. That's certainly not the case these days. Even a college degree is not a guarantee of getting a great job anymore. The figures in the accompanying chart point out that there is a close, positive link between education and income, but a college degree is increasingly treated as the minimum necessary credential to earn even an average income these days.

EDUCATION AND TRAINING PAY OFF
(Year-round full-time workers aged 25 years and over)

Unemployment rate in 1998		Median Earnings in 1997
1.3%	Professional degree	$72,700
1.4%	Doctorate	$62,400
1.6%	Master's degree	$50,000
1.9%	Bachelor's degree	$40,100
2.5%	Associate's degree	$31,700
3.2%	Some college, no degree	$30,400
4.0%	High school graduate	$26,000
7.1%	Less than high school	$19,700

Source: Bureau of the Census: BLS

Knowledge—or a recognized symbol of the ability to compete in a knowledge-based world, such as a college degree—is demanded of those who wish to make headway in the fast-moving marketplace of the third millennium. The old chant was "Stay in school. High school dropouts rarely get ahead." The new chant is "Stay in school. People without a graduate degree rarely get ahead." In a knowledge-based economy, even one in which services are playing an increasingly significant role in wealth production, educational preparation is paramount.

Ten years ago analysts were heralding the onset of the third wave economy—that is, the transition from the first wave (agriculture) and second wave (manufacturing) to the new, third wave (services). Their prediction proved true. Look at the evolution of the U.S. employment structure. At its peak in the eighteenth century more than 80 percent of the nation's work-force was employed on farms. In 1900, 28 percent of the labor force worked in farming, fishing or forestry. By 2005, though, less than 3 percent of work-ing Americans will toil in such first-wave endeavors. Instead, half of the twenty fastest-growing occupations will involve computer technology, health care and education. Almost 98 percent of the 19.5 million new jobs expected to be created between 1998 and 2008 will be service jobs.[1]

Naturally, the nation still needs to produce goods. However, the same number of people occupying production jobs in 1950 (20 million) will be serving in such capacities at the end of this decade—although they will pro-duce more goods.[2] The service sector is where the action is—today. But if you want to look down the road and understand where things are headed, don't put all of your eggs in the service basket; you've got to anticipate the coming of the experience economy.

The Experience Economy

Two economists, Joe Pine II and James Gilmore, have led the charge regard-ing comprehension of the winds of the economy. They recently showed how the new shift is from services to experiences. Experiences, rather than serv-ices or goods, represent the largest percentage of our economic growth and are the elements of the economy that are least sensitive to downward price pressure. If services were the third economic wave, then experiences consti-tute the fourth wave.

Pine and Gilmore have amassed data that convincingly suggest that perhaps the service economy has peaked and that the fourth wave is well on its way to ascending to the economic throne.[3] Beginning in the 1970s, serv-ices rose in importance in our economy. Although many analysts fretted that the failure to produce tangible goods could not sustain a huge eco-nomic base such as that of the United States, the service economy morphed into a blended sector in which commodities became desirable and differen-tiated on the basis of the service associated with those products. Companies such as Nordstrom, Starbucks, Saturn and IBM marketed products that were not unusual, but the companies experienced tremendous success thanks to the service elements wrapped into those products.

Mere service is no longer enough, though. Heightened consumer expectations, combined with innovative technologies, have raised the bar of economic offerings to demand the product, plus service, plus a rich and compelling experience. Bored with mere price reductions, attractive packaging, carefully crafted retail environments and reliable old-fashioned service, people are learning that they can have it all—product, service and entertainment, all wrapped up into one easily accessible package. This new set of expectations has even revised the traditional view of pricing, moving businesses beyond the limited considerations of time and cost to incorporate a dollar figure assessed on the typical consumer's perceived value of the experience.

From this vantage point, organizations such as Disney and America Online (AOL) are well positioned for future success, since they sell commodities and service within the context of a unique and desirable experience. The experience may be emotional, physical, spiritual or intellectual and thus prevents imitators from instantly copying the component accessed by consumers. The successful business of the future must be original and proactive. The bottom line is profound but quite simple: Entertain people while they purchase related goodies, or struggle for survival as the fourth wave washes over the economic landscape. Quality, novelty, value and convenience will constitute the hallowed foursome of economic necessity.

Futurist Watts Wacker reviewed the argument underlying this theory and emerged convinced that "work is theater, and success will come from creating experiences and pushing the envelope by staging every interaction as a once-in-a-lifetime event."[4] In this economic fourth wave, the goal is to have brand presence and distinction while turning a hefty profit by giving consumers something memorable and fresh. Even common products and services will be promoted in relation to compelling events that are staged by actors in a marketing environment in which you satiate the desires of guests rather than mere customers.

Think about many of the more recent entries into the marketplace that have fared well by capitalizing upon the desire for experiences. The Hard Rock Café and even McDonalds are examples. McDonalds, despite fierce competition, has matured beyond a mere fast-food stop to a model experience vendor. Thousands of their shops include brightly colored play areas for children. Their successful Happy Meal is a family staple for millions, largely attributable to the toy that accompanies the burger and fries for the kiddies. Talk to children across the nation and they are not just familiar with the Golden Arches, but it is their restaurant of choice—primarily because of the experience they have at the nation's original drive-thru hamburger joint.

The Hard Rock Café is more than a restaurant—it delivers a music-based experience to its patrons. Rock music blasts from speakers strategically located throughout the venue. The floor often includes a stage for live performances. Music videos are projected from video walls and almost every available inch of wall space is turned into mini-shrines to rock heroes or events, displaying authentic rock memorabilia. Each restaurant generates significant revenue from the sale of T-shirts and other products, causing a number of outlets in the chain to stay open for longer hours than the food area of the establishment. Oh, yes, they also provide meals for those who wish to eat.

The Fifth Wave

Pine and Gilmore argue that the experience economy is just one stop along the road until we arrive at the ultimate economic destination: the transformation economy. Transformations are a natural extension of experiences. After all, the best experiences are not only memorable but also help you become a better person.

Why are transformations the final economic offering? Because transformation represents the endpoint in a natural progression. That chain starts with raw commodities manipulated into consumer goods; then those goods are delivered in unique ways through services, which are then re-engineered so that they are delivered as experiences, which become temporal transformations if sufficiently memorable and, finally, permanent transformations that are everlasting.[5] Translated, this means that only God can deliver on the promise of a permanent transformation through the power of Jesus' life, death and resurrection. The ultimate, eternal transformation is freely given by God, having been bought at a price no one else could pay and provided as a gift based on an experience with Christ, producing the final, perfect transactional transformation.

Unfortunately, an experience economy does not always lead to the eternal, Christ-based transformation that is possible. Pornography, gambling, prostitution and many other vices provide seductive experiences and transformations, creating economic growth alongside of moral deterioration. Transformational offerings glorify their particular worldview, however ugly or heinous the result. The power of experiences, no matter how debilitating, is evident in the thousands of people who make international journeys to Southeast Asia every year for experiences that involve pedophilia and homosexuality. These experiences facilitate transformation but not of an uplifting, enhancing nature.

As the national economy chugs along toward its transformative endpoint, imagine the possibilities related to genetic engineering and gene manipulation when there is money to be made and euphoria to be achieved. In a nation that has essentially lost its moral moorings, you have to wonder if the Church is prepared to provide moral direction that opposes the opportunities for people to prosper by feeling good. In fact, for the local church to maintain a place in people's lives, the experience economy raises the specter of having to provide evermore compelling spiritual performances that tickle people's ears, dazzle their eyes and titillate their minds. Will there be a place for Jesus to move in their hearts when all else is based on bigger, better, glitzier moving experiences? Will we retain the capacity to discern the still, small voice of God's Holy Spirit moving within us in the context of a loud, bright, professional, captivating life of experience after experience? We are not advocating a rejection of engaging and exciting worship and learning environments but a thoughtful and reasonable understanding of the implications of ministry in

> In the midst of spiritual performances that tickle people's ears and dazzle their eyes, will there be a place for Jesus to move in their hearts?

an age when the economy itself is fueled by the pursuit of transformational experiences.

Unleashing the Information Economy

There is a part of economic thought called the "economics of information" that relates to how businesses facilitate and complete transactions through the accumulation, analysis and application of information. We will spare you the details but will note that for businesses to get the right information, when and where it is needed, typically it has been a very expensive proposition. For instance, it has been estimated that taking the paperwork out of the health-care process would save $60 billion a year in the U.S. alone!

Information transfer has been one of the largest costs involved in economic transactions. Ronald Coase, who won a Nobel Prize in economics for his work in the area of transaction costs, has motivated people to reexamine recent shifts in the economy in light of what it takes to incorporate relevant information in common marketplace transactions.[6] One of his key arguments is that as markets become more efficient, organizations downsize, outsource and decentralize their operations. Such ruminations have helped to fuel interest in the Internet as an economic vehicle, since transactions fostered electronically drives transaction costs associated with the delivery of information almost to zero.

Ivory-tower theorizing on such matters can have some very personal implications for you. In *Unleashing the Killer App,* authors Larry Downes and Chunka Mui claim that when you combine Moore's Law (computer processing power doubles every 18 months) with Metcalf's Law (the value of a network increases significantly each time a new node is added) and Ronald Coase's theories on transaction costs, you get the "Law of Diminishing Firms."[7] Good-bye to the massive firms employing giant portions of our labor pool; hello to smaller, faster and nimbler firms. Companies will get smaller either because technology expedites procedures that used to be labor intensive or because it is becoming cheaper to outsource aspects of transactional processing. Finding qualified specialists to take on those tasks is getting easier and cheaper by the day. Either way, the results are the same: more efficient, focused and profitable companies using fewer employees to produce more output.

This trend does not mean that many of us will be out of a job, but it does mean that a large share of the newly created jobs will be in small companies. In fact, many new positions will come from within the freelance economy.

The Freelance Economy

The aforementioned "law of diminishing firms" is made possible by increasing the ease and speed with which we can transmit electronic communications and by wiring the world in entirely new ways for engagement in work. Smaller firms are multiplying in number partially due to advances in telecommuting, which enables people to accomplish more and more without leaving home.

When a new technology hits the scene, our first inclination is to use it to slightly modify the way we have been doing things. For example, television was initially used as a way of broadcasting a picture of radio shows, giving viewers a look at the talking heads in the radio studio. Television's pioneers simply took the new potential and tried to integrate it into the known, existing arena of activity, following the path of least resistance—and least benefit.

The invention of the telephone suffered from the same myopic deployment. Alexander Graham Bell told an investor that his device would eventually enable a businessman in New York to talk to another businessman in Boston. The incredulous investor asked why any businessman in New York would want or need to talk to someone in Boston when all of his associates were in New York. Since it had never been possible to talk to someone in Boston, the investor was confident that he and everyone like him would get along fine without this new device. Discouraged but not devastated by the rejection, Bell then raised money for his invention based on the idea that the "killer app" for the telephone would be enabling live concerts to be played in one city and listened to in another. Bell predicted that people would call in to listen to concerts, speeches or religious revivals. People were unable to think "outside the box" long enough to envision the true value of the invention.

We are on the precipice of a new economy that requires new ideas about labor and staffing. In the past, firms staffed for peak or near-peak utilization. The strategy made sense because it was expensive and time consuming to find (and orient) qualified workers when they were needed. Indeed, in a second wave (i.e., manufacturing) economy, physical presence and production are necessary. Finding workers required advertising, interviews, background checks and other resource-depleting activities. An alternative was to retain a search firm or employment agency to provide qualified staff, but that drained an average of 30 percent of the value of the worker from the company's revenue base.

The new era operates on different practices and principles. If you need a specific talent or skill in your business, you may quickly dip into a huge electronic pool of freelance talent and find the person you need by searching online databases of individuals who are available for hire, either on a permanent, short-term or project basis. The search can be done quickly, efficiently—and at way less than 30 percent of the employee's first year of compensation. Most large companies already use the Internet to facilitate hiring.

Resumé automation software enables an employer to capture the vital information of a potential hire. Soon companies will be instantly staffing projects by reaching into a pool of millions of service providers with a request for proposal. What effect will this have on the economy?

Take a real-life example. Suppose you need someone to design a promotional character for your company. A few years ago you would have called some friends or looked up designers in the phone book. The result would have been a list of maybe a half-dozen people in your area that you would then have to contact and interview regarding their availability, experience, quality, interest in the project, fee structures and the like. The process was very hit-or-miss, and it consumed substantial resources just to find someone marginally qualified. In the new era, however, you might simply post a description of your desired specialist on a website such as Ants.com. The result might well be 40 qualified specialists bidding to get the job (after hundreds of e-mails went out to potential designers). In the case in point, one of the responses was from a Pulitzer Prize-winning cartoonist—and he lived within 10 miles of the organization seeking the help. In no time at all, the new approach had enlisted the assistance of an eminently qualified specialist while consuming minimal resources. You would never have located that person otherwise: he was not listed in the Yellow Pages—and certainly not advertised as a Pulitzer Prize-winning cartoonist—was not in your friends' circle of acquaintances and was not shopped out for work by recruiting agencies. Welcome to the world of diminishing firms.

The existence of continually updated and growing databases of millions of potential service providers, combined with the electronic flow of hundreds of thousands of temporary projects getting posted, parsed and shipped out to this talent pool quickly and inexpensively, is turning the industrial revolution on its head. We are moving into the first decade of the Digital Counterrevolution.

Soon, millions of knowledge workers will begin to live their lives differently. "Live where you want, work where you live" will become the cry for the freelance lifestyle. Ants.com set up shop in Santa Barbara, California because its employees wanted to live what they preached. Santa Barbara has one of the best year-round climates in the country, with pristine beaches at hand and easy access to LA, San Jose and San Francisco. This trend, reflecting merely hundreds of organizations today, will be a wave of the future as people use technology to reshape how they think about and engage in gainful employment.

We will be fleeing the cities for the wired family farm.

This trend may lead us to choose the communities where we live based on cultural values and worldviews. Many of us will work primarily from our homes, making a physical appearance at a central office maybe two or three days a week, as required. (Both authors already engage in this practice.) "Live where you want, work where you live" will become the battle cry for reversing the industrial revolution. That revolution caused our great-great-grandparents to flee the family farm for the city. These days we will be fleeing the suburbs and cities for the wired family farm.

Consider the consequences for one's lifestyle when telecommuting replaces physical commuting. The average amount of time an employee is willing to commute to work has not changed since the start of the industrial revolution; the longest daily commute deemed tolerable by millions is 90 minutes, each way, per day. That was the distance New York factory workers were willing to walk to work at the turn of the nineteenth century, and it represents the amount of time many Los Angeles commuters drive today. (The average commute for Americans is much less—roughly 25 minutes each way.) At the outside, then, five days of commuting per week, at three hours per day, equates to a maximum of 15 hours spent in transit—the equivalent of one-third of a typical work week! Imagine the new possibilities opened up for such people if they are able to work from home three days a week. Consider the impact on quality of life when meetings are conducted by teleconference or videoconferencing, rather than in person.

Freed from the tyranny of office location, many people will choose where they raise their children and what community they live in independent from who they work for or where the office is located. They will have access to forms of entertainment, lifestyles and even churches that were not possible just 10 years ago. Expect to see both positive and negative outgrowths of this shift, including new versions of communes and other social experiments.

Sometimes you will be the victim of the freelance economy. The scope of global competition for freelance positions will be enormous. Specialists living in places you've never heard of may beat you out of jobs for which you are completely qualified—simply because those foreign competitors respond faster, can be hired for less or market themselves more effectively.

Sometimes you will be the beneficiary of the freelance economy. Let's say your child wakes you up at 2 A.M. with an earache. What will you do in the future? You will probably hook up your home medical diagnostic kit to your Internet device and call up a 24-hour Internet medical help line. And you'll have choices as to how to handle your dilemma. You could wake up a local physician at $200 an hour plus charges for after-hours service. You could contact the U.S.-trained physician in India who charges $80 per hour and has a few minutes between patients. You could use your automated medical camera, loaned to you by your health company in anticipation of such moments, to take a digital photo of your child's ear and submit it to an on-line computer diagnostic software routine for a diagnosis that may run about $10. The choice is yours; you are the beneficiary of good news, in this scenario.

Granted, nobody is protected from competition in this new economic jungle. Will these changes lead to a global labor depression? Hardly. If analysts are correct, this is likely to introduce a global economic boom. It has taken our government years to realize that they have been tracking productivity numbers so poorly that the economic policies they have implemented have essentially served as a brake on U.S. economic performance and potential. Recent innovations in computers, fiber optics, telecommunications, the Internet and biotechnology provide the opportunity to minimize the government's shortsightedness.

In the example above, when your child contracts the earache, you might have waited until the next morning, trudged to the doctor's office with your agonized child in tow and paid the $100 to have your doctor run basically the same diagnosis that you could have run for $10 on-line. If, instead, you engage in the on-line alternative diagnosis, then the $100 dollars you would have spent to eliminate the earache would be reduced to $10 dollars, resulting in a savings of $90 which you will then spend on something else. Throughout recorded human history, when we have freed an economy from more mundane economic requirements, labor-saving devices have been created, improved living standards have resulted, and creativity has flourished.

Where Are We Headed?

The days ahead are both exciting and frightening. New skills will be required to compete successfully in the knowledge world. Upgraded training will become a regular routine in people's lives as we strive to remain competent in the new economy. The flow of the economy will look different and new measures of the strength of the economy will slowly be adapted. Inevitably, many individuals and government officials will resist change and attempt to fight innovations and progress. Their success at doing so will be to the detriment of our society. Here are some other coming economic and business-related realities for which you should be prepared:

• Education will continue to be the most important determinant of potential employability. Competition for entrance into the best schools will become even fiercer. At the elementary and secondary school levels, after-school study centers will multiply, sales of educational software for consumers (i.e. digital tutors) will skyrocket, and children will be forced to study harder and longer.

- The gap between what the average professional makes and the average high school graduate makes will widen.
- Services will continue to drive growth in the U.S. economy. The age of manufacturing driving the national economy is over.
- Computer-related jobs will continue to lead the expansion of our job market, followed closely by positions in health care (because we are a graying society) and education (because we live in a knowledge society).
- Experiences will become an important growth industry. People will pay more for experiences than they will for their groceries. The travel and entertainment industries will continue to grow.
- Adventure travel, cruises and new forms of experiences (like educational adventures) will be created.
- People will extend the concepts of personal trainers and coaches into one-on-one language, music, dance and other forms of self-improvement. The best and most charismatic coaches will be in high demand.
- Las Vegas will continue to grow. Increasing competition in Las Vegas will develop with the offer of more explicit vices, the advertising and promotion of which is likely to develop through the Internet.
- There will be fewer large companies. Many companies will reduce their number of employees while increasing total sales and profitability.
- Layoffs and downsizing will increase dramatically, but most of the people affected by those cuts will land on their feet economically and be equally or more satisfied with their new employment.
- It will seem like everyone is freelancing. Programmers for large corporations will take projects on the side (evenings and weekends) to make extra money. Being a "consultant" will not always mean you are between jobs looking for something permanent. Many will prefer this lifestyle choice.

- Some knowledge workers will relocate to less expensive locations. Others will choose their homes based on the values of their neighbors. A few will move out of the country at least for part of the year. (Baja California's winters will look mighty attractive to a growing number of flexible workers.)
- The number of female-owned businesses will continue to climb beyond the current 38 percent to close to half of all businesses by the end of this decade. A majority of the newly minted female-owned companies will be small, home-based operations that provide women a challenge, income and flexibility.
- Hispanic-owned businesses will also flourish in this decade as the Hispanic population continues to blossom, investment capital for such businesses expands and second- and third-generation Hispanics launch their own enterprises in their adopted culture.
- Consumer-direct marketing, driven partly by on-line transactions, will exceed $1 trillion in sales by 2003 and may double again by the end of the decade.
- Impulse buying will grow significantly as people get swept away by the entertaining presentations related to services and products and as buying provides relief from stress. Currently, one-fourth of all women shop in order to release stress. That figure—and the associated sales revenues—will increase as the decade progresses.
- Companies will struggle to find young, talented, hard-working employees to raise up within the company. This will become increasingly difficult based on the mind-set of young adults: they want money, benefits, authority and a life. One common solution will be businesses raiding the executive and midlevel ranks of competitors to quickly gain access to proven talent and productive capacity.

What Can You Do?

Christians will find the transformation of the economy fraught with ethical and moral challenges. It will be a decade when being a Christian presents almost constant opportunities to live Christianly.

Because of the intensified significance of a college education, believers must acknowledge and prepare to battle the forces of secularism that have taken over on college campuses. Christian colleges are one alternative. Demanding that America's youth have exposure to Christian values, Christian historical perspectives and different types of intellectual role models is another alternative that we must be willing to support.

We can offer free or low cost after-school programs for homework and training sessions to children whose parents work or to children of single-parent homes. We can offer this service while explicitly teaching God's Word to these children. This is a tough call as it may encourage some parents to choose a bigger home or nicer car over the well-being of their children. On the other hand this is the path our society is headed down, and we may be able to redeem more than we lose by reaching out to these children.

Encourage your legislators to provide religious schools with the same benefits accorded to public schools and other private educational institutions. Families that rely upon Christian schools deserve the same tax credits as do parents who make different educational choices for their kids.

There is a fine line to be walked by Christians between teaching their children the value of education and marketplace achievement versus life-long reliance upon the provision of God and a view of wealth that is not based on getting ahead at all costs. Christians have a responsibility to work and to perform well in their jobs and to live in a financially responsible manner, but they must also set their sights not on material wealth but on spiritual riches.

If your church chooses lay leaders for elderships and deaconships, avoid the temptation to select individuals on the basis of their success in the world's eyes. Seek people who earnestly follow God and apply their spiritual gifts to all that they do—inside the church and outside of it as well. Avoid the natural and widespread tendency to assume that someone who is financially secure has his/her act together. (When business guru Tom Peters was asked if someone could have a balanced life and be highly successful, he said his research and experience suggested it is not possible.)

Intentionally build great experiences for your family. Camps, vacations, travel and other experiences shared by the family provide fond memories, deeper relationships and a broader worldview as well as wonderful teaching moments. The American way—sending each individual in his/her own direction to satiate personal experiential appetites and preferences—often undermines the strength of family and the absorption of Christian values.

Get involved in transformational opportunities with your family and friends. Bible studies, accountability groups, worship and faith-based community service projects are examples of the transformational activities in which we are called to participate. We must be careful, in the coming economic transitions, not to prioritize the entertainment aspect of events over the substantive component, but also not to minimize the potential value of building excitement into faith-building experiences.

Prepare to assist family and friends to get back on their feet after their current employer releases them. (This will be especially prevalent among those who work for large corporations.) Protect yourself and your family against the winds of economic change by setting aside enough savings to withstand at least six months of unemployment. Further protect and prepare yourself by developing transferable and sought-after skills.

If your situation allows for it, consider the possibilities of living in a community that has values similar to yours. While not everyone has the flexibility or financial capacity to move to such a place, such a relocation may be enormously helpful in facilitating a stronger and more viable family life.

Remember that the economy moves in waves: Every boom time is followed by a compensatory downswing. During the good times, save up for the coming harsh times. As a person of faith blessed by the goodness of God, be prepared to share your good fortune with family and fellow believers who have not been so foresighted. Those opportunities may be some of your most powerful witnessing moments.

Notes

1. *Occupational Outlook Handbook* (Indianapolis, IN: JIST Works, Inc., 2000), p. 5.
2. Lester Brown and Christopher Flavin and Hilary French, *State of the World 2000: A Worldwatch Institute Report on Progress Toward a Sustainable Society,* ed. Linda Starke (New York: W. W. Norton and Company, Inc., 2000), p. 170.
3. B. Joseph Pine II and James H. Gilmore, *The Experience Economy* (Boston, MA: Harvard Business School Press, 1999).
4. Source unknown.

5. Pine and Gilmore, *The Experience Economy*, p. 206.
6. R. H. Coase, *The Firm, the Market and the Law* (Chicago, IL: University of Chicago Press, 1988), n.p.
7. Larry Downes and Chunka Mui, *Unleashing the Killer App* (Boston, MA: Harvard Business Press, 2000), n.p.

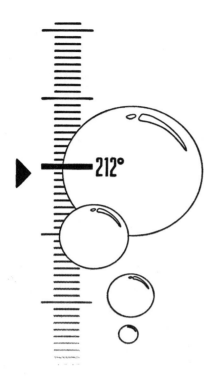

CHAPTER NINE

WHAT AMERICANS REALLY BELIEVE

Future Glimpse

Jill looked at her boss, the hotel manager, in disbelief. "But changing that policy is in direct conflict with the instructions that Corporate sent last week. I know it makes more sense to do it your way, but isn't that just asking for trouble?"

He smiled at her. "Come on, Jill, you know what the Bible says: 'It's better to seek forgiveness than to ask for permission.'" He chuckled to himself as he left her tiny office.

Jill shook her head in amusement. Her boss was an avid church goer, and she sometimes marveled at how he brought his faith into his life choices. She thought back to some of the other nuggets of wisdom from the Bible that he had integrated into his decisions and conversations at work. "God helps those who help themselves" was one of his favorites. "Don't sweat it, God wants you to be happy" was another gem she had filed away in her mind for the next time he asked her to take on a particularly odious task. His dismissal of such ancient notions as the devil, a Holy Spirit or even heaven and hell had also caused her to think. "Those are just literary devices used to communicate a concept—stuff like evil, power or separation from God," was how he'd explained it.

His clever summaries of heavy Bible principles usually made her smile— and almost always made her feel better about herself. Jill had little direct experience with the Bible, and she couldn't bear to listen to those radio and TV preachers; they were always yelling about something. She absorbed spiritual principles from movies, television and her friends. She really appreciated how some people—Oprah in particular—made religious ideas practical. She found so much of the dialogue in TV shows and movies more inspiring and useful than church sermons because the media presentations made the important ideas easy to remember, they made logical sense and brought her peace. That was what religion was all about, after all—helping people to understand how God could help them to become comfortable and happy and to achieve a sense of meaning and purpose in life.

Jill glanced at the small, round wall clock that hung above her desk. It was that time of day when the influx of guests checking in would be heaviest, and she would be expected to help at the front desk. It was the most dreaded part of her job. She was so far behind in the bookkeeping and she hadn't even started on the filing. She weighed her options for a minute then decided: She would stay here and get her work done rather than trudge downstairs to the front desk to help with the arriving guests. *After all*, she thought to herself as she broke out in a big smile, *even God knows that it's better to seek forgiveness than to ask for permission.*

The Defining Nature of Faith

You are defined by what you believe. Your behavior, your relationships, your lifestyle, your worship, your values, your choices, your goals—everything about you is influenced by your beliefs about what is right and wrong, good or bad, appropriate or inappropriate, meaningful or meaningless and so forth. Consequently, your life is driven by your faith, which is the summation of your beliefs.

Americans are a people of tremendous faith. But our faith is multidimensional—and often outside the realm of spirituality. Think of how we express our real faith, day after day, through demonstrations of trust and belief. When we drive a car at 70 miles per hour, we believe that the brakes will stop the car within just a few seconds—and at least a few inches short of the car in front of us. We trust that everyone will obey the traffic lights and not randomly plow into us because they don't feel like waiting. We believe the nightly news crew conveys real incidents from a relatively objective point of view. We trust banks to return the money we deposited—maybe even with a little bit of interest—when we demand it. We believe doctors and surgeons know what to do to improve the health of our bodies. We trust the floor under our feet not to cave in and the roof over our head not to crash on top of us. We board airplanes and trains in the belief that they will deliver us safely and quickly to our desired destinations.

You get the idea. We endlessly demonstrate faith in ourselves, in the people that we know (and many we've never met), in nature and in the objects that we have created (many of which we don't completely understand). Why is it, then, that we seem to have so much difficulty trusting the Creator of it all, who has revealed and proven Himself to be loving, reliable and omnipotent, when He spells out for us relatively simple ideas about truth, faith and lifestyle?

In short, it is because we live in an age of spiritual anarchy. Our worldviews typically inform us that there is no absolute moral or spiritual truth (or that if there is, that truth is not highly significant), that a person's faith is personal and can be customized to his/her needs without consequences, and that we alone are the final arbiters of appropriate thought and behavior. The rejection and elimination of universal standards and accountability that has wormed its way through every segment of society since the mid-'60s has empowered us to follow our own whims and will. The result is that more and more Americans have accepted the responsibility of crafting their own religious paradigm. Some people have done this consciously and intentionally, while others have done it without realizing that is what they were doing. However people have arrived at that place, though, Americans today are alarmingly relaxed and comfortable about their theology. The predominant belief is that it doesn't matter what you believe as long as you believe something and feel good about it.

Nothing could be further from the truth.

Spiritual Anarchy

Anarchy is a state in which there are no rules, limitations or order that directs people's lives; chaos and confusion reign. America is in a state of spiritual anarchy today. People adopt religious labels for themselves that bear no relationship to what they believe or how they live. Millions of adults say they believe in and worship God, but they have no idea what worship means, who God is, what He stands for or what He expects of those who wish to relate to Him. Importantly, nobody cares about the inconsistencies embedded within our faith philosophies, creeds and practices. At the beginning of the third millennium, America is a land where you may call yourself what you want, believe whatever you want, live however you wish and do what you will with religion, faith and spirituality. All that's required of you is that you're comfortable with your choices and that they do not infringe on someone else's exercise of their choices.

> **Religious labels do not reflect what people believe or how they live.**

Think about the Christian Church in the U.S. Spiritual anarchy is rampant. People wholeheartedly believe things that are antithetical to what the Bible teaches—and nobody challenges them or imposes sanctions on them for their beliefs. In fact, we have become so theologically complacent that nobody really knows what anyone else believes because we're too busy doing our own thing. We cannot really call the faith of American Christians a Bible-based faith. It is a synthetic, syncretic faith.

Twelve years ago I began speaking and writing that syncretism had become America's faith of choice. Syncretism is a fluid combination of disparate and sometimes opposing religious ideas that have been combined into something completely new and sometimes illogical. Living in this era of information surplus, people are regularly bombarded with theological perspectives that a discerning mind will not filter; without a clear understanding of theological foundations and implications, every doctrine sounds just as valid as the next. Labels, such as "Christian" or "New Age," simply become generic categorical descriptions; for example, the label "Christian" no longer means beliefs and practices associated with the Christian faith, but instead means elements related to the religious realm.

Here's how it works. People observe, hear or read something related to spirituality and faith that they like. They then integrate it into their theological framework, whether it is consistent with God's Word or not. That process repeats itself day after day, resulting in a theological foundation that is being continually reshaped, without any document or touchstone that serves as the filter through which every new idea or principle is evaluated. The filter is exclusively personal: does the idea feel right, does it appear to offer positive outcomes for me, does it square with my past experience? Before you know it, the average born-again,[1] baptized, churchgoing person has embraced elements of Buddhism, Hinduism, Judaism, Islam, Mormonism, Scientology, Unitarianism and Christian Science—without any idea that they have just created their own unique faith. In most cases the act of compromising biblical foundations is not done intentionally or even knowingly. As we say in our society, it just happens.

When I first conveyed this message, most church leaders smiled and shook their heads, rejecting the possibility that such silliness would occur on their watch. The idea that lifelong, church-attending, born-again believers would embrace theology that emanated from L. Ron Hubbard, Shirley MacLaine and Maharishi Mahesh Yogi was laughed off as foolishness.

Nobody's laughing today.

Let's be honest. Most of us do not have enough theological training, enough time for reflection and a sufficient thirst for spiritual purity to screen out the unbiblical theological messages that are thrust upon us every day. The world of entertainment and mass communications—through television, radio, contemporary music, movies, magazines, art, video games and pop literature—is indisputably the most extensive and influential theological training system in the world. From commercials to sitcoms, from biographies to hit songs, from computer simulation games to talk shows, God's principles are challenged every moment of every day, in very entertaining, palatable and discreet ways. Few Christians currently have the intellectual and spiritual tools to identify and reject the garbage.

Does it really matter? you ask. Absolutely! Since your life is a direct reflection of the values, principles and truths in which you believe, and because those elements are greatly impacted by your religious beliefs and convictions, the substance of your faith matters a great deal. It mattered enough for Jesus to take every opportunity He had to expound on those principles and truths. It mattered enough for God to make sure that humanity would have His Word as an enduring guide to holy living—a guidebook that implores us to embody those principles and truths and energetically purge our lives of false principles.

What We Believe

In 2000, 85 percent of all adults concurred that their religious faith was "very important in my life." The allure of faith is exhibited by the fact that even two-thirds of the unchurched contend that their religious faith is very important to them. But what exactly do Americans believe? And where do those beliefs come from?

Most adults submit that their spiritual views come largely from the Bible and from the teaching they get from their church (which, presumably, is Bible-based). Interestingly, more than 4 out of 5 adults say that they know all the basic teachings of the Bible. (In a few minutes, after we have taken a guided tour of America's theological perspectives, you may beg to differ.)

An examination of what people think about the Bible itself, though, is revealing. About half of the people who call themselves Christians but are not born again—a group that constitutes a majority of churchgoers—have a "low view" of Scripture, contending that it has interesting religious information but that it contains errors and falsehoods. Even one-fifth of the born-again crowd believe that the Bible contains errors. That may help to explain why many of the fundamental stories and lessons in the Bible are recalled or interpreted differently by the public at large than by the pastors who strive to communicate God's truth to the people.

Here's what we, as a nation, believe.[2]

Beliefs About the Bible

The nation is divided on what to make of the Bible. Four out of 10 adults firmly agree that the Bible is totally accurate in everything it teaches—not necessarily inerrant, mind you, but infallible. (An additional 1 out of 5 offers moderate agreement with this notion.) That fits with the finding that 6 out of 10 adults believe that the Bible is without error (one-fifth say it is the actual Word of God and can be taken literally, and one-third say it is the inspired Word of God and contains no errors, although some of the substance is symbolic, not literal). The remaining 4 out of 10 assert that the Bible may be inspired but includes factual errors (one-fifth), is neither inspired nor accurate (one-eighth) or is just another religious book (1 out of 12 adults).

So, if 9 out of 10 adults own at least one Bible, most of them read on their own during the course of a year, most of them say they know its contents pretty well, and the majority endorses the view that the Bible is reliable, then how come so few understand some of its fundamental principles? For instance, three-quarters of all adults believe that the Bible teaches that God helps those who help themselves. That, of course, is the exact *opposite* of what the Bible teaches: Jesus had to die on the cross for humanity, because we are incapable of helping ourselves. Even most born-again Christians get this one wrong: 7 out of every 10 believers attribute the principle that "God helps those who help themselves" to Scripture.

This case of mistaken perception is more than just a theological blunder: It is the very cornerstone of contemporary American theology. Sometime within the past two decades we decided that if life is going to work out as we'd like, we had better take things into our own hands and essentially restructure the order of the universe.

Toward that end we determined that we can and will determine our destiny and have thus demoted God to the role of Senior Assistant to Humanity. The world used to revolve around the principles and admonitions of the Creator God; now, He must work around our agenda. We used to strive to please Him, but now we strive for self-satisfaction with the assumption that if we can make ourselves happy, God will find joy and pleasure in that as well. Rather than worrying about how our thoughts, words and deeds are perceived by God, we simply focus on how to make the most of what's available to us and have the faith that He will recognize and appreciate a good effort when He sees it.

We now believe that whatever is good, positive, meaningful or satisfying in our lives will be the result of our own efforts. If we work hard enough, do enough good deeds, conceive clever or effective strategies, have laudable intentions, meet our goals—in essence, if we do whatever it takes to get where we want to go—then God, as if by divine necessity, will bless our efforts. We have relegated the Almighty to the role of pasting His heavenly seal of approval on our best work, certifying those efforts as universally acceptable and worthy of commendation. In other words, we are now at the center of things, and God is on the periphery. If life is to be worth living, we must make it so; God will watch, applaud and may even help us along in some unseen and perhaps unexpected ways, but it is our initiative and capacity that makes life fulfilling.

WHAT AMERICANS BELIEVE

KEY: ASt = agree strongly; ASw = agree somewhat; DSw = disagree somewhat; DSt = disagree strongly; DK = don't know; BA = born-again Christian; NBA = not born-again Christian

	ASt	ASw	DSw	DSt	DK	BA	NBA
Beliefs About the Bible							
It's totally accurate in all of its teachings	43%	17%	18%	15%	6%	85%	43%
The Bible teaches that God helps those who help themselves	53%	22%	7%	14%	5%	68%	81%

Beliefs About Deity and the Trinity

Statement							
When He lived on Earth, Jesus Christ committed sins	20%	19%	9%	43%	9%	24%	49%
The Holy Spirit is a symbol of God's presence or power, but is not a living entity	41%	20%	8%	25%	7%	53%	66%
After He was crucified and died, Jesus Christ did not return to life physically	29%	11%	11%	41%	8%	30%	48%
Jesus Christ was born to a virgin	71%	10%	6%	6%	8%	97%	73%

Beliefs About Spiritual Power

Statement							
Angels exist and influence people's lives	49%	32%	8%	7%	5%	92%	71%
The universe was originally created by God	74%	13%	4%	5%	4%	99%	77%
All of the miracles described in the Bible actually took place	56%	14%	14%	10%	6%	91%	58%

Beliefs About Truth, Morality and Integrity

Statement							
The Bible provides us with absolute moral truths that are the same for all people in all situations, without exception	50%	18%	15%	12%	6%	85%	54%
Whatever is right for your life or works best for you is the only truth you can know	16%	16%	28%	34%	7%	26%	35%
The way things are these days, lying is sometimes necessary	7%	25%	15%	51%	2%	24%	40%
Viewing pornography is a matter of taste, not morality	12%	20%	13%	50%	6%	19%	42%

Source: Barna Research Group, Ltd., Ventura, CA. Based on nation surveys of 1,000 or more randomly sampled adults 18 or older.

Thus stands another contradiction in life. We believe in God, but we have effectively neutered Him by making Him our slave or part of our entourage. We believe in the Bible, but we interpret it to say that God has passed the baton of power to us. We argue that the Bible is accurate in its teachings, but we exhibit selective recall when we recite the Bible principles by which we live and the universe operates. If God wants to be part of the activity, He needs to get on our bandwagon because we're on a roll.

Beliefs About Deity and the Trinity

More than 9 out of 10 adults say they believe in God. But if you dig a bit deeper you discover that not everyone is referring to the same deity. About two-thirds of adults believe in the existence of the God described in the Bible. One-third define themselves as God or accept other theistic views (pantheism, naturalism, etc.).

Our views about Jesus Christ are even more convoluted. While most people agree that He was born to a virgin, only half of the country says that He actually had a physical resurrection or that He lived a sinless life. Consider the implications of these assertions. One hundred million Americans are denying the divinity of Jesus Christ and trashing the biblical claims to His power over death. These numbers, by the way, are growing. And it is not just the pagans and heathen who promote these views. One out of every 4 born-again Christians states that Jesus sinned while on Earth. Three out of 10 born-again adults reject the narrative of His physical resurrection.

The capstone on this revisionist theology is the astounding fact that more than 6 out of 10 adults claim that the Holy Spirit is a symbol of God's presence or power, but not a real entity. Even a majority of born-again Christians deny the existence of the Holy Spirit! Once again, this puts a major dent in the idea that the Trinity exists or that God is alive in His followers through His Spirit or that Scripture can be trusted when it talks about miracles, power or how God works. Think about the implications of praying to a God in whom we don't fully believe, calling on His name with faith less sizable than the proverbial mustard seed.

Beliefs About Truth, Morality and Integrity

Here's another point of confusion and contradiction evident in our theology. On the one hand we discovered that two-thirds of all adults agreed with the statement that the Bible provides us with absolute moral truths that are the same for everyone, without exception. But when we asked people if there are any moral absolutes that are unchanging or if moral and ethical choices depend on circumstances and personal preferences, confusion emerged. One-third said they believe moral truth is absolute and unchanging. Slightly fewer said moral truth depends on the individual and his/her circumstances. The remaining one-third admitted that they had no idea.

WHAT AMERICANS BELIEVE

KEY: ASt = agree strongly; ASw = agree somewhat; DSw = disagree somewhat; DSt = disagree strongly; DK = don't know; BA = born-again Christian; NBA = not born-again Christian

	ASt	ASw	DSw	DSt	DK	BA	NBA
Beliefs about Sin, Evil and Salvation							
Personal responsibility to tell other people your religious beliefs	31%	17%	22%	29%	3%	72%	31%
The devil, or Satan, is not a living being but is a symbol of evil	40%	18%	9%	27%	7%	47%	65%
If a person is generally good or does enough good things for others, they will earn a place in heaven	31%	20%	11%	31%	7%	31%	65%
All people experience the same outcome after death, regardless of their spiritual beliefs	28%	13%	16%	36%	7%	29%	50%
There are some crimes or sins people commit that God cannot forgive	20%	10%	15%	50%	5%	23%	35%

KEY: ASt = agree strongly; ASw = agree somewhat; DSw = disagree somewhat; DSt = disagree strongly; DK = don't know; BA = born-again Christian; NBA = not born-again Christian

	ASt	ASw	DSw	DSt	DK	BA	NBA
The whole idea of sin is outdated	7%	6%	15%	68%	5%	8%	17%
People who do not consciously accept Jesus Christ as their Savior will be condemned to hell	29%	8%	18%	37%	8%	65%	19%
All people will be judged by God after they die, regardless of their belief	73%	12%	5%	7%	4%	96%	81%
After death, some people are reincarnated in another life form	10%	13%	14%	15%	12%	10%	26%

Beliefs About Life

	ASt	ASw	DSw	DSt	DK	BA	NBA
You can lead a full and satisfying life without pursuing spiritual maturity	19%	24%	16%	37%	4%	28%	55%
You are certain that God wants you, personally, to help the poor	45%	24%	14%	8%	8%	84%	59%
God is ultimately responsible for allowing suffering in your life	14%	10%	17%	55%	5%	27%	22%
It is important to you to experience spiritual growth	69%	19%	5%	6%	2%	96%	81%
You are still trying to figure out the purpose and meaning of your life	23%	20%	15%	40%	2%	36%	49%
It is more important to please God than to achieve success or acceptance	58%	20%	11%	4%	6%	91%	68%
All religious faiths teach the same basic principles	23%	24%	13%	37%	4%	30%	55%

Source: Barna Research Group, Ltd., Ventura, CA. Based on national surveys of 1,000 or more randomly sampled adults 18 or older.

Probing further, we found that one-quarter of the people who believe absolute moral truth exists admitted that they could be persuaded otherwise. Likewise, two-thirds of those who said they believe truth is relative let on that they, too, could be persuaded otherwise. Where does that leave us? One-quarter of the population firmly believe that absolute moral truth exists. One out of 10 adults is convinced that truth is relative. One out of 20 leans toward believing truth is absolute, 1 out of 10 leans toward believing it is relative. The remaining *half* of the population has no real stand on one of the pivotal perspectives for life!

The prospects of straightening out this mess in the near future are limited. Only one-third of the public claim that figuring out the answer to this dilemma is very important to them—and three-quarters of those people have already staked out a definitive stand on the issue. In other words, grappling with the issue of truth stimulates a massive yawn from most people.

Perhaps it is this indifference to moral truth that has led one-third of Americans to believe that sometimes lying is "necessary" and one-third to argue that viewing pornography is a matter of taste, not a moral issue. (Note, by the way, that at least 1 out of every 5 born-again adults endorses each of these views.) Earlier in this book, in our discussion of moral anarchy, the existence of such wayward thinking may not have seemed feasible. In light of people's confusion over the existence of moral truth, whether or not it is even important and whether one's faith is related to such issues, the environment for extreme independence on the matter is clearly in place.

Beliefs About Sin, Evil and Salvation

There is good news regarding sin and judgment. People believe that sin is still a relevant concept and that all humans will be judged by God.

Unfortunately, most people expect the Judge to go easy on the sentencing. In fact, most adults have unwittingly embraced a tri-furcated theology, stating that you may either gain entry into God's eternal presence (i.e., heaven) by accepting His grace available through Jesus Christ, by completing a sufficient quantity or magnitude of good deeds or by relying upon God's boundless and forgiving love. Incredibly, more than one-third of all born-again adults have adopted this synthetic evangelistic stance: "You can enter heaven by grace, as I will, or you can choose one of the alternative paths God has provided for you." This explains why there is so little passion for evangelism in America. We have squeezed God's truth through our own interpretive filter and concluded that He has provided us with options to choose from—just the way we like it. We can choose grace, works or universalism, but we can rest assured with the false premise that all paths lead to heaven.

We have further reduced the pressure to acknowledge and confess our sins and to trust in Jesus as the only way to salvation by denying the existence of Satan. Just as we have pooh-poohed the existence of the Holy Spirit, so have 6 out of 10 adults determined that the devil is just a symbol of evil. Again, massive numbers of born-again believers—half!—concur that Satan is not a reality. The enemy of God is clearly winning the battle for the hearts of tens of millions of Americans, including many who earnestly seek to serve the King, but are not spiritually equipped to do battle on His behalf.

Beliefs About Life

Interestingly, Americans are three times more likely to say that you can live a full and satisfying life without pursuing spiritual development and maturity than they are to say that their spiritual life is not important to them. In other words, spirituality matters, but it is not necessary to maximize your life. Spirituality is a value-added element in our society, an extra attachment that we embrace when it makes sense or happens comfortably, a lifestyle choice; but almost half of the nation feels that it can get along just fine without spirituality, if necessary.

This must certainly be related to the discovery that almost half of all adults are still struggling to figure out the meaning and purpose of their life. Notice in the accompanying chart that slightly more than 1 out of every 3 born-again individuals is trying to ascertain the meaning and purpose of their life. One would have thought that, since most of those individuals accept the authority and infallibility of Scripture, the purpose of life would be crystal clear.

However, the spiritual chaos of the age is fostered by notions such as that held by the half of the population who maintain that it really doesn't matter what faith you align yourself with since all of the major religious groups teach the same basic principles. Other surveys we have conducted even pointed out that most people believe that Catholics and Protestants have the same beliefs regarding salvation and that Mormons are Christians.

Beliefs About Spiritual Power
There can be no denying it: Americans love a good show of power. We root for the underdog, but we always side with the winner. (If you want evidence, study the ascendancy of modern-day heroes like Michael Jordan, Mark McGwire, Steve Jobs, Ronald Reagan and Tom Hanks, and note the point at which each of them transitioned from being appreciated wanna-bes to heralded champions of the people.) The spiritual realm is a good showcase for power.

SPIRITUAL PERSPECTIVES

	Agree	Disagree
God is the all-powerful, all-knowing and perfect Creator of the universe who still rules the world today	68%	26%
A person's most important task in life is to take care of his/her family	56%	36%
The apostle Paul was originally a leader in the Jewish group responsible for Jesus' death	37%	38%
Jesus taught there are some situations in which divorce is permissible	39%	43%
People are blessed by God so they can enjoy life as much as possible	72%	21%

Source: Barna Research Group, Ltd., Ventura, CA. Based on national surveys of 1,000 or more randomly sampled adults 18 or older.

People accept the existence and influence of angels. (Yes, it's inconsistent with our rejection of the Holy Spirit and Satan.) They accept creationism as valid. They even buy into the miracles reported in the Bible. (How odd that they don't accept the Resurrection.)

You might want to again look over the tables outlining our beliefs, this time trying to imagine how the introduction of non-Christian principles—

whether they are New Age, cult-based or from other world religions—has mutated God's perfect principles. (For example, the popular self-help movement and motivational speakers of our society are largely based on Eastern philosophies that assert that you are divine and powerful and can therefore determine your destiny by strength of will and other tricks of the mind and spirit. Such beliefs have clearly diminished the percentage of people who describe God as the only true deity and it has made a mockery of Satan's existence.)

Changes over Time

Although our theology changes only a bit from year to year, those tiny shifts add up to something significant over the course of time. In the '90s alone the percentages of people who shifted away from Bible views to unbiblical views increased substantially. Belief in God as described in the Bible declined by 8 percent while the proportion of adults who strongly believe that Satan does not exist jumped by 14 percent. The number of those who maintain that the Bible is totally accurate in all that it teaches shrunk by 14 percent. Belief in the personal responsibility to share their faith with others eroded by 9 percent. The idea that good people can earn their way into heaven is accepted by 28 percent more people today than just a decade ago. Clearly, our theological foundations are being rapidly eroded by the constant battering they take at the hands of a theologically inept society.

Part of the change process relates to the emergence of new generations. Over time each generation mellows a bit from its radical youth views to more mainstream biblical views. But the theological starting point for young people entering adulthood is less and less bibliocentric. When Boomers were in their 20s, almost half of them firmly believed the Bible was totally accurate; among today's Busters and Mosaics, barely one-third hold that same stand. A decade ago, slightly less than one-third of 20-something Boomers strongly agreed that Satan does not exist. Among today's teens and 20-somethings, the figure is about two-fifths. Busters and teenagers are 32 percent more likely than Boomers, Builders and Seniors to strongly believe that a good person can earn entrance into heaven. Similarly, the younger generations are more likely than the older segments to hold strong but incorrect beliefs about Jesus' having sinned, the nature of God, creation, the fulfillment possible without spiritual development and the responsibility to share one's faith.

The long-term outcome, of course, is that we will continue to see biblical truth lost in the cacophony of feel-good messages that fill the marketplace and seduce our people. Jesus' exhortation for us to be in the world but not of it must include the commitment to provide people with His truths and principles in every forum available. Our studies show that the greatest theological influences in people's lives are their family, their peers and the mass media. Certain church experiences when people are young (typically preteen) may also leave lasting impressions. The evidence is mounting that the Church, if it chooses to retreat to a Sunday-morning offensive, will continue to lose its share of people's minds and hearts.

Contradictions and Confusion

If you are still unconvinced that spiritual anarchy is in process, take a look at just some of the points of theological confusion and ignorance we have just highlighted:

- People say they know the basic teaching of the Bible, but are typically in error on such simple matters as divorce, the reason for God's blessings, the primary purpose of life and whether God helps those who help themselves.
- We claim the Bible is accurate and trustworthy, but we doubt the existence of moral truth and don't care that much about getting it right anyway.
- We accept the deity of Jesus, but reject his sinless nature and His physical resurrection.
- We allow for angels but not for the Holy Spirit or Satan (a fallen angel).
- We endorse the miracles of the Bible as having taken place as written, but we deny the physical return of the Lord and the gift of the Spirit.
- We accept sin as relevant to modern life, but we lean toward situational acceptance of lying and pornography.

- Huge numbers of people who say their salvation is by God's grace alone nevertheless allow that others might find salvation through other means.
- Most adults acknowledge that God wants them to reach out to the poor, but relatively few make any real effort to do so.
- Three out of 4 believers note that they have a responsibility to share their faith with nonbelievers, but most of them rarely, if ever, do so and make almost no effort to facilitate greater involvement in evangelism in the future.

Does that strike you as a lineup that characterizes a body of individuals who have a common and deep commitment to a life-changing cause?

It is also striking how many tenuously held beliefs we possess in comparison to how few firmly held convictions we claim. We have strong convictions about God creating the world; the existence of angels; the relevance of sin; the forgiving nature of God. We have merely flimsy hopes that salvation by grace is real; the Bible is reliable; that there is eternal damnation; that God wants a relationship with us; that spiritual maturity matters or that we have a significant spiritual responsibility. In a nation widely regarded as the most religious on earth—and, until recent years, thought to be the most solidly Christian—you would expect to find a much deeper set of Bible-based spiritual convictions.

Where Are We Headed?

The great tragedy is that now that the genie of syncretism has been let out of the bottle, the chances of capturing that genie and jamming it back in the bottle are slim. Yet, until we curb our appetite for culture-based, self-defined theology, we will see the continued demolition of biblical truth.

Here are some of the outcomes we are likely to experience in people's beliefs during the course of this decade:

- Ecumenism—the uniting and joint ministry of churches with disparate theological traditions—will flourish this decade as people celebrate relationships, diversity and cooperation rather than clarity of conviction and unity without co-optation.

- New tools for Bible learning will be developed. You may expect several courageous and creative organizations to launch new product lines which essentially amount to the reinvention of the Bible, accomplished without changing the content of God's Word.

- New teaching strategies will be adopted across the country as churches struggle to capture and maintain people's attention while imparting and implanting truth. Just as public school and college education is being radically reshaped by technology, physiology, politics and cultural expectations, so will church-based training venture into new methods.

- Bible knowledge will continue to decline. Unless a cataclysmic event occurs to drive people back to a genuine acceptance of Bible-based truth, our casual commitment to God's ways will become even more casual and self-directed.

- A growing number of churches will confront biblical illiteracy by starting their own theological training schools. While this will help churches to have individuals in lay ministry who have a better sense of Bible content, the volume of people educated in these schools will not be able to keep up with the rate of population growth or the volume of the culture's competing messages.

- Non-Christian faith groups will gain an increasingly large foothold in the U.S., since their theological foundations will be less and less disturbing to people. The new groups will gain ground by emphasizing their response to high profile felt needs such as positive relationships, self-improvement, integrity, good health, purposeful living, retaining control, achievement without stress and having fun.

- Pragmatic Christian principles will be reduced to sound bites. (For example, Jesus' teaching on conflict resolution found in Matthew 18:15-17 might be reduced to "Say your piece and then get on with your life.") Consequently, these pithy euphemisms will lose even more of their life-transforming power through such trivialization. In some cases, after several iterations of dumbing down

God's words, the very essence of the message may be distorted. (For example, in Matthew 6:25-34 Jesus taught His disciples not to worry about things they cannot control and that are already managed by God but to focus on what's important—Kingdom priorities. Such a teaching is likely to evolve into the "Don't worry, be happy" catch phrase.)

In short, look for spiritual anarchy to accelerate. The environment is conducive to such growth.

What Can You Do?

In short, Americans have a variety of beliefs, but they don't make much sense and they certainly do not coincide with God's guidelines. The Church is rotting from the inside out, crippled by abiblical theology.

But we cannot give up in despair, of course. If the Church is serious about restoring its theological purity, then we must commit to several major steps.

1. Let's acknowledge that we are in a state of spiritual anarchy. People are perfectly comfortable defining theology for themselves and ignoring any attempts to be taught differently. Christians are typically indistinguishable from non-Christians, theologically or behaviorally, which neither fulfills our scriptural mandate nor brings honor to God.

2. Let's admit that turning this situation around will take a massive, concerted, long-term effort. People's minds are made up, their ears are closed and their hearts are hardened. Breaking through is going to take a move of the Spirit. We must pray for God's guidance and power to bring about the reformation that He undoubtedly desires for America. It may well be, too, that to usher in an era of theological sanity we will have to adopt new approaches to educating people about God's Word and new tools to facilitate growth. Rather than giving people disjointed

morsels of spiritual truth each week, we must have a systematic method of enabling people to buy into a biblical worldview that transforms their life. The desired outcomes of this effort, as well as some of its procedures, will be countercultural and therefore controversial. So be it.

3. The effort will not make any inroads unless accountability for one's beliefs is front and center. We've been teaching (presumably) good theological perspectives in the Church for years, but people have instead adopted viewpoints from other places. They have been allowed to foster and nurture those offbeat views while calling themselves by the name of Christ, and even spreading heresies within the body, to no account. As any decent parent will tell you, if there is not a clear set of enforced parameters, children will push the limits and do what they can get away with. The result is disastrous for all involved.

With all of these considerations in mind, here are a few practical steps you can take.

1. Get a good book of basic biblical theology. Use the Table of Contents to identify the core principles covered in the text (e.g., sanctification, holiness, salvation). Thoughtfully write down your current beliefs and perceptions related to each of those core principles. Then carefully study the book, consulting the scriptural passages alluded to in the text. Make a new list identifying the items on which your predispositions were different from the biblical view, and consider the ramifications of those differences in your daily life.

2. Work on developing a clear, comprehensive and Bible-based worldview. That worldview should serve as a filter for all of your decisions, enabling you to live in concert with God's principles.[3]

3. Have a discussion with your family members about what they believe in relation to core biblical principles. Identify areas of confusion, and challenge your kin on beliefs they possess that do not conform to Scripture. Interact with your family in rela-

tion to what differences their spiritual beliefs make in their daily thinking and behavior.

4. Get involved with a group of mature Christians who will hold you lovingly but firmly accountable for your beliefs. Treat that group as your safe place in which to ask all of your "dumb" questions and to struggle with the application of theology to lifestyle. When you get to a point at which you are pretty confident in your ability to blend biblical perspective and daily application, look for other people whom you can mentor in the art of such thinking and living.

5. Learn more about the fundamental beliefs of non-Christian groups such as Scientology, Mormonism, Christian Science, TM and Jehovah's Witnesses.[4] Contrast their views with what the Bible teaches and figure out how you could counteract the teaching or evangelistic efforts of people from those faith groups. As time progresses, those groups are likely to become more aggressive and prevalent in the U.S.

6. Search for instances of contradictions in your own faith and behavior. Think about the principles that you accept from the Bible and then examine your day-to-day activities to identify examples of conflict between your biblical views and how you live. Make a commitment to change your ways to conform to God's principles.

7. Pray frequently that God's truths will become better known and accepted by American society. Pray that the teachers in your church will learn how to more effectively convey those truths. Pray that God will raise up an army of journalists, writers, producers, directors and media executives dedicated to cleansing the mass media of unbiblical messages.

Since spiritual anarchy has taken hold of our society, each of us has probably bought into it in ways we have not recognized. List all of the connections and commitments you have made to your community of faith and evaluate how consistently you work within the parameters adopted by that community.

Notes

1. In all of our research and throughout this book, the term "born again" is based on asking people's response to two survey questions. In the first question we ask people "Have you ever made a personal commitment to Jesus Christ that is still important in your life today?" If they answer yes, we then pose the second question, which relates to what they believe will happen to them after they die. One of the seven options we offer is "After I die, I know I will go to heaven because I have confessed my sins and have accepted Jesus Christ as my Savior." We then classify people who provide that answer as born-again Christians. We do not ask people if they consider themselves to be born again. We also do not truly know who is born again—only God does—but we use this process of estimation to give us a sense of what is happening spiritually among those who rely on God's grace rather than works or universalism for their salvation.

2. The data described in this chapter are all drawn from nationwide surveys of adults based on random samples of 1,000 or more people that were conducted between 1997 and 2000. Most of the data are from several surveys conducted between November 1999 and July 2000.

3. For more extensive reading about the development of a biblical worldview, take a look at Charles Colson and Nancy Pearcey, *How Now Shall We Live?* (Wheaton, IL: Tyndale Publishers, 1999); W. Andrew Hoffecker, ed., *Building A Christian Worldview* (Phillipsburg, NJ: Presbyterian and Reformed Publishing, 1986); Thomas Oden, *John Wesley's Scriptural Christianity* (Grand Rapids, MI: Zondervan Publishing, 1994); James Sire, *The Universe Next Door* (Downers Grove, IL: InterVarsity Press, 1988); and Arthur Holmes, *Contours of a Worldview* (Grand Rapids, MI: Eerdmans Publishing, 1983).

4. There are many resources that will help you to better understand other faith groups. Among the most helpful are Walter Martin, *The Kingdom of the Cults* (Minneapolis, MN: Bethany House, 1985); and Dean Halverson, ed., *The Compact Guide to World Religions* (Minneapolis, MN: Bethany House, 1996).

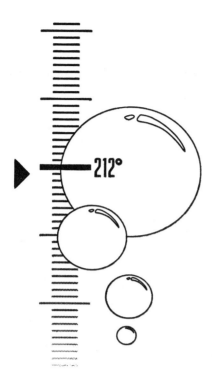

CHAPTER TEN

FAITH IN PRACTICE

Future Glimpse

"Excuse me, ma'am. My family and I will be staying until Monday, and we were wondering if there's a good evangelical church in the area that you'd recommend we visit on Sunday." Jill never knew how to best answer these church questions from hotel guests. She gave the inquiring guest the standard response: Check the list of churches in the guest directory in their room, and if you don't like what you see, try the Yellow Pages.

Like most people, Jill and Carl believed that spirituality was an important dimension of life. Everyone has a spiritual nature that guides them in time of need and sensitizes them to God. Intuition, conscience, feelings—all of that seemed somehow wrapped up in spirituality. At least, that's what they had gleaned from their experience with churches. They considered themselves to be Christian, kind of, although they weren't too sure what to make of the Bible or things people do in churches. They liked the idea of being part of a group of people who encourage each other and share a common spiritual experience, but they were leery of organized religion because of its formality, excessive rules and frequent irrelevance. Jill viewed most Christians as hypocrites: people who agreed to one set of rules on Sunday but lived according to their own rules the rest of the week. Unless a faith was going to help them become wiser or better people, Jill and Carl didn't need it. There were too many other worthwhile things clamoring for their attention already. God would understand.

Even their experiences with the youth groups at churches hadn't worked out too well. Jill wanted Jackson to have exposure to religious values and perspectives, but the two churches he'd attended left a sour taste in his mouth.

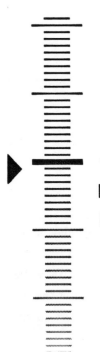

"Christian" no longer denotes being a devoted follower of Christ.

He felt like an outsider. His tattoos, shaved head, nose ring, baggy pants, perpetual sunglasses and skateboard may have had something to do with it. But she agreed with her son: If they couldn't accept him for who he was, he didn't need whatever they had. Carl's girls had been involved in a church group for a while, but they grew tired of the activities and cliquishness, and Brittany felt that her parents' divorce had made her an outcast and a subject of gossip.

So Jill's church involvement was pretty much limited to attending special events (weddings, funerals or concerts) or to times of high stress or extreme curiosity. At this point she was just as likely to visit a New Age discussion, a Catholic retreat or Buddhist temple as a Protestant church. It was all the same to her: Supernatural power and inspirational ideas related to that particular religion's deity and sacred literature.

In the end, she didn't really care where hotel guests went to church or if they went at all. She figured they'd probably be better off taking a hike in the mountains and seeking spiritual truth in the beauty of nature.

The Fixture in American Culture

It's not easy to remain a player in this era of overnight change. Once-hot commodities ranging from Ross Perot, Ted Kennedy and Michael Jordan to Michael Jackson, Donald Trump and Lee Iacocca have lost their luster and are now merely Trivial Pursuit fodder.

But then there's God. Now there's Someone with real staying power.

God remains a fixture in American culture. Who He is and how we relate to Him varies greatly, but almost all Americans acknowledge that God, in some form or another, exists. Among His characterizations are the omnipotent, triune Creator described in the Bible, the generic "Man upstairs," Buddha, our self-actualized self and a variety of other divine entities. No matter: More than 9 out of 10 Americans say they believe in God, more than 4 out of 5 say their religious faith is very important in their lives today, and about two-thirds even define themselves as "religious."

During the last 15 years there has been a high and stable level of interest in faith and spirituality. Consistent with our shifts in values and attitudes, though, the traditional religious labels don't fit as snugly as they used to. "Christian" no longer indicates being a devoted follower of Jesus Christ. "Protestant" no longer means much of anything to people under 40. "Catholic" is a term that describes a person's religious leanings but without much theological content or church history associated with the term. "Fundamentalist" has become synonymous with judgmental and narrow-minded. "Evangelical" is misinterpreted to encompass anyone who is committed to Christianity, spiritually outspoken and politically conservative. "Born again" is typically ascribed to bothersome proselytizers.

Religion has certainly become a high profile category for journalists to cover. There have been remarkable religious leaders—Billy Graham, Mother Teresa, Pope John Paul, Charles Colson, the Dalai Lama—whose stories have touched many. There have been ample drama and conflict ranging from the ordination of women and gays, clergy misconduct and Supreme Court rulings on religious freedom to lawsuits against churches, church bombings, spiritual revival activities and monumental mission efforts. Television networks, magazines, radio stations and newspapers discovered that salting their menu with a noticeable portion of religious offerings is a wise strategy to pursue.

The Stake in the Ground

Gallup surveys conducted between the mid-'40s and mid-'70s show that there was substantial change in America's religious affiliations. The percentage of people who called themselves "Protestant" declined by some 15 percent; those who aligned with Catholicism grew by more than one-third; Judaism declined in its share of the religious landscape by 60 percent; and atheists and agnostics appear to have increased fourfold between the early '50s and mid-'70s.[1] During a period of development and self-definition, those transitions are crucial to understanding the values, motivations and goals of post-war America.

In spite of all the religious activity, spending and ferment reported in recent years, people's basic religious affiliations—Protestant, Catholic, Jewish, other—have changed remarkably little since the Carter Administration. Six out of every 10 adults align with a Protestant church; 1 out of 4 is Catholic; the remaining 15 percent or so are strewn throughout the religious world. That does not mean that people's religious dimension has been ignored or that religious affiliations are insignificant; it does imply that either we have been relatively satisfied with our existing affiliations or that our energy has been devoted to changing other components of our religious experience.

Amazingly, even the attendance levels and general patterns of change related to specific Protestant denominations evident in the '70s and '80s continued to be relatively consistent throughout the '90s. Charismatic and evangelical Protestant churches drew bigger crowds than they had before, mainline Protestant churches continued to lose followers, and the numbers of people associated with Catholic churches, Judaism and eastern religions remained stable. Currently, in the Protestant camp, about one-third are

Baptist, one-third are from mainline churches and one-third attend a vast array of other Protestant churches (predominantly evangelical in nature)—certainly a shift from the Eisenhower era, but generally descriptive of the religious domain since the days of President Carter.

During the past decade charismatic churches and nondenominational evangelical congregations experienced the greatest growth in church affiliation and attendance. Their growth comes from a combination of factors such as the attraction of immigrants and previously unchurched people along with the influx of the dissatisfied from mainline churches. The quest for independence, for relevant and productive spiritual experiences and for sensitive, rapid-response ministries diminished the appeal of many churches and denominations that have been around for a long time. The independent churches—whether charismatic, evangelical or fundamentalist—have grown because they met a specific set of needs harbored by a growing segment of people—needs such as vision for life and ministry, strong leadership, clear, firm and defensible theology and value-added experiences (e.g., meaningful worship, genuine community). They have been aggressive in their growth strategies and programmatic activity.

The very absence of those characteristics largely explains the decline among the mainline denominations (especially the Episcopal, Presbyterian and United Church of Christ churches).[2] These churches constituted half of the Protestant population in the '50s, but have dropped to just one-third of the total today. Distracted by internal theological and polity skirmishes, suffering from the absence of ministry vision, strong leadership and experiential relevance, millions of people have fled the mainline churches for other options. The hemorrhaging slowed during the '90s, partly due to stopgap measures (e.g., services with contemporary music, needs-oriented programs), but until those churches can address their underlying weaknesses, their decline will continue.

Most Americans call themselves "Christian" but what about the one-sixth of the population who do not? The largest segment, interestingly, is not an alternative faith group but the atheist/agnostic contingent. About 10 percent of all Americans say they have no religious faith or are simply indifferent to the faith dimension. That's a substantial increase from the 2 percent that Gallup reported in the '50s and '60s and indicative of the direction that people's faith is taking: More and more people say they are spiritual but are not associated with a church or denomination.

A smaller portion of the population—about 5 percent of the adult public—is comprised of individuals aligned with other faith groups. The largest of those are Jews and Mormons, both of which maintained a small but constant share of the religious pie by attracting enough new members to replace those they lost from deaths and defections. There are signs of a slight turnaround within the Jewish community, as greater energy is being put into building up pride, knowledge and community among Jewish people in America. The Mormon church has been quite aggressive in its marketing ventures in the U.S., but after brief spurts of growth in the past two decades, its greatest marketing challenge is the retention of those who commit to the Mormon faith. Turnover in the Church of Jesus Christ of Latter-Day Saints appears to be the highest of any church in the U.S.

You have probably heard that the Muslim church is the fastest-growing religious body in America. That may be true—on a percentage basis—but realize that the rapid growth is primarily because the base number of Muslims in the U.S. is so tiny (and, therefore, it takes relatively few additions to generate a large growth percentage). In this age of spin doctors and analysis by anecdote, you must carefully choose the statistics you ingest; many are stretched beyond recognition and accuracy. Muslims, like adherents of all the eastern religions combined, represent less than 1 percent of the adults in America.

Personal Participation

Expressions of interest in religion and spirituality are one thing, but such words mean little until they are backed by action. During the '90s, truly a period of contradictions and paradoxes, we saw a simultaneous increase in people's openness to religion and decrease of personal involvement in religious activities. Church attendance dropped to about 4 out of 10 adults attending on any given Sunday, and among church attenders, the norm went from three appearances per month down to two. Both church volunteerism and Sunday School involvement dropped from 1 out of every 4 adults to about 1 in 5. Bible reading dropped from half of all adults down to 1 out of 3, before rebounding during the last three years of the decade to about 4 out of 10 adults. Giving levels, in constant dollars, dipped while fewer people bought into tithing: Just 8 percent of all born-again believers were giving 10 percent of their income to their church in 2000. The frequency of prayer and participation in a cell group or small group remained consistent.

Many of the traditional assumptions about faith activity have been altered beyond recognition. Notions such as the necessity of daily Bible reading, the importance of serving in or becoming a member of a church, and the sinfulness of missing a weekend worship service have all gone the way of the Edsel. Instead, most people's sense of religious responsibility begins with personal felt needs and desires and ends with convenience and simplicity. If it takes too long, requires too much effort, costs too much money, seems too complicated or causes too much discomfort, then the chances are good it won't make the day's agenda. The rule of thumb is that religion exists to serve people's needs, not God's purposes; anything religious that asks too much cannot be a legitimate extension of authentic spirituality since it does not overtly please, satisfy or fulfill us.

PATTERNS OF RELIGIOUS INVOLVEMENT

	1991	2000	2010
In a typical week:			
Attended church service	49%	40%	35%
Read the Bible	45%	40%	32%
Attended Sunday School	23%	19%	17%
Volunteered at church	27%	21%	18%
Prayed to God	88%	83%	78%
Attended a small group	15%	17%	19%
In a typical month:			
Used Internet for religious purposes	*	10%	24%
Donated money to a church	42%	54%	47%

(*indicates less than one-half of one percent)
Source: Barna Research Group, Ltd., Ventura, CA

The projections in the accompanying table show that there will likely be a small but noteworthy decrease in the percentage of adults who are active in a local church. Significantly, many churches will not realize that the culture is gradually slipping farther away from Christ because the increase in the total adult population will numerically compensate for the relative decline in church influence and appeal. In other words, because the nation's population will grow by close to 25 to 30 million people during the triple-zero decade, the impact of a declining share of the population will occur simultaneous with a net gain in numbers of people from which churches can draw adherents. Rather than focusing on the fact that an ever-increasing number of people are distanced from a genuine relationship with Jesus, many churches will draw comfort from the relative stability (or, in some cases, apparent growth) in their attendance figures.

For instance, an average of 40 percent of all adults—roughly 80-85 million—attend worship services on a typical weekend in 2000. Although the percentage will drop to about 35 percent in 2010, the rise in adults will place about 75-80 million adults in churches on a given weekend. Since we also anticipate an increase in the number of new churches, the decline in average church size will be attributed largely to planned dispersion rather than unintended reduction, thus sidestepping the root cause of the challenge.

The biggest area of growth in religious activity will be in people turning to the Internet for religious information and experiences. Already, 1 out of every 10 adults (and an even higher percentage of teenagers) use the Net for religious purposes. That will jump to about 1 out of 4 adults by the close of this decade in response to greater Net penetration, usage of the Net for a broader range of life needs and interests, the aging of the two digital generations, the explosion of Net-oriented products that will appear and the increased reliance on the Net as a communication vehicle by churches. However, many who use the Internet for religious endeavors will engage in nontraditional pursuits such as holding theological discussions, participating in real-time worship, joining with others from around the world in real-time prayer and taking religious education courses on-line. For some people, the Internet will supplement what they receive from their local church; for millions of others, the Internet will replace it.

Another critical dimension of the spiritual temperature of the nation relates to people's involvement in serving others. The key aspects of such service relate to evangelism, mentoring or discipleship, assisting at the church and helping the needy. The Bible is pretty clear that serving others is not an option, but one of the signs of a true believer. Jesus taught the importance and substance of this principle through both His words and lifestyle.

Perhaps surprisingly, only about half of the individuals who associate with Christian churches are actively involved in anything beyond Sunday morning fare. The busy-ness of people's schedules, the perceived lack of skills or training and the absence of appealing, well-managed opportunities for service are the main reasons people give for their failure to be more active.

Apathy, of course, is another reason—but one that few people admit to. Some church observers have mocked congregations where leaders spend time celebrating, encouraging and pumping up—i.e., motivating—people to get them involved in ministry and spiritual growth. But whether we like going to such great lengths or not, we minister in a culture that necessitates such effort. Our research shows that the typical lay leaders are not completely sold on their faith or church, and they are extremely busy and greatly distracted from the church's agenda. To persuade them to focus on and commit to the church's needs takes more than simply asking people to do what is right and appropriate or exegeting the Scripture verses that command us to do the work of the ministry. (Remember, even a majority of the lay leaders in Christian churches do not believe the Bible is absolute truth.)

Religious Media

Several decades ago we transitioned from a written culture to a visual culture. Rather than communicating truth, values, beliefs and principles to the masses via the printed word, the masses began taking their primary cues from visual depictions of current and future reality. First television, then videos, then computer games, then CD-ROMs, then the Internet. The written word is still a powerful communication medium, through books, magazines, newspapers and other formats, but it has lost its supremacy to the visual media.

As time marches on and technological breakthroughs are made, expect to see more visualized information. Whether it will be picture phones, ubiquitous displays for streaming or practical applications of virtual reality, the mass media, with customization opportunities, will continue to shape the media environment.

What will that mean for the Church? Visual media and digital media will represent the growing edge of the spiritual communication frontier. Talking-head TV programs and televised church services will continue to lose market share because such options are not competitive in the new media and entertainment environment. Even educators are recognizing that to stimulate people's minds in an overstimulated culture requires a dose of entertainment added to factual content.

Christian radio is likely to remain a fixture in many people's lives. In 2000, we know that about 4 out of 10 adults listen to some type of religious radio broadcasting in a typical month. The nature of their preferred programming is changing, though. Broadcast sermons are less appealing to today's listener than is a Christian talk show or a Christian music show. These latter presentations have both content and entertainment value. Whether they are effective at helping people to grow spiritually is a different matter, one that has some evidence on both sides of the argument.

Are Christians Spiritually Healthy?

The goal of spiritual activity, of course, is obedience to God's calling to people to know, love and serve Him. Jesus explained to His followers that the mark of a believer was the fruit that comes from his/her life and ministry. Involvement in activities like Sunday School, worship and small groups are not ends in themselves, but are means to two grand ends: glorifying God and experiencing personal life transformation through the application of faith.

How are we doing? Well, the good news is that many Christians are trying their best even though there is room for improvement. The bad news is that there is *so much* room for improvement. Indeed, the concentrated efforts of the Church in recent years to call people to pray for revival and renewal could not have come at a more opportune time; millions of Americans desperately need the guidance and power of the Holy Spirit to revitalize their lives.

One way to assess the state of the Church is to look for the signs of spiritual health and reawakening. The signs that we might search for are drawn from Scripture and from the experience of our nation during its times of past spiritual revival. Here are seven signs that seem to be present during times when America has undergone a serious spiritual awakening. These signs may therefore serve as a benchmark against which we can judge the spiritual health and vitality of the nation[3]:

1. Acceptance of the authority of Scripture.
2. Belief in the centrality of the death and resurrection of Christ.
3. Increased devotional life and a commitment to personal holiness.
4. Extensive and intensive evangelism and discipleship.
5. Cultural change is evident and is attributable to widespread individual spiritual transformation.
6. Wickedness grieves and humbles Christians.
7. The Church is focused on pursuing and achieving ever-greater spiritual depth.

Let's briefly consider how well we are doing in relation to each of these signs of spiritual health and vitality.[4]

The Authority of Scripture

God's Word sells—if not in our hearts, at least in our stores. More than $600 million worth of Bibles are sold in the U.S. each year. It remains the top-selling book in the nation, year after year and resides in more than 9 out of every 10 households in the country. When we asked adults to identify the most influential book in human history, more than 4 out of 5 adults named the Bible. Most people feel they know its content quite well and most of them assert that it remains relevant for us today. Just 1 out of every 5 adults argues that the Ten Commandments are not relevant for people these days.

Unfortunately, owning copies of the Bible and truly possessing the truths of Scripture are two different realities. Americans have taken physical ownership of the Book but have not taken spiritual ownership of its content. For instance, only 4 out of 10 adults even read the Bible during a typical week, other than when they are in church. Those who read the Bible spend an average of roughly one hour during the entire week reading the Scriptures. That's less time than they will devote to watching TV in an average day. People are more likely to memorize their growing list of telephone numbers—home phone, cell phone, spouse's cell phone, modem line, business number, business fax, spouse's business number, second home phone—than to memorize Bible verses. Reading, studying and reflecting on—much less applying—God's Word is a highly regarded idea, but it is not a top priority for most people.

Only 2 out of every 5 adults strongly agree that the Bible is accurate in all that it teaches. Our lack of conviction about, and confusion related to, the Bible can be seen when we correlate that perspective with our views on the veracity of Scripture. When asked to describe their views on the Bible, one-fifth said it is the actual Word of God and can be taken literally; two-fifths said it is the inspired Word of God without errors; 1 out of 5 said it is the inspired word of God but contains mistakes; and 1 out of 5 said it is simply a religious book by human beings. Combine that with the fact that only 1 out of every 10 adults is convinced that there is absolute moral truth—and that only 15 percent cite the Bible as the dominant influence on their thinking about truth—and you get a sense of just how lightly we take the Bible.

The Death and Resurrection of Christ

Few Americans doubt the existence of Jesus Christ. In fact, almost 9 out of every 10 adults believe that Jesus died, rose again and is alive today and even that someday God will judge every person. Three-quarters of all adults state that forgiveness of sins is possible only through Jesus Christ. We may not be a "Christian nation," but at least most people acknowledge the life and eternal presence of Jesus.

But whether or not His death was meaningful is another issue. Six out of 10 adults do not have any assurance of their own eternal spiritual salvation through a personal reliance upon God's grace, given through Jesus' act of atonement on our behalf. In fact, a majority of adults say that eternal salvation, if they believe such a state exists, is based upon earning a reprieve from God. (Amazingly, 9 out of 10 Americans do believe that they will go to heaven when they die—and most of them are convinced that they have earned the privilege by their stellar earthly performance.) Half of all adults argue that in the end it doesn't really matter anyway, since a person's religious beliefs will make no difference to their eternal condition.

Most astounding of all, perhaps, are the findings that more than 65 million adults believe that Jesus committed sins; and an even greater number argue that He died but never had a physical resurrection. As we noted in the previous chapter, these errant views are held by millions of born-again Christians, too. Jesus remains a revered teacher and miracle worker, but He has yet to truly and permanently penetrate the hearts of millions of people who call themselves "Christian" and attend Christian churches.

Devotional Life and Personal Holiness

One of the signs of spiritual vitality in a culture is when people commit themselves to becoming more Christlike. This would be exemplified by a meaningful and growing commitment to prayer, Scripture and meditation on God's Word, resulting in a desire to seek greater personal holiness.

Some of the raw material for seeking a deeper connection with God and living a holier life is certainly in place. Two-thirds of adults discuss moral or ethical situations with friends during a typical week and half of all adults turn off a TV program they were watching because they find the values or views presented to be offensive. One-third of all adults are currently involved in some type of discipleship or intentional spiritual growth process, whether it be through involvement in a small group, a one-to-one mentoring relationship or some other focused developmental process.

Several million Americans are striving to live consistently with their spiritual values by putting pressure on corporate America through economic boycotts. (The high-profile efforts are those against corporations that distribute, produce or otherwise support pornography or abortion; but millions of people are boycotting organizations that produce, distribute or promote a variety of immoral media products or corporate policies.) This direct response to immorality is related to the sizable increase measured in the proportion of people who say their religious faith is very important to them.

But cracks in the spiritual armor are evident when we evaluate the most serious or significant problems and challenges people say they are facing in life only to find that few individuals cite the need for a better relationship with God, the need for God's forgiveness, the need to grow spiritually or a desire to achieve eternal salvation or acceptance. In a recent survey we even asked people to identify their goals in life and discovered that less than 1 percent mentioned anything related to holiness, righteousness or purity. In a different survey we asked people to describe their priorities in life and found that only 3 out of 10 adults said that having a satisfying spiritual life is a top priority in their lives today.

Most people see spirituality as an addendum to their lives.

The commitment to seeking greater holiness would imply that we recognize our failings and confess those to the only One who can provide forgiveness and the strength to change our shortcomings. However, we learned that the typical believer does not confess his/her sins to God during an average year, much less during a typical week. The concept of brokenness does not sell well in our culture; strength, capacity and individualism are the kinds of characteristics we cherish. Busy schedules and the absence of clear priorities have led most people to see spirituality as an addendum to, rather than the core of, their lives.

Evangelism and Discipleship

If ever there was a time for consistent outreach, this is the time. There is a greater level of interest in spiritual matters and in discovering meaning and purpose in life than has been seen at any time in the past 50 years. A large number of people are open to being spiritually mentored by a mature peer. A large majority of born-again Christians believe that they have a responsibility to share their faith in Christ with people they know who are not believers. Most churches, of course, encourage such outreach.

But even on something that seems as clear-cut and simple as following the Great Commission—that is, to "go and make disciples of all nations"— just 1 out of every 6 adults always thinks of himself/herself as a representative of the Christian faith. Most Christians believe that evangelism is important but also assume that it is someone else's job to spread the good news.

While prayer has become a more significant ministry in churches during the latter half of the '90s, the fact remains that only a small number of Christian churches have any type of ongoing prayer for the souls of nonbelievers. In fact, most churches have no formal type of training or preparation for their people to equip them for evangelism. The result we have found in study after study is a nation of churches filled with people who are dispassionate about evangelism, theologically incapable of accurately representing God's principles and standards, and relationally and methodologically unable to lead a person to Christ. One way of evaluating the evangelistic commitment of churches is to note that they will spend more money on buildings and maintenance this year than on evangelism and follow-up—by a factor of more than 4 to 1!

Churches, like the people within them, have become so busy with programs and other business affairs that many seem to have lost a sense of why they exist. The area of introducing Christ to the non-Christian segment of the community is a prime example of this problem. Although evangelism is the ministry priority most frequently mentioned by senior pastors, it is not ranked as one of the three highest ministry priorities by even half of the senior pastors of Protestant churches in America. And when someone shares his/her faith in Christ with a nonbeliever and the person makes a decision to follow Christ as his/her Savior, we also discovered that most of them become nominal believers—they do not become truly devoted followers of Christ because there is not an effective follow-up ministry to help them grow and mature in their faith.[5]

Does all of this seem unbelievable? If so, then ask why the average size of churches has actually decreased from slightly more than 100 adults attending the typical church to just 90. (Remember, this is in the midst of a population that continues to grow and whose interest in spirituality has blossomed in the past decade.) Ask yourself why it is that more than 4 out of every 10 people sitting in churches on weekends are not born again—even though most of them have been attending churches for decades, and have been at the same church they presently attend for several years. Without a doubt, the most accessible mission field sits in church pews on Sunday morning!

Here's another way of slicing the data. In 2000, we asked a national sample of unchurched people about their experience with Christians. Most of them have never been invited to a church by a Christian. Most of them have never been told by a Christian what it means to be a believer in Jesus Christ or invited to embrace Jesus as their Lord and Savior. Our interviews with believers also showed that fewer than 1 out of every 5 believers knew a non-Christian well enough to share their faith with that individual in a context of trust and credibility.

Cultural Change, Spiritual Transformation

When God changes people's hearts, the culture in which they live will be altered in tangible ways. Having read the preceding chapters regarding America's values and lifestyles, you may already have a sense that faith-driven cultural reformation has not overtaken the United States. But there are some reassuring changes that have occurred that deserve consideration.

For instance, through the work of Prison Fellowship and other associated ministries, a number of prison systems are allowing spiritual development to become a cornerstone of their reform programs—and are experiencing tremendous success. Crime levels, overall, have decreased in the last half-decade in several categories of crime.

Our nationwide surveys, as well as those by Gallup, Yankelovich and Wirthlin, have seen a growing number of adults identifying the moral decay of the nation as one of the top two or three priorities that must be addressed by the nation. Some states have responded by passing laws that deal with moral issues such as marriage between homosexuals, pornography, divorce and doctor-assisted suicide. Concern over morals and values has fueled the explosive growth of homeschooling that has occurred in the last two decades. Concerted efforts to encourage youth to abstain from sex until marriage have touched the lives of many young people. Similar efforts to awaken the soul of men, through the work of Promise Keepers and other ministries, have rejuvenated the spiritual life of thousands of men around the country.

But we all know that much of the cultural change that has occurred in the last 10 years or so has not been for the better. Cohabitation, divorce, sexual promiscuity and deviance and birth outside of marriage are increasing. Sales of pornographic material on the Internet surpass the cumulative sales of all other products sold on-line. The nation was dragged through President Clinton's moral scandal but the most scandalous outcome of all was that his reported sexual adventures and deceitful replies to investigators disturbed so few people. Most types of crime continue to escalate. People are shirking their financial obligations in record numbers, hiding behind the legal protections of bankruptcy laws. Parents cannot trust the mass media to provide wholesome content for their children. We are increasingly comfortable with homosexuality as a lifestyle, divorce as an immediate solution to troubled marriages, allowing personal choice regarding abortion, ignoring "white lies," instigating lawsuits, hoarding wealth, facilitating segregation, cheating when it's convenient and stealing when we "need to."

Much of this can be attributed to the heart condition of Americans. More than two-thirds of all adults define "success" in life as the acquisition of sufficient money, education, material possessions or career prestige; only 7 percent relate success to their faith condition and its influence upon their life. In a culture that prides itself on being successful and providing people with the opportunity to become successful, we pursue whatever we define as "success." Today, few people see a connection between the evolution of their faith and the achievement of success.

Rejecting Wickedness

A distinguishing mark of authentic Christians is their distaste for evil. Because we serve a holy and righteous God, One who can neither accept nor be in the presence of wickedness, our challenge is to adopt the same hatred of sin and evil. Jesus' death and resurrection was for the purpose of facilitating God's forgiveness for our improper behavior; our gratitude and maturity are demonstrated by a consistent drive to distance ourselves from the disease of sinful living.

America shows signs of awakening to this need to choose between God's way and Satan's way. Our rising level of concern about the moral decay of the nation is such a sign. The acceptance of laws and their enforcement insinuates that we recognize the need for parameters in life. Our rejection of harmful or immoral behaviors (e.g., suicide, looting) is evidence of God at work in people's minds and hearts. Even the ongoing debates on moral issues such as abortion, pornography, adultery and euthanasia are signs that we are not a completely depraved society.

And there have been many exhilarating instances of believers falling to their knees before God and seeking His forgiveness and direction. Prayer summits and areawide fellowship meetings among pastors have modeled spiritual authenticity for congregants since the mid-'90s. Several dozen Christian colleges, parachurch ministries and local churches have experienced times of intense repentance among their members. The Promise Keepers event in Washington, D.C., that attracted several hundred thousand men, was perhaps the largest gathering of Christian men in American history, and acknowledgment and repentance of sin was a core element in the event. The extended revival meetings at several churches across the nation have produced positive, discernible spiritual fruit. God is neither silent nor preoccupied; He is at work among Americans.

> **Ongoing debates on moral issues indicate that we are not a completely depraved society.**

But we truly have a long way to go before we can assert that Christians are sincerely grieved by sin—even their own sin—and are humbled before a holy God by their own indiscretions and moral failings. As evidence, realize that most Christians do not confess their sins to God even as infrequently as once a year. While slightly more than half of all adults claim that their spiritual beliefs affect their behavior, even they admit that such influence is occasional at best. These weaknesses are not helped much by churches: The proportion of churches that incorporate a time of private or corporate confession into their worship events has declined substantially in the past 20 years. Things are no better in the home: Fewer than 1 out of every 5 Christian husbands and wives prays and confesses together—ever. Accountability is one of the most glaring shortcomings within Christian circles.

Americans are incredibly independent and self-reliant, rather than dependent upon God. We bask in our autonomy and defiance rather than seek humility and strive for obedience. We define success according to material possessions rather than spiritual brokenness.

Perhaps the most heartbreaking evidence of this was a study Barna Research conducted in 1999. Using interviews with more than 6,000 adults randomly drawn from across the nation, we divided that base into born-again Christian and non-born-again adults. We then compared the two groups on 65 common nonreligious behaviors and values to gauge how Christians differ from their non-Christian counterparts. We discovered that there were a number of cases in which believers were a few percentage points different, but no instances in which Christians were substantially different. We concluded that Christians have a limited influence on American society because we do not live differently and thereby model an alternative lifestyle for others to emulate. The fundamental indictment of that report, however, could have been phrased this way: Christians fail to transform the culture in which they live because they are neither grieved nor humbled by their own sin.

Seeking Spiritual Depth

The American Christian Body is certainly not beyond reproach. But the question is, Do we care? Or are we content to emulate the spiritually lukewarm church of Laodicea that drew the wrath of the Lord?[6]

There is indeed evidence that the Church is not comatose. More than $50 billion is donated to churches every year. The Bible remains the best-selling book in America, several centuries after its initial release date. The Bible is just the tip of the iceberg, though, as Americans shell out in excess of $3 billion annually for faith-related products and resources ranging from Bible reference books to day-glow "Jesus Loves Me" pens. More people attend church services on the lowest-attendance weekend of the year than watch the Super Bowl. There is a growing interest in genuine worship, growth in spiritual mentoring and a resurgence of laity in church leadership roles. Prayer for revival and renewal is more common today than at any time in the past two decades. Cooperation among churches is more likely than ever as competition has given way to a spirit of common mission. The explosive expansion of Christianity on other continents has even caused many Church leaders to consider new models for how ministry might be more effective.

But there is no denying the numerous weak links in the nation's spiritual chain. Most believers are only moderately committed to their faith. Just 8 percent of born-again Christians tithe. People are far more likely to pray for material desires than for the souls of others or the spiritual restoration of our culture. Fasting remains a lost art. Pastors tend to be preachers, not the visionary leaders who can motivate and mobilize people around God's grand vision for His Church. Our schedules are too busy to permit regular times with God and His Word, and our priorities are too worldly to reform our schedules.

Perhaps they will know we are Christians by our love, but more likely, they will know we are Christians by our divisiveness over theological, doctrinal and methodological issues. All people may be equal in God's eyes, but in the Church we separate people on the basis of color, age and gender. Too often it seems that our attention is diverted from the key principles of God to the finer workings of earthly matters.

Where Are We Headed?

Thankfully, as devoted followers of Jesus Christ we know that He will prevail and that He will protect those of us who cling to Him as our only hope from the eternal abandonment we deserve. Beyond that we can also draw some conclusions about where the country is headed spiritually.

- There will be a steady decline in traditional religious activity as alternatives materialize, some of which will be absorbed by the cyberchurch. We are also likely to see a simultaneous reduction in people's current levels of interest and investment in spirituality. This reconfiguring of religious activity will also result in a significant increase in unchurched people, although a larger than usual percentage of unchurched folks will be active in religious interaction and development through technological means.

- Congregations will become older, on average, as the decade progresses. This will be attributable to a large percentage of young adults—Busters and Mosaics—avoiding physical churches for alternative church models (e.g., house churches, cyberchurches) and many engaging in spiritual anarchy (i.e., doing whatever works at the moment, without any sense of parameters or obligation to belong to an organized group of like-minded people).

- A rising proportion of Protestant churches will focus their teaching and ministry activity on basic Christianity, in recognition of the weak or nonexistent theological foundations of most people under 40.

- There will be a bifurcation of spiritual intensity, with an increase among the spiritual zealots (currently less than 10 percent) and among the spiritually ambivalent (currently around 6 percent).

- There will be greater diversification in the faith groups accessible to people. New non-Christian faiths will start up, although few are likely to flourish on a grand scale. They will owe their existence to the cultural appreciation of customization, independence and diversity.

- Fewer people will join churches to become formal members. More and more churches will dispense with membership as a formal process. Instead, they will redefine membership to include forms of regular involvement in the ministry.

- The primary emphases in church-based ministry will vary by the denominational affiliation of the church. The needs that will overlay all Christian congregations, though, will be for more meaningful community, true worship experiences and one-to-one peer development.

- Personal holiness will be a forgotten concept as the nation buckles under the weight of moral—and spiritual—anarchy.

- Evangelism will become tougher and tougher among adults since a larger number of them will have made a first-time decision in the past but have been abandoned after that decision, and thus fallen away from the faith. Reviving their interest in Christianity will prove to be extremely difficult.

- Evangelism among children will flourish as churches finally recognize that the only significant chance we have of reaching a person is when he/she is young. Youth workers will incorporate evangelistic ministry into their Sunday School, Vacation Bible School and other programmatic responsibilities.

- New approaches to evangelism will be developed to exploit technology and our increasing understanding of postmodern thinking and behavior. Socratic forms of evangelism will finally start to gain a foothold and will bear significant fruit.

- People will regularly rotate among different churches rather than remain loyal to one church for a long period of time. The average length of time a person will include a given church in their rotation will be two to four years.

- Pockets of revival will continue to emerge as the Holy Spirit finds open hearts in various communities. The fervor over praying for and preparing for revival will evaporate by mid-decade. Nobody can predict revival, and the country is certainly ripe for widescale revival, but the Church is neither mobilized nor equipped for it. From a human vantage point, nationwide revival does not seem likely.

- Churches will reap record-breaking amounts of donations this decade. This will be due to Seniors and Builders leaving portions of their estate to churches, the growth of the population and the desire of people to give to local organizations whose spending of their donations can be more easily tracked.

- Tens of thousands of Sunday Schools will close down in favor of small-group and Net-based ministry.

- Churches rather than seminaries will increasingly provide the theological training of elders, lay leaders and future church pastors. There will also be alternative training institutions using the

Internet, video conferencing and other technologies to expedite such training.

If the Church in the '80s was shaped by the seeker movement, and the purpose-driven approach and revival thrusts dominated the '90s, look to the Church of the triple-zero decade to be characterized by a return-to-basics effort. A handful of new leaders, armed with focused, no-nonsense content, will emerge to champion this "roots revolution" as a necessity for a culture that has so completely lost its sense of theological moorings.

What Can You Do?

Church as you have always known it will still be available in 2010, but it will no longer be the only viable option in town. The faith world will be reshaped along with everything else in our culture. Here are some challenges that might help you to make the most of the likely changes that will come.

- Study the Bible to figure out what is required of you by God in terms of a church or corporate faith relationship. Some of the options available in the future may not be legitimate—but you will only know for sure if you examine God's Word for yourself and anticipate the changes and opportunities before they have a chance to seduce you.
- Identify God's expectations in terms of commitment. What is lukewarm Christianity and how can you avoid it? What are your priorities in life and how do your faith and God's expectations fit into that scheme?
- What does personal holiness mean and how will you respond to the possibility of achieving holiness in a culture—and sometimes, in a church—that has lost its compass and is pursuing whatever seems right at the moment?
- If you engage in evangelism—and you should—consider the ways of integrating meaningful and effective follow-up into your evan-

gelistic relationships. Sharing the good news with people, seeing the Holy Spirit lead them to ask God to save them, and then abandoning them does them little good. Are you truly committed to finishing the task of helping the people not only to embrace Christ but also to grow in spiritual maturity?

- Continue to pray for spiritual revival and renewal in your community, your church and your own life. It is a journey, not a destination, so reliance on God's power to guide you and strengthen you on that journey makes all the sense in the world.

- Examine your spiritual life to determine who holds you accountable and how that process works. Continual self-evaluation and submission to the examination of others who love you and are looking out for your best interest is one of the greatest gifts the Church can provide to you. Don't neglect it.

- In the midst of people's demand for a better and better worship experience, keep in mind that the experience is a submissive relationship with God, not a feel-good time of music and clever teaching. How often do you experience the presence of God when you worship? How often do you seek to worship Him outside of a corporate worship event?

- Think through the process by which you determine your "home church." Is it legitimate to change churches? Is it legitimate to attend more than one church on a rotating or regular basis? What are the criteria by which you select your primary church? What is your responsibility to that church?

- Have you clearly identified your worldview? If not, this is the ideal decade in which to do so. As more teaching and resources focus on what you believe and why; how biblical principles intersect and interact and what it all looks like in practice, this will be the era of narrowing your spiritual energy to build a deeper foundation.

Expect to be challenged this decade in how you participate in the Church. That's not a bad thing, but it can be uncomfortable. And if you're not up to the challenge, it can ultimately be devastating for your spiritual well-being.

Notes

1. These figures are found in *The Gallup Poll-Public Opinion, 1935-1997,* CD-ROM ed. (Wilmington, DE: Scholarly Resources, Inc., 2000). This resource contains a wealth of insight into how people's opinions have changed over the last 60 years.

2. In our analyses, we include the following churches in the mainline category: American Baptist, United Church of Christ, Episcopal, United Methodist, Evangelical Lutheran Church, Lutheran Church Missouri Synod and Presbyterian Church USA.

3. Some of these indicators are drawn from a study of revival described in Tom Phillips, *Revival Signs* (Gresham, OR: Vision House, 1995).

4. Numerous statistics will be alluded to in this section. Unless otherwise noted, the data comes from nationwide, random sample surveys of 1,000 or more adults conducted by the Barna Research Group in 1998, 1999 or 2000. For specific statistics, visit the Barna Research Group website, which includes an archive of statistics and a library of recent mini-reports on our research findings. These statistics and reports are available at no cost. The website is *www.barna.org.* If you would like to receive free e-mails every two weeks notifying you of the latest report, the topic and the highlights, you may sign up for The Barna Update on the home page of the website. There is no charge for that service.

5. Several years ago, research we conducted discovered that a majority of people who made a first-time decision to follow Jesus Christ in response to a gospel presentation in a church service were no longer associated with that church—or any other—within eight weeks of having made that decision. The problem was lack of personal follow-up with the new followers. More discussion of this can be found in George Barna, *Evangelism That Works* (Ventura, CA: Regal Books, 1995).

6. The plight of the Laodicean church is described in Revelation 3:14-22.

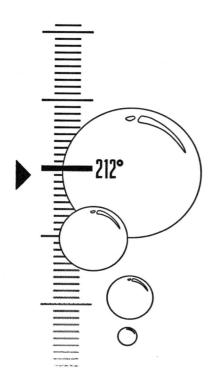

212°

CHAPTER ELEVEN

THE LOCAL CHURCH AND ITS FUTURE

Future Glimpse

Carl and Jill were slumped on the living room couch, peering passively at the TV while Carl flipped through the 70-plus channels they received. "So many channels, so little to watch," he muttered while Jill suppressed her frustration at his two-second attention span and the trigger-happy thumb that was relentlessly working the remote. Suddenly, he got up, gently tossed the remote into Jill's lap, and said he was going to check his e-mail since there was nothing on worth watching. He had stopped on a channel showing a documentary about major religious figures of the twentieth century.

Jill watched the images of religious leaders pass before her eyes—Billy Graham, two popes, Mother Teresa, Martin Luther King, Mahatma Gandhi and others she did not recognize. *What had happened to the Church in this country*, she wondered silently. She was no student of Church history but it seemed to her as if the Christian Church in America had fallen apart. It had gone from a handful of denominations with clear distinctions to dozens of interchangeable groups. The message of the Church had become fuzzy and was overshadowed by all the factionalism and infighting. And it was pretty much impossible to think of anyone whose life was so influenced by faith that the person was unarguably a true Christian. Most church people talked, looked and behaved just like everyone else. What had happened, indeed.

The TV camera panned the main streets and churches of a town whose name she didn't catch. It reminded her of her hometown. It caused her to think about the churches in her Denver suburb. What churches were there? She couldn't recall the name of a single one. There was the big brick one they had visited, Community or Cornerstone or Crossroads, something with a C; they all sounded alike these days.

She recalled her last visit to a church. It was a huge place, reminiscent of some of the basketball arenas she had visited. She liked the pastor and the people seemed nice enough. It was wonderful being able to check it out under the cover of anonymity that the sheer size of the congregation provided her. But she'd left the place confident it was not right for her. First of all, they kept referring to people like her as lost—what an insult! And their primary means of ministry seemed to be in small groups that met during the week. Who had time for that? And it sounded kind of scary—baring your soul in front of a group of peers. Not at this stage in my life, thank you.

Carl, aware of her frequent musings about spiritual things, had turned her on to a few religious websites—e-churches, he called them. She had to admit, some of the discussions and streamed presentations were stimulating. Her friend at work, Fran, had invited her to a forum that was held occasionally at a nearby coffeehouse. Jill went once and found it, too, to be appealing—free- flowing, open, genuine. Fran called it her "church." That had startled Jill—there were no organs, pews, hymns, sermons, Sunday

School—not even a pastor, from what she could tell. But Fran explained it was a collection of people earnestly seeking to understand and apply the Bible, and they just had a different way of growing. Whatever.

During her reverie the program had reached its conclusion and the credits now rolled down the screen. Jill took Carl's place thumbing through the channels. Meanwhile she wondered what *had* happened to the Christian Church and where it was going.

The Pulse of the Church

The Church, manifested largely through the local church, is God's chosen instrument for people to experience a taste of His kingdom on Earth and to prepare the way for the return of Jesus before ushering in God's perfect and unassailable rule throughout all creation. It is a primary means through which we are to be ministered to and through which we may minister to others. The local church is to be a source of strength and continuity, a place of love, safety, security and growth for all who follow Jesus—and all who wish to explore the possibilities.

Frankly, the local church in the U.S. has come on hard times. Not financially—it reaps more than ever—but in terms of its image and influence. To understand how the church could lose its edge during a time when interest in spirituality is breaking records, while people are spending literally billions of dollars on faith-related products, and seminaries are experiencing record-breaking enrollment levels, you have to look at the bigger picture. The preceding chapters gave you a taste of America's theological morass and the lotta-talk-little-action spirituality of Americans. The spread of spiritual anarchy has diminished the role and weakened the impact of the local church. But there's more to it than that. To get the big picture and the related challenges, let's summarize the state of the local church.

The Current State of Christian Churches
In spite of the nation's population increase and a climate of rising interest in spirituality, Christian churches actually decreased in size during the '90s.

They went from an average of 99 adults attending on an average Sunday in 1990 to 90 adults present on a Sunday in 2000. The reasons for the shrinkage include the opening of several thousand new churches (which often start out with fewer people than the average existing church has); an increase in the number of unchurched adults; and the decreased frequency of attendance among churchgoers. Claims of prolific church growth have been grossly exaggerated; not only are most churches not increasing in size, but those that are expanding are doing so at the expense of other churches. More than 80 percent of the adults who get counted as new adherents and thus as part of the growth statistic are really just transplants from other churches—religious consumers in search of the perfect, or at least more exciting or enjoyable, church experience. Disturbingly little church growth is attributable to new converts. All in all, it was not a good decade for church growth.

The '90s ushered in three challenging attendance trends that still plague churches: irregular attendance among the regulars (a behavior especially prevalent among Boomers), multiple-church attendance and the development of megachurches. The first of these trends is a reflection of people's increased spiritual options, busy schedules, diminished sense of obligation and general boredom with the predictability of the Sunday morning event. The second pattern describes the one out of every six adults who selects a group of churches (usually anywhere from two to five congregations) and attends each of them sporadically, rather than just one of them all the time. We will address the megachurch phenomenon shortly.

Consider how pastors describe their churches. Most of the senior pastors of Protestant churches say their church is theologically conservative (79 percent) and evangelical (83 percent). Half say that their church is seeker sensitive; somewhat fewer (one-third) claim to be seeker driven. One-quarter describe their church as charismatic, and one-quarter say their ministry is Pentecostal. (About one-third who say they are charismatic do *not* consider their ministry to be Pentecostal and vice versa.) One-third embrace the label "liturgical"; not surprisingly two-thirds of all mainline congregations accept that term. Four out of 5 maintain that they are consistently serving the needy people of their community. However, only 2 out of 5 say that their church is consistently engaged with social and political issues.

As you can see, during the past two decades churches have been giving their images a complete makeover. Among the characterizations that churches are more comfortable adopting these days are seeker sensitive, evangelical, charismatic and theologically conservative. It is no longer fashionable to be liturgical, traditional, liberal or denominational. Even if you are one of those types of churches, you search for a more appealing way to describe it.

The focus of local church ministry has also shifted between a variety of needs and interests over the last few decades. In 1990 pastors told us their church's most pressing ministry needs were addressing people's time commitments and apathy toward ministry (25 percent), demographic changes and challenges (8 percent), evangelism (8 percent) and raising more money for ministry (7 percent). Other significant priorities included congregational resistance to change (5 percent) and the deterioration of existing values and morals (5 percent).

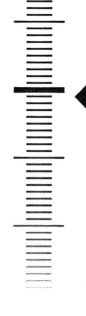

It is no longer fashionable for churches to be liturgical, traditional, liberal or denominational.

As the times changed, so did the top 10 issues on church agendas. By the start of the new millennium, ministry priorities had shifted to getting the church to engage more consistently and effectively in evangelism (30 percent—a huge reawakening from the 8 percent level of 10 years earlier); enhancing the spiritual depth or growth of believers (11 percent); addressing the needs of children and teenagers (9 percent); identifying community needs that the church can address (9 percent); and increasing people's involvement in the life of the church (8 percent).

Consider this: At no time in the past decade (including the data from surveys conducted in the intervening years) have pastors placed areas such as worship, leadership development, holistic stewardship or effective assessment of the ministry among the church's top priorities.

Churches Might Surprise You

Contradictions and surprises abound in the church world, as they do elsewhere in our culture. The assumptions you hold regarding churches may be outdated—or, perhaps, were never accurate in the first place. Here are a few correlations we discovered that might catch you off-guard.

Many people believe that churches are large and growing because of the focus on the megachurches. The truth is that only about 2 percent of all Protestant churches have 1,000 or more adults attending in a typical week. Most churches are small—and getting smaller!

Pastors are among the best-educated folks in town (60 percent are seminary graduates) but their average compensation package is barely above that of a newly-degreed college student starting his/her first (entry-level) job.

True followers of Christ expect the nation's network of Christian churches to ignite and sustain a moral and spiritual revolution. But successful revolutions take money. Although Americans donate more than $50 billion to churches each year, the average ministry outpost is staked to just $120,000 to finance the local revolution. (In constant dollars, that is a 13 percent increase from the budget level in 1987, but still a relatively paltry bank account given the scope of the challenge.)

Churches claim that ministry to kids is one of their top priorities, and more than 9 out of 10 churches have ministry programs for kids of all ages. However, fewer than 1 out of every 4 Protestant churches has a full-time, paid youth worker to lead that ministry.

Nine out of 10 churches say they are evangelistic, but the typical church spends less money on evangelistic outreach than on maintaining its facilities.

Mainline Protestant churches are widely characterized as bastions of theological liberalism. However, 60 percent of mainline senior pastors call their church "theologically conservative" and just 28 percent say they are "theologically liberal."

Black churches are thought of as congregations of poor people. The reality is that the average black adult donates more money to his/her church than people of any other racial group donate to their churches. In fact, black churches have the highest annual operating budget of any churches in the country.

The great interest in spirituality among Baby Busters is assumed to have led them to embrace churches as their second home. Actually, Busters have the lowest level of church attendance, church giving, Sunday School involvement, small group participation, church volunteerism, Bible reading, discipleship involvement and use of Christian media. In short, in spite of their interest in spiritual matters, Busters are the single most disengaged population group in relation to organized religion.

Owing to their rapid population growth and commitment to cultural assimilation, many people assume that Hispanics represent the fastest-growing group of born-again Christians in the nation. Actually, if there was any degree of spiritual revival during the '90s it was most likely among Asian-Americans. While 5 percent of Asians were believers in 1991, that figure ballooned to 27 percent in 2000—a 440 percent increase in nine years.

Complaints about the length of sermons are common. Most people believe that the sermon consumes most of the worship service program. In reality, the average service lasts 70 minutes, and the average sermon is 30 minutes long—perhaps too long for a culture in which people under 30 have an average attention span of less than 10 minutes, but less than half of the morning's event. (Those who think a half hour sermon is interminable would never have lasted during the pastorate of renowned eighteenth century New England preacher Jonathan Edwards. His sermons were reported to have lasted as long as five hours—and his audiences returned to listen to him again and again.)

Mainline Protestant churches—American Baptist, United Church of Christ, Episcopal, Evangelical Lutheran, United Methodist, Presbyterian Church U.S.A.—are often thought to represent a large sector of the population. They may have attracted a majority of Protestants in the '50s, but today they claim just one-third of all Protestant churchgoers. The competition for parishioners has gotten fierce: There are now more than 200 Protestant denominations in the U.S.!

What's Happening in the Pastorate?

Nine out of 10 churches have a full-time, paid senior pastor heading the ministry. Four out of every 5 times, that pastor is the only paid minister in the church. He (pardon the pronoun, but the pastor is male in 95 percent of our churches) works more than 60 hours per week for a relatively paltry compensation package valued at less than $40,000 per year. In fact, the package the typical pastor receives is worth 2 percent less today (in constant dollars) than he was making in 1992. So much for appreciation!

Ministry is tough on the pastor's family life: 94 percent are married, most of them have children and a large proportion of these clergy admit that the emotional demands of the ministry, combined with the stingy compensation and long hours, have caused their family life to suffer. (To their credit, only 15 percent have experienced a divorce—substantially lower than the national norm.) While the average pastor has been in full-time ministry for 17 years, he has served at his current church for just five. Both of these figures represent a rebound from the trend of the '80s, when pastorates were shorter and the average career in full-time church work lasted 14 years.

Most pastors find their work meaningful and fulfilling. Although the stress levels they admit to experiencing are higher than the norm, the rewards seem more satisfying than those achieved by other professionals. Perhaps their appreciation for their high-pressure position relates to the ability to use their spiritual gifts so often. Two-thirds of senior pastors say that their primary spiritual gift is teaching or preaching. No other gift is mentioned by even half as many pastors as this one. Naturally, having spent years in seminary honing their communication abilities and having the opportunity to exercise that skill every week, most pastors always have at least one rewarding and energizing experience to look forward to each week.

Are Christian Churches Healthy Spiritually?

In a recent survey among a nationwide sample of Protestant pastors, we asked them how well their church is performing its ministry duties in each of 10 key areas. Two insights emerged from the study. First, most churches do not have any objective or regular process for evaluating how well their ministry is faring in any given dimension of ministry. Second, among the churches that assessed their quality in an area of ministry, a majority (ranging from 53 percent to 89 percent) rated their church as doing an excellent or good job in each of the 10 dimensions examined.

Are those self-assessments accurate? One way to find out would be to examine how the church is doing in the "six pillars of ministry"—that is, the half-dozen aspects of church-based activity that constitute the heart of the church's work. The pillars are well-known to all Christians: evangelism, worship, discipleship, stewardship, fellowship and service to the needy.[1] Let's take a brief look at some measures of health in relation to each of these ministry pillars.

Worship

Indisputably, worship is among the highest priorities of God. The weekly worship service is, for most churches, the focal point of each week and, for most pastors, the personal highlight of their ministry because they get to preach. Churches have excelled in providing people with a greater variety of worship experiences and delivering learning aids (e.g., study notes, audiotapes) that are designed to help them capture some of the information provided during the teaching time.

Yet, we also know that each weekend, millions come but few understand. Two-thirds of regular churchgoers cannot describe what worship means. Our research shows that a majority of those who attend worship services in any given week (more than three-quarters of adults in attendance) do not experience the presence of God during worship. In fact, half of all churchgoers admit that they have not felt connected to God or in His presence at any time in the past year, in spite of their regular attendance at church. Even so, only 4 percent of Protestant senior pastors list facilitating or enhancing worship as a top priority for their churches. Among those who are concerned about their worship events, energy is being put into determining the best style of music, the appropriate forms of technology (e.g., video screens, PowerPoint presentations), and how to pack out the worship center.

Evangelism

Things have improved in evangelism in the past decade. Presently, about half of all born-again adults say that they have shared their faith with a nonbeliever in the past year. That's a considerable jump from the one-third who had done so a decade ago. The population groups that have shown the most positive response to evangelistic efforts have been Asians, the affluent and people over 50. The toughest groups to penetrate with the gospel have been Hispanics, Baby Busters and people residing in the Northeast and the West—the two regions traditionally least susceptive to Christianity.[2]

Our studies have also discovered another highly significant fact: Evangelism is most effective among preteens. The survey data show that people from ages 5-13 have a 32 percent probability of accepting Christ as their Savior. Young people from the ages of 14-18 have just a 4 percent likelihood of doing so, while adults (ages 19 through death) have only a 6 percent probability of making that choice.[3]

Most Christians have never had any formal training in how to share their faith with a nonbeliever, and most born-again adults do not currently have a personal relationship of consequence with more than one nonbeliever. Since only one out of every seven people who accept Christ as their Savior do so at a worship service or other church event, one-to-one evangelism is crucial to the spread of the good news about Jesus.

Discipleship

There is some serious effort being made by millions of Christians to become devoted followers of Jesus Christ. Currently, one out of every six people who attends a Christian church is involved in being discipled, primarily through small groups that meet during the week to study the Bible, pray and build Christian community. It is important to note that women are almost twice as likely as men to be involved in a discipleship process. That fits the general pattern we discover through almost every research project we conduct: Women serve as the backbone of the American Church, demonstrating greater commitment to their faith than do the men who are associated with Christianity.[4] Other groups that have been particularly hard to motivate to engage in serious spiritual growth pursuits have included those with less than a college education, Catholics and Baby Busters. Adults in their twenties are only half as likely as the rest of the population to engage in discipleship efforts.

One of the most disturbing weaknesses of the Christian community is the infrequency with which believers live their faith. Several studies previously described in these pages have demonstrated that believers are rarely distinguishable in their thoughts, words or deeds from those who have no relationship with Christ. One recent study we completed showed that the values and goals of believers place commitment to Christ and their church in the middle and lower echelons of their life priorities.

The lukewarmness of people's spiritual commitment is at least partially attributable to the fact that, even by their own reckoning, less than 1 out of every 10 born-again Christians possesses a biblical worldview, and partially due to the struggle most believers have of converting head knowledge into behavior. The ultimate consequences of these struggles are that believers lack the power to deal with life's moral and spiritual challenges and that Christians are unattractive models of the Christian faith for those who are seeking spiritual truth.

It may come as a shock to discover that less than 1 percent of America's senior pastors list better teaching, the provision of worldview-based teaching or the development of a life in which faith and behavior are integrated as a top priority for their church. This may be a nonissue to pastors because 94 percent of them believe that "the people who attend my church are consistently exposed to preaching and teaching that intentionally and systematically lead them to develop or embrace a biblical worldview."

Almost half of all churched adults sense that promoting discipleship is among the highest priorities of their church. The fact that a majority of those individuals are aware of the exhortation but ignore it speaks volumes. (Five out of every 6 active churchgoers are not involved in an intentional discipling process.) The fact that 4 out of every 10 individuals currently involved in a Christian discipling process contend that there is no such thing as absolute moral truth underscores that good intent is not enough.

Stewardship

Compared to people from other nations of the world, Americans are generous, donating more than $120 billion every year to the million-plus charities and churches in the country. The greatest share of that money—almost half—goes to religious organizations, especially churches. Most people get into the act: More than 8 out of 10 adults gave away money last year and two-thirds of all adults donated to a church or religious center during the year.

But the generosity and sense of commitment is not universal. About one-third of all adults—and 1 out of every 6 born-again Christians—gave no money to a church last year. In spite of the widespread teaching and emphasis upon tithing, only 8 percent of born-again Christians tithed their income to churches last year. The median donation by Christians to their churches was approximately $1,000 per household, or a bit less than 3 percent of their gross household income. Interestingly, the smaller the church, the less money the typical individual donates.[5]

But stewardship is not simply about tithing or giving money on a regular and generous basis. It is about a mind-set or lifestyle as much as anything. Again, research confirms that American believers are looking for simple formulas and freedom from sacrifice. Often, if the church campus looks good and the church budget is being met, then believers feel they have accomplished all they need to with the resources God has entrusted to them.

Congregational Relationships

One of the areas in which churches do best is providing individuals opportunities to connect with other like-minded people. In a society as mobile and as isolated as ours, having the chance to connect with such people is a gift. More than 4 out of 5 church attenders describe their church as friendly.

There are difficulties related to internal relationships, of course. While most attenders cite their congregation as a friendly group of people, far fewer suggest that their church is a "caring" congregation. Relatively few churches have ministries that connect families and mentor them. Even marriages are a shambles within the church: 27 percent of born-again adults are currently or have previously been divorced compared to 24 percent among adults who are not born again.[6]

The current emphasis upon small groups is the church's latest thrust at building true community within the body. Participants in groups typically give high marks to their groups for enabling them to feel as if they are part of a deeper community of faith.

Serving the Needy

"They will know we are Christians by our love" is one of the themes that churches across the nation embrace, and service to the needy is a core method of demonstrating that love. A large majority of Protestant senior pastors rate their church as doing a good job in community outreach. Perhaps that is why pastors buried helping the poor toward the bottom of a list of ministry priorities for their church.

Amazingly, survey statistics reveal that only 1 out of 5 adults actually gives time and money to any activities designed to assist the disadvantaged during the past year. Ministry to the community, it turns out, is one of those image-building programs that everybody wants to highlight but nobody really wants to serve. Our studies show that people like to mention the outreach programs of their church, and many unchurched people list such efforts as among the most important characteristics they look for in a church. However, when asked what ministries they personally get involved in, the vast majority have to do with taking resources from the ministry, rather than investing personal resources (time, effort, money) in activities designed to help others.

Ministry Leadership

While this is not one of the six pillars of the local church, we have found that the presence or absence of strong leadership is one of the traits that distinguishes the highly effective churches of America from those that are doing well-intentioned religious activity. One of the most significant findings from our research is that most churches have a mismatch between the expectations the church has of their pastor and his/her gifts and skills. By their own admission, most senior pastors are neither gifted in nor excited about leadership. Fewer than 1 out of every 20 senior pastors can identify the unique vision that God will entrust to His leaders on behalf of the churches they pastor. Less than 1 out of every 8 claims to have the gift of spiritual leadership.

Our work with highly effective churches has also shown that those churches prioritize leadership development. Their congregations have successfully identified the lay leaders God inevitably brings to a congregation and equipped them to use their gifts and abilities to lead the ministry. Highly effective churches typically have more than double the number of gifted and trained lay leaders in service compared to the average American church. The recognition, preparedness and deployment of those leaders are the primary reasons why their churches make serious spiritual progress.

In spite of this, only 2 percent of Protestant senior pastors name personal or lay leadership development, vision clarification and vision communication or strategic development of the ministry as top ministry priorities. In fact, despite (or maybe because of their exposure to) all the books and conferences focused on leadership concerns, fewer pastors identify leadership as a major challenge than was true at the beginning of this decade. Almost every pastor across the country—an astounding 96 percent—contend that "the people in my church would describe me as an effective leader."

Assessing Church Health

Having considered these factors, then, the result is a mixed report card. There are certainly many incredible and wonderful things happening in thousands of churches throughout the nation. God is worshiped, His people are studying His Word and striving to become better disciples, resources are freely given to the work of the church, the gospel is being shared, needy people are being helped, and the members of the community of believers are encouraging and stimulating each other to grow.

Healthy churches are more often the exception to the rule.

On balance, though, there are many areas in which churches simply are not healthy. The examples of spiritual health are more often the exception to the rule. Nobody likes to admit this. But, as addiction clinics tell their patients, the first step to recovery is to admit that they have a problem and that they need help. One must wonder if we have been addicted to religious rituals and assumptions for so long that we, too, have an addiction that needs to be healed—an addiction to empty, self-deceiving, unhealthy church practices.

Megachurches: Curse or Panacea?

In the midst of all of the changes taking place in the Church world has been the emergence of the large church, commonly known as megachurches. Some analysts (including the authors) consider megachurches to be those attracting 1,000 or more adults to weekly services, while others use 2,000 people as the criteria. Regardless, these large ministry centers have been increasing in number and have been the primary focus of media attention during the past decade. You might be surprised to learn that in spite of all of the attention and hoopla surrounding megachurches, they constitute barely more than 1 percent of the nation's 324,000 Protestant churches. Perhaps the attention is given to them because they draw close to one-fifth of the nation's churchgoers!

Megachurch ministry has become attractive because of the economies of scale that can be realized in a large ministry. People can have access to a broader range of programs, events and styles of ministry; individuals can pursue a variety of niche interests or simply maintain their anonymity; financial and human resources, as well as facilities, can be used more efficiently; talented people have opportunities to focus on their areas of giftedness and the church can afford to hire a greater quantity and quality of top-of-the-line personnel; and the bulk of the church permits it to have greater influence in its community. The icons of the Protestant church world have become the pastors who preside over the largest churches.

One of the dangers facing the Church in this new decade is that the complexity and pace of life motivates Americans to seek quick and easy solutions. The lust for megachurches represents such a condition. There is nothing inherently wrong with a large church, of course, but the dangers of seeking size are that we prioritize quantity of attenders over quality of spiritual life, and we depersonalize the ministry in order to provide a broader menu of programs from which people may choose. In essence, the attraction of megachurches has caused the typical suburban and urban church (and a few rural congregations) to redefine what it takes to be a successful ministry.[7] The more people, programs, money and square footage the church accumulates, the more "successful" it has become in the eyes of many.

Church leaders have responded to some of these concerns by gearing themselves toward getting big by becoming small. That strategy calls for churches to provide some measure of intimacy and relational connection in the midst of the thousands of strangers attending a church's worship services and programs by facilitating weekly or biweekly small-group (aka "cell group") meetings. These meetings consist of anywhere from 5 to 20 people who meet regularly, usually in someone's home, for any of a wide range of purposes, such as relationships, religious education, prayer, community service and worship. At the opening of this decade, 1 out of every 6 adults in the country—and about 1 out of every 3 born-again adults—was involved in a small group. Oddly, those figures have not changed since the early '90s, in spite of the emphasis churches have placed on small-group involvement.

Small groups became the hope of the local church during the '90s. Seventy percent of senior pastors informed us that their small-group ministry is "central to the overall success" of their church's ministry. Perhaps because so much energy was devoted to recruiting participation in groups, the ministry promise of small groups (i.e., results) has yet to be fulfilled. The spiritual depth and accountability that is so desperately needed for Christianity to be anything more than a temporary fix or feel-good experience has not yet been delivered.

Participants generally report great satisfaction with the relationships that have been developed in their minichurches, but research has also shown that there has been negligible growth in Bible knowledge, the application of scriptural principles or overall spiritual maturity. What's missing? Our preliminary research identifies the absence of strong leadership within the group, effective teaching methods and firm accountability to be the dominant soft spots. Since tens of thousands of Protestant churches have staked their future on the success of small groups to deliver effective ministry to their adherents, and to enable their march toward megachurchdom to succeed, the triple-zero decade will be a make-it-or-break-it period for both small groups and the megachurch concept.

Leadership at the National Level

Here's a test. What are the three things that these people have in common?

Billy Graham	Bill Bright	Charles Stanley
Chuck Colson	James Dobson	Donald Wildmon
Pat Robertson	Chuck Swindoll	Paul Crouch
Jack Hayford	James Kennedy	R.C. Sproul
Pope John Paul II	Robert Schuller	John Stott
Peter Wagner	David Yonggi Cho	Lyle Schaller

Answer: they're all major leaders or agents of influence within the American Church, they're all men and they're all in their sixties or beyond.

During this decade the American Church will experience a massive turnover in Church leadership. Many of the individuals who have shaped the Church as we know it today will pass the baton to successors. Some of those choices have already been made public. Billy Graham has appointed one of his sons to continue his evangelistic ministry. Bill Bright has chosen his second in command to lead Campus Crusade for Christ. More of these transitions will become news in the next few years.

If history is a guide, though, the impact of many of the personality-driven ministries will fade as the primary personality departs the scene. We might expect a new cadre of leaders and associated ministries to arise and fill the vacuum they leave behind. Some of the new faces have already assumed places of prominence (e.g., Bill Hybels, John Maxwell, Rick Warren), while other young leaders are just ascending to positions of influence. You can bet that another dozen or so fresh names will emerge in the next five years to provide direction, continuity and personality to the Church of the twenty-first century.

Innovative Church Models

Not only will there be a new class of national Church leaders casting vision and providing direction, but Americans will experience a growing range of church alternatives from which they may choose. For several hundred years, if a person wished to participate in the life of the Christian Body, the only game in town was the local church and its standard menu of options:

Sunday morning worship service (available in one of two or three flavors: traditional, contemporary, blended), Sunday School, a few midweek programs and an annual stewardship effort.

The new America does not understand standardization without options; it demands a pallet of possibilities from which to choose and resents efforts to curtail its breath of choices. The church is the last frontier within our culture to resist the progression of multiple choices. But that resistance is about to dissolve into a catalogue of opportunities. Some of the new choices will be minor variations on existing themes, such as churches offering congregants additional worship services that provide a different style of music, or denominations and large churches planting new churches designed to reach specific demographic target groups. The more intriguing creations, though, are those that will emerge independently of mother organizations in an attempt to meet an unmet need.

Why the sudden rush of new possibilities? Because American life is now defined by concepts such as diversification, experience, customization, intimacy, authenticity, reliability and quality. Having been given these elements in a wide range of other products, services, resources and events that are common to our daily existence, people expect such choices in all realms of life. The failure to provide such choices causes people to lose interest in the offering. As the dictators of our own destiny, we do not trust any organization or cause that tells us what, how, when, where or why to do a prescribed activity.

Here are some of the innovations in "doing church" that you will find at your disposal.[8]

House Church

Popular in other countries, especially Southeast Asia, thousands of independent faith groups will meet for a complete church experience and expression within living rooms and garages. Driven by the need for intimacy, spontaneity and control, this option will appeal to individuals who are especially interested in restoring authenticity, community and simplicity to the church.

Cyberchurch

The Internet is changing the way Americans experience God in many ways. As the decade evolves, expect more people to rely upon the Internet for all of their spiritual input and output; we're projecting that the Internet will encompass the aggregate spiritual expression of 10-20 percent of the population by 2010. You will find worshiping communities, confessing communities, dialoguing communities and faith-driven relational communities that exist entirely through digital communication. The benefit of such a ministry medium is the reach it affords, along with the potential for honesty (driven by the protection of anonymity), widespread prayer support, and opportunities for personal expression and the development of relationships. The greatest downside is the possibility of spiritual heresy gaining credence as biblical truth.

In addition, of course, most of the standard bricks-and-mortar churches will integrate websites, e-mail, audio streaming, video streaming, outreach and chat rooms into its existing ministry operations.

Event Church

Frustrated by the politics, structures and general hassle of living within a standard church, growing numbers of entrepreneurial believers will leave the standard congregational church to be the impresarios of infrequent communitywide worship events. These events will occur in public places—theaters, auditoriums, public parks—and feature the best musicians, dramatists and speakers that the impresarios can find (and afford). The purpose: Have a no-strings-attached, high quality, focus-on-God-alone event that elevates worship to high art and life-changing personal experience.

Boutique Church

Thousands of unidimensional churches will spring up, offering people one type of ministry experience—e.g., worship, discipleship, fellowship, community service—on a regular basis and done with excellence. The key to making these churches effective is that they will be part of a network of boutique ministries that enables individual Christians to select a group of boutique ministries that will fulfill their personal needs and round out their spiritual experience. Thus, a typical boutiquer might select a worship church, a discipling church, a community service church and an outreach church as part of the menu of churches from which he/she will choose whenever they feel the need for a spiritual experience. (By the way, providing just a single dimension of ministry will be intentional at these churches, unlike the thousands of existing churches that currently provide only one viable dimension of ministry although they dabble in a variety of dimensions.)

Communal Church

The back-to-basics, return-to-the-simple-life movement will give birth to communal faith groups. This is a throwback to the '60s, when hippie communes were popular. They will arise again, but this time with greater structure and purpose, not so much as an angry response to "the military-industrial complex," but as a means of rediscovering many of the more simple pleasures of life. The pivot point of these communes will be their monastery-like devotion to Christian maturity and introspection, within the context of a broader, shared community life.

Dialogical Forums

The predisposition of the Busters and Mosaics is to grow through dialogue, not propositional teaching. Much like Paul's experience at Mars Hill (see Acts 17) there will be a national smattering of regular meetings that take place for the purpose of having a Socratic dialogue on spiritual matters. Often held in casual environments such as coffeehouses or condo complex meeting halls, these groups will be less concerned about developing a structured ministry than about grappling with the substance of faith matters.

Compassion Clusters

The desire to couple beliefs and social action will produce these relatively small aggregations of socially conscious individuals. Their primary focus will be on making their faith real through acts of service. These formations are likely to be of limited duration, measured perhaps in months rather than years and generated around the energy of individuals who develop the group through word of mouth.

Prayer Shelters

Individuals who love to pray will come together on a regular basis to share some thoughts from Scripture, to sing psalms to the Lord, to share prayer burdens and to spend hours together in prayer. Rather than devote themselves to the life of a standard church, these are individuals who have felt that prayer was undervalued as a ministry within the local church and who take great joy being in the presence of others who lose themselves in prayer.

Marketplace Ministries

The pace of life and the demands of standard church bodies will motivate a growing number of people to team with work associates or recreational buddies to develop a ministry to the people whom they encounter in that segment of the marketplace. Rather than encourage their work or recreational acquaintances to attend a standard church, these people will serve as the ministers to their associates, engaging in evangelism, discipling and service ministries. Rather than connect with a local church, these people will float in and out of churches for the aspects of spiritual experience they cannot replicate on their own (e.g., corporate worship) but will exploit the freedom they have to be a roving ambassador of Christ to the world they regularly inhabit. By the way, examples of all of these new forms of the Church exist today. The coming decade will afford each model a chance to expand and mature—or die trying.

Where Are We Headed?

As you can imagine, given the elements described in this chapter, the triple-zero decade will radically reshape the Church in preparation for a very different culture. We have already described a few of the major changes coming:

- At least three major denominations are likely to experience splits during the decade in reaction to the structural, theological and methodological stands of the denomination. The upstarts who depart in controversy will start their own denominations and will grow in response to their clarity of vision and passion for their convictions.

- Dozens of church associations will emerge, formalizing and facilitating the networking of churches that share practices and dreams in common. It will not be uncommon for churches to trumpet their affiliation with such associations rather than their connection to the old-line denominations. Dozens of denominations will realize that they must make a shift away from being centralized bureaucracies to service bureaus.

- Charismatic churches will flourish as they emphasize power, emotion and experience. Those elements will resonate with the population.

- New ministry priorities will capture the attention of church leaders. Among those will be the need to facilitate genuine worship, not just to provide worship services; the need to facilitate a biblical worldview, rather than teaching disparate, unconnected truths from Scripture; and the necessity of improving children's programs.

- Society at large will embarrass the Church into taking community service more seriously. As government agencies distance themselves from service to the needy, churches will be expected to pick up the slack.

- The Catholic Church will plateau in terms of growth and will experience a time of programmatic uncertainty after the passing of Pope John Paul II. That period of ambiguity will change once the personality and vision of his successor become clear.

- The Muslim faith will grow in the U.S., primarily among blacks who are seeking an alternative to Christianity and a more politically aggressive association. Mormonism will continue to attract hundreds of thousands of new adherents every year but will see minimal net growth in the U.S. because of the high turnover ratio within the LDS church. Mainline churches will see their decline level off during this decade.

- Churches will refine their small-group ministry procedures to include better training of leaders, superior development of study and discussion content for groups and better tracking of individual spiritual development.

- There will be an influx of men in their mid-forties to late fifties who become staff members and even senior pastors at Protestant churches. These individuals will be the "Second Half" class—men entering full-time ministry as a second career. Their business expertise will bring a more professional, structured orientation to the Protestant community.

- People will lose their focus on megachurches as the plethora of new church models gains momentum and public awareness. Megachurches, while no longer the darling of church analysts, will remain a potent force in the Church world, in spite of their loss of luster.

- Thousands of churches will default on their buildings, constructed during the capital campaign boom of the '90s and early triple-zero decade. There will also be more churches selling their properties and facilities to other churches to accommodate fluctuations in church size. Campus swapping will become one of the prevalent activities in reaction to the unpredictable and rapidly changing loyalties of congregants.

- The notion of being "Protestant" will lose meaning and cachet in the new decade. Most young adults have no sense of what their church has been protesting about and thus will choose a more conciliatory, positive or substantive label with which to describe their faith allegiance.

What Can You Do?

Although this chapter has been mostly devoted to organizational and structural trends, here are a few challenges that those shifts raise for you.

Take the time to clarify your understanding of what the local church is about and your obligation to it as a Christian.[9] Issues such as loyalty to a church, what you can expect to get from a church, what you should expect to give to a church, the role of the Internet in a community of faith—all of these and more will be issues to ponder as you clarify your own philosophy of personal responsibility to the Church. Make sure you base your conclusions on Scripture, not the leanings of the culture.

Examine your own spiritual maturity and experience in relation to the six pillars of the church: worship, evangelism, discipleship, stewardship, relationships and community service. No matter what church (or churches) you attend, you are responsible for growing in these dimensions. How well are you doing?

If you are not currently involved in a small group associated with your church, consider getting involved in one. If you are involved already, examine the value you are getting from that commitment and how you could help raise the standard for your group.

Notes

1. For a more detailed exploration of how the most effective churches in the nation are focusing on these areas, see George Barna, *The Habits of Highly Effective Churches* (Ventura, CA: Regal Books, 2000). In the book I describe the results of our research that identified the nine ministry habits of churches where spiritually based life transformation is consistently occurring.

2. A more complete discussion of recent evangelistic outcomes can be found in "Asians and Affluent Are Increasingly Likely to be Born Again," a report from May 30, 2000 that is in the News Release Library at http://www.barna.org (accessed August 2000).

3. This research was described in a summary report, "Teens and Adults Have Little Chance of Accepting Christ As Their Savior." That release, originally published November 15, 1999, can be accessed through the News Release library at the Barna Research website at http://www.barna.org (accessed August 2000).

4. Recent research on both discipleship and the commitment of women to the Christian faith can be accessed at the Barna Research website. Two reports, in particular, may be of interest: "Women Are the Backbone of the Christian Congregations in America," released March 6, 2000, and "More Than 20 Million Churched Adults Actively Involved in Spiritual Growth Efforts," released May 9, 2000, and are located at http://www.barna.org.

5. More detailed statistics on giving patterns are found in "Evangelicals Are The Most Generous Givers, But Fewer Than 10 Percent of Born-Again Christians Give 10

Percent to Their Church." That report was released April 5, 2000 and is contained in the News Release Library on the Barna Research website at http://www.barna.org.

6. The details of this research are found in "Christians Are More Likely to Experience Divorce Than Are Non-Christians," released December 21, 1999, and available through the News Release Library at http://www.barna.org (accessed August 2000).

7. For a more detailed discussion of our research on how churches define success in ministry, and how they evaluate whether or not they are successful, consult the audio and video presentations of George Barna's seminar session, *Ministry Evaluation*, available from Barna Research at http://www.barna.org (accessed August 2000) or call 1-800-552-2762.

8. There is a more extensive discussion of some of these innovations in chapter 13 in George Barna, *The Second Coming of the Church* (Nashville, TN: Word Books, 1998).

9. Libraries of books have been written on the basics of the Church. If you're not sure where to start, consider these: Max Anders, *The Church in 12 Lessons* (Nashville, TN: Thomas Nelson Publishers, 1997); David Watson, *I Believe in the Church* (Grand Rapids, MI: Eerdmans Publishing, 1978); Charles Colson and Ellen Vaughan, *The Body* (Nashville, TN: Word Publishing, 1992).

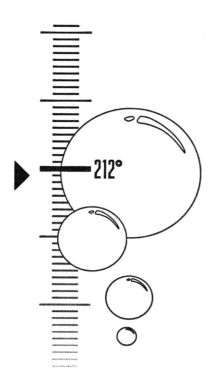

CHAPTER TWELVE

THE GLOBAL ECONOMY

Future Glimpse

Jill used to enjoy watching the evening news with Carl. But things had changed. The news was now packed with what seemed like esoteric financial tidbits: monetary fund security leaks, international electronic fund transfers, trade deficits, national debt battles, labor supply reports, multinational inflation statistics and so on. Whatever happened to the good ol' days when a half-hour national newscast was littered with stories about celebrities shacking up, rude comments made by public officials and the inappropriate behavior of sports heroes? It took her only a second to realize the answer to her own question: That was no longer news because those examples were the normal behavior nowadays. She lamented the realization that she'd probably better get used to the financial doublespeak pouring forth from her flat-screen, high-definition TV, since that was what life in the new millennium had evolved into.

As Carl chomped on some peanuts and soaked in the news of the day's financial undertakings, Jill glanced at the living room table, where her purse lay. It was tiny—smaller than she'd ever had in her life. The major reason was that she no longer had to carry around a multitude of credit cards, forms of identification and cash. Three cards—her global ID card, her medical summary card and her money card—were all she, or anyone, really needed. All of them were electronic and made life so much easier. She could go anywhere in the world and any time of day or night she (or whomever possessed the cards and her security codes) could gain access to everything vital about her. Sometimes she wondered about the security of it all, but Jill was one who hated to ask too many questions if things were working okay. She was like most Americans in that regard.

She rarely journeyed to the bank anymore since most transactions—her bill paying, her salary payments, her in-person transactions at stores—were carried out electronically. Sure, every once in a while you'd hear about a person suddenly discovering that they were $10 million in debt, but those digital glitches were worked out (she assumed) quickly. And all that talk about international debt loads and the like—meaningless to her. Let the political bigwigs work out their needs without cluttering her mind with the details. The end result was always the same, anyway: They'd just send her and everyone else the bill—electronically.

She sighed in relief at the realization that Carl, a pretty amazing amateur investor, would be able to take their retirement funds and invest them in a few momentarily hot trading options. His track record was good so far. She just hoped she could continue to persuade him not to "bet the house" with their nest egg and not to get too heavily immersed in the on-line gambling schemes that seemed omnipresent.

Carl got up at the commercial break to go to the bathroom. Jill seized her chance. She grabbed the remote control and switched to a more engaging channel, escaping the tedium of the day's financial news. *Much better*, she thought, *nothing like a good Maglev (Magnetic Levitation vehicle) race to take my mind off the world of high finance.*

Anticipation—The Global Neighborhood

We've discussed a myriad of changes that are likely to occur in the United States during this decade—transitions related to demographics, generations, values, morality, lifestyles, religious beliefs and practices and church life. Isn't that enough to think about—and to get ready to handle? It seems like that's plenty to take on! Why should you care about esoteric matters like the global economy? Who cares what will be going on half a world away in places like Tokyo, London, Moscow, Lagos, Bombay, Rio de Janeiro or Beijing?

The answer relates to something we noted in the introductory chapter: Success in the new world depends upon anticipation, not reaction. What may seem esoteric today will be mainstream reality tomorrow. As we get deeper into this decade, you will find that all the talk about global this and worldwide that has become a reality: We really will be an interrelated, if not wholly integrated, global economy. And that's just the beginning. The intricately linked global economy may well be the high-octane fuel that propels the coming movement toward a one-world government, truly global corporations and an international labor pool.

Competing Among 6 Billion People

To get some perspective on the scope and personal impact of the globalization process, consider what it takes to get a job these days. You learn about an opening, you contact the firm, you submit the applications and support documents, you go through interviews and wait to hear. You know you're up against a few dozen, maybe even a few hundred people, some of whom are undoubtedly more qualified than you. Depending on the nature of the job, your competition might be limited to people within a 10-mile radius of the employer's location, or their recruiting net might be as wide as the entire

United States (through a significant advertising and headhunting campaign).

If you thought competing for jobs was tough in the past, just wait until your competitors are some of the best and brightest living in places all over the world who may be able to ship or electronically deliver their work. If your pool of competition is now X, a few years from now your competition may easily be $12X$, or whatever the multiplier will be to encompass the aggregate scale of the wired world. If you own a business, count on your competition expanding like a brushfire, too. Each year more than 150,000 new businesses come into being in the U.S. alone, creating nearly a million new jobs (i.e., tougher competition for that labor market). Layer on top of that the fact that a competitor is no longer someone whose business is nearby. With the Internet touching virtually every person in the nation these days, a savvy upstart in Nowheresville, Wyoming, has just as good a shot at attracting customers (or employees) as a long-standing, upstanding, outstanding corporation in Los Angeles.

In a global economy, your competitors will be the best and the brightest in the world!

Maybe you've already been affected by the globalization of the employment market. Between us authors, we can identify a number of personal friends whose careers have been altered by globalization.

One friend recently lost a recording job in his hometown of Los Angeles to someone living in Poland. Instead of paying the daily union minimum for a recording artist in Los Angeles (roughly $300), the producer hired someone in Warsaw for $30 who recorded the music in Poland and electronically transmitted his work overnight.

A very talented creative friend lost an illustrator job for Fox when the studio instead hired a parcel of Japanese animators who worked longer hours for less pay. (Fox is simply following the established trend in computer design; the major movie and television studios send millions of dollars of such work overseas, mostly to artists and studios in southeast Asia.)

A family member recently lost out on a contract for software design to a European professional who has never met anyone in the company commissioning the work, will never have a face-to-face meeting with any representatives of the firm, nor has any experience even working in the industry of the company that is hiring him.

Another friend, who operates a clothing manufacturing plant, is on the brink of bankruptcy because he cannot compete with the labor costs of Third World nations.

A former colleague at Barna Research, who now heads up a business school in the South, notes that major corporations are no longer limiting their hiring of new college graduates to those emanating from top U.S. schools. Many now send recruiting teams to India, Japan, South Africa, Singapore, Malaysia, Australia and a host of other nations to discover and snare the best talent available—at the most reasonable wages payable.

To be fair, realize that the sword cuts both ways: You lose some opportunities, but the same process opens up an entire world of new options, as well. One of the authors oversees a dot com company that brokers talented professionals and jobs via the Internet, matching hundreds of skilled Americans with talent-starved foreign companies. Thanks to the Internet, telecommuting and other recent (and soon-to-be) technological innovations, American workers and corporations have unprecedented entré into foreign markets. Millions of us will be inexpensively marketing goods and services overseas or selling our skills and knowledge to higher bidders in other nations.

Is your head spinning yet, just thinking about the challenges and opportunities that are coming down the road? Realize that nobody is forcing us to exploit these new conditions. Americans will zealously go after these options of our own free will because they seem like a natural extension of the free market economy that we have championed for so many years. The global economy will bring both benefits and hardships: some goods and services will be cheaper, better and faster as a result, while some employees and organizations will suffer from the intensity of the competition.

International Financial Stability

Many of these changes are merely a continuation of surging forces and transformations that began many years ago. Our world already experiences the most integrated markets in history. The transnational movement of money—global liquidity—has reached unprecedented levels. As an example, from the time a barrel of oil is extracted from the ground until the time that it is pumped into your gas tank, that resource is typically bought and sold nine times, mostly by people who never had any intention of personally using that oil but who figured it was a good thing to own for a short while. In other words, economic trading has become unbelievably complex. Governments and corporations trade with dozens of other governments and corporations every day. The world's economies have become inextricably intertwined, creating financial (and political) strengths and weaknesses never before experienced.

The U.S. has fared well in the early stages of globalization. The American economy is still, by far, the largest economy in the world. California by itself is the world's seventh largest economy and Southern California is the ninth largest economy in the world. So it still remains true that when the U.S. economy sneezes the rest of the world catches a cold.

But in times of fast and fundamental change, nothing is forever—and that is doubly true when money and power are involved. Regional economies now wield tremendous influence. Just a few years ago we endured the collapse of the Japanese and Asian economies that sent a ripple effect through much of the rest of the world and certainly affected the U.S. (It was often called "the Asian Flu" because their economies sneezed and the whole world caught a financial cold.) Since that time, rather than isolate ourselves from such effects, we have become even more tied to the health of foreign economies—as they, in turn, have become more susceptible to ours.

Over the next 10 years you will see national economies continue to become a more unified and integrated system. There will be significant trade increases and an escalation of international-trade policy agreements and enforcement procedures. One of the nation's founding fathers, George Washington, once argued that the United States should avoid foreign entanglements. What a different world he lived in!

If you want a preview of how complicated it all becomes, just review the recent history of the relations between the United States and China. This is a good example of foreign policy being shaped by monetary interests as these two superpowers jockey for economic and political supremacy. The importance of economics is underscored by the shift in the focus of the policy debates. Recent discussions hinge less on concerns about morality, ethics and philosophy than they do on trade volume, categorical restrictions and deficit trading. Fewer Americans care if China is under communist rule than whether it will be a reliable trading partner. The debate rarely turns on who made the goods—exploited children, prison labor or persecuted Christians—than on whether we can get large quantities of good quality, inexpensive goods. We're not too interested in their government's views on mandated abortion, family planning, or religious freedom as long as we're allowed to export the latest Hollywood fare across the ocean, without restrictions and editing. Artistic freedom, it seems, transcends physical and religious freedom in importance.

More than ever before, international policies are being determined in the boardrooms of the largest corporations throughout the world. The financial powerbrokers increasingly manipulate national policy debates and actions. The greatest punishment exacted upon a nation may no longer be accomplished with guns and bombs, but with trade and monetary restrictions. (Financial traders openly speak of punishing those organizations or nations that have the nerve to mess with the market. For instance, when it was discovered that Mexico was printing money to pay its civil workers in international currency, traders zeroed in on the Mexican currency until it was virtually worthless, proclaiming that the Mexicans deserved to be punished for their inappropriate actions. This caused the "peso-crisis" of 1994-1995.) The ability of international banks to devalue a nation's currency, to undermine its ability to get loans or to engage in competitive trading has escalated, while the ability of a nation's chief executive or central banking authorities to manage their own economy has been diminished. Freedom has been harnessed by the loan makers' economic leash.

In the midst of the whirlwinds of change that are reshaping high finance, the economic conditions of many of the less stable nations are still susceptible to an old-fashioned nemesis: theft. This is a systemic problem that is especially prevalent in underdeveloped nations. In some cases, although many of the people are distraught over the constant deception and robbery, they have almost come to accept the practice as inevitable, resulting in a culture of theft. Every year you read about millions of dollars of government payments, loans and other investment capital disappearing, allegedly into the hands of those who already have substantial power, wealth and connections. The filching of public and private funds robs those nations of valuable assets and of their ability to deliver on promises made, effectively destroying the nations' hope of true progress.

The former Soviet Union is a prime example of this cycle. During the past decade, the one-time superpower has gone through incredible highs and lows. After the promise of freedom and democracy, the nation has slid back into the throes of a corrupt and inept government that is undermined by rampant criminal behavior. International investments into Russia have slowed to a dribble as investors have watched the nation fall prey to graft, byzantine rules, outright theft, underground economies and an internal economic system that is unpredictable. Perhaps the most frightening possibility is that the unhealthy economic patterns evident in Russia could not only become permanent in that country, but also a precursor of coming economic disaster in China, many African nations and most of Latin America.

> **The unhealthy economic patterns in Russia could be a precursor of coming economic disaster in other countries.**

A robust international economy is predicated upon trust, accepted international law and follow-through. Not surprisingly, the adoption of Judeo-Christian ethics in a nation tends to improve the transparency of its monetary actions and to reduce the culture of theft, enabling the nation to experience a strong economy. By adopting and enforcing laws that reject graft, manipulation and theft as acceptable practices, the propensity to suffer from such vices is lessened. Alternatively, when the brightest, most powerful or wealthiest individuals in a developing nation lie, cheat and steal to get ahead, they send a powerful message to their compatriots. In effect, their example trains their countrymen that such underhanded behavior is the only means to success. The triple-zero decade may well be the one in which nations teetering on the economic edge—e.g., Mexico, Russia, Columbia, Brazil, Nigeria, Thailand and even China—determine their economic and political destiny for generations to come.

International Debt

The financing of international growth or floating the economic development of a nation through debt instruments can be a useful means of improving the well-being of millions of people in that country, provided that the debt is used productively and effectively. Schools, bridges and roads are some of the traditional deliverables financed by debt that produce high, long-term returns.

Unfortunately, the process of financing national debt is a tricky and sometimes treacherous business. The one rule of thumb is that the funds typically flow from the economic "haves" to the economic "have nots." A second rule is that such loans do not come without strings attached. The lending nations or organizations (i.e., International Monetary Fund, United Nations and World Bank) usually impose a host of expectations—some of which are non-monetary in nature—upon the fund recipients. Thus, nations receiving the economic injections may have to acquiesce to morals, family planning policies or other programs that make sense to the lending entity.

Sometimes, these rules or impositions are invaluable, helping to promote order, continuity, consistency and compatibility, all of which benefit the receiving nation. Other times, though, the rules unwittingly generate social unrest, moral confusion and policy problems that are as bad or worse than what would otherwise have been experienced. Even apart from the oftentimes incompatibility of western and Third World values, the bottom line is that many underdeveloped nations are buckling under the weight of the debt that they are incurring in their efforts to become economically viable. All the loans in the world will do little more than bury the country in financial paper until infrastructural transformations occur (e.g., significant improvements in schools, roads, health care, food production and distribution). What is happening today amounts to the economic enslavement of nations in the Southern Hemisphere to those in the Northern Hemisphere. (As it turns out, almost the entire industrialized world lies in the Northern Hemisphere and much of the Third World lies in the Southern Hemisphere.) Unless there is a massive change of heart among the industrialized nations to embrace the concept of debt forgiveness, there will be all manner of civil unrest in the underdeveloped nations crippled by their debt and mismanagement and the disenchantment of the lending entities with the unlikelihood of their ever being paid back.[1]

Centers and Sources of Wealth

Few things influence the direction of power and impact in the world more than the creation of wealth. But as the world becomes simultaneously smaller and more complex, there will be more variety in the ways in which wealth is created. During this decade there will be new wealth emerging from new trading blocks, the sale of natural resources, revenues generated by manufacturing, services, innovation and patents, the reliance on physical labor and the development of new monetary laws. These methods can be divided into the old-school and new-school approaches to wealth creation.

Old-School Wealth Creation

Perhaps the most traditional route to economic ascension is through the use of physical labor. In much the same way that families on the American frontier sought to get ahead by having many children and using their energy to work the family farm, so do many underdeveloped nations seek to grow economically through this population growth strategy. Unfortunately, as Karl Marx pointed out, the full value of labor does not always accrue to the person whose labor is being utilized. Typically, the laborer will capture some portion of the value that his/her efforts generate, but this is a very slow, long-term approach in a world that moves at warp speed. This strategy often works in tandem with a heightened focus on manufacturing that produces desired goods at a competitive labor rate to satisfy the consumption needs of wealthier nations.

Another of the more traditional approaches to wealth creation is the accumulation, refinement, packaging and sale of natural resources. This process is somewhat more stable, assuming that the resources—land, oil and minerals—are in demand by nations that can afford to pay for those resources. This path to financial security is fairly common within the Third World and has boosted a number of resource-rich nations to economic viability in spite of numerous other weaknesses within the nations.

A somewhat more sophisticated means of creating wealth is through the development of trading blocks. These are international agreements through which the participating nations have opportunities to optimize their wealth creation through the trading of goods and services with other partners inside that block. Reducing internal barriers to competition within the trading block gives rise to wealth creation. This strategy is a good, short-term boost for a national economy, but history has shown that trading blocks improve the economies of those inside the trading block only to a point. In fact, there is evidence that in the long run this approach may well diminish potential wealth creation by excluding countries outside of the block from full participation in the economic activity and by limiting the emergence and fiscal value of innovation. Overall, reliance on trading blocks is helpful if it encourages a country to lower or reduce barriers to economic competition without also injuring some of its own people or institutions through increased competition. Even so, the secondary economic growth stimulated by this strategy—such as secondary industries having a larger market for their goods and services—may sometimes compensate for a few of the more overt challenges.

Finally, a traditional means to creating wealth is through the crafting of a nation's laws. Legal strategies can create wealth through the reduction of theft, fraud and other illegal activities, and they can sometimes spark new efforts within high-potential but moribund industries. History also shows that if a law-based plan is not carefully and appropriately executed, new laws can distort the distribution of wealth through the unwarranted preferential treatment given to specific industries or companies who capture value by the creation, manipulation or sustaining of a particular law. Visit almost any Third World nation and you will witness evidence of companies and individuals who initiated and then exploited laws for their benefit.

One of the clear lessons of the twentieth century was that free markets are much more efficient creators of wealth than any other economic system. Many have recently hypothesized that it is the combination of democracy and free markets that truly stokes the engines of innovation and wealth creation. The Chinese seem to be taking a different course in that they are attempting to create a capitalistic system contained inside a dictatorial political system. It's doubtful that this will be nearly as productive as an open and democratic political system, but the early signs suggest that their strategy may succeed at producing wealth nevertheless.

It's worth noting that such success is likely to have severely negative consequences for religious freedom and, especially, for the Christians inside of China. The communist system in the former USSR was ultimately unsustainable because its attempts to control the economy failed. If, however, a communist system is somehow maintained by freeing up the economy while maintaining rigid political control, then this overtly antireligious system may be able to sustain itself for a long time. This is not good news for those who may be hoping that the Chinese will follow the Soviet path out of communism.

As a side note of interest, realize that we have only recently reached the same threshold of international trade on a percentage basis that we had prior to the Smoot-Holly Act in the late 1920s. The lesson might be that the intertwined nature of international commerce may significantly increase the interdependence and reliance we have on our trading partners. A major blow to anyone will be felt by all in the system and could lead to another global depression.

New-School Wealth Creation

One of the most prolific new strategies being deployed to generate wealth is really an old-school strategy dressed up to look new. The United States is on the forefront of leaning upon the provision of services as the new mechanism for wealth creation. Of course, the service sector of the economy has existed for hundreds of years. But what has made this strategy so novel and new-school is the magnitude and creativity with which it is being pursued.

Services have replaced manufacturing as the largest employer in the United States. We now live in what is termed a service economy. Services are capable of creating wealth—everything from health-care benefits and legal and tax advice to housecleaning, gardening and food preparation. Increasingly, the higher value version of those services will be contained in a class of services called "knowledge work." Highly advanced economies are the ones where most people work in the services sector. There remains some debate regarding the sustainability of a truly service-based economy. Expect that debate to be settled during this decade.

PERCENTAGE OF THE LABOR FORCE IN:

Country Group	Agriculture	Industry	Services
Low Income	69	15	16
Lower Middle Income	36	11	37
Upper Middle Income	49	27	52
High Income	5	31	64

Source: *Global Shift,* p. 447

Perhaps the most interesting wealth creation strategy—and the least predictable—is innovation. This approach runs the gamut from simply rearranging the inputs in a manufacturing process, altering the way a service is delivered or completely repackaging existing resources to inventing something that has never before existed. Either path may lead to increased user satisfaction, increased product functionality or a reduction in the overall cost of final goods or services.

In the case of inventing something new, a key element in the process is a patent. These are legal protections that enable the patent holder to capture a great deal of the value of the idea in the first 20 years of that idea's life. The genius of patents is that they create an incentive for innovation. Those who hold the most valuable patents will become very wealthy and will be further motivated to continue their innovative efforts. Others who possess creative impulses may also be motivated to compete in the world of innovation, encouraged by the security that the patent process provides.

One of the dangers, of course, is a world in which the rights of the patent holder are disregarded by a society that lacks moral integrity. The onset of moral anarchy is, ultimately, a major threat to economic progress through the disintegration of legal measures such as patents. Untold billions of dollars of value were lost when patents, copyrights and other legal restrictions were ignored in Thailand, and brand-name goods were copied and sold at bargain basement prices throughout the '80s and '90s. While international economic pressure brought that practice to a halt (mostly), the ever-shifting morals and power balance may enable such challenges to rise again during this decade.

True Wealth

The most insidious problem associated with the creation of wealth is that of an individual, organization, nation or world replacing God in the center of our thoughts and lives with the pursuit of money. This is not a new threat—just read the Old Testament to get a sense of how decadent some cities became in their lust for riches. Or you can read *Time*, *Newsweek* or any other current news magazine in the U.S. to see the modern-day danger we face in trying to balance reasonable wealth creation and an inappropriate love of affluence. The unbridled pursuit of wealth creates enormous pain and suffering in its wake and inevitably leads to spiritual destruction.

Attempts to replace God with money, security, happiness and pleasure are futile, but they sure are alluring. True wealth is found in the inner peace, joy and contentment that emanate from knowing God intimately and understanding our position in relationship to Him. Seeking fulfillment in the riches of this world cannot be achieved; money, financial influence and the other baubles of monetary ascension are little more than fool's gold. Human history is packed with stories of people who placed their energy into the accumulation of meaningless riches, and yet we persist in our drive to possess them. It doesn't take much of a futurist to confidently predict that during this decade there will be millions of people who will suffer personal destruction because they placed their trust in the goodies of this world rather than focusing on the only true wealth we will ever experience: a sincere, growing relationship with God.

Electronic Money

To many people, the promise of "electronic money" sounds too far-fetched to be of much interest or concern. A number of respected Christian financial experts contend, however, that the emergence of electronic money signals the start of the global system the antiChrist will use to force many into submission. If global economic integration drives us to a one-world government, the strength of that government will be determined by its ability to control electronic forms of value exchange.

Electronic money is money that one can move around the globe via wire transfer or some other form of electronic communication. The ease with which one can move money around the globe today is unprecedented. You can literally log on from anywhere on the globe, access your bank accounts and move money from one fund to another—from a savings plan into a stock purchase plan, in and out of the market at will—in a matter of seconds, with a minimum of hassle. Not long ago this was unimaginable.

Just 40 years ago, most major retailers in the U.S. would only accept paper money and an occasional check, as long as that check did not exceed a particular maximum, was written by a local resident and was drawn on a local bank—and if you didn't look suspicious. In 1960, American Express traveler's checks and credit cards were still innovations being tested in New York City. Compare that to today, when college freshmen wade through an avalanche of credit card offers made to them during their first week on campus! Direct deposit, electronic banking and electronic bill payment enable us to conduct the bulk of our economic life without even touching money.

So what is money, really? The key attribute of money is a concept called "fungibility." Fungibility is what enables us to transfer our efforts at creating value—our labor, physical goods or services—into a form that has stored value, which is where the notion of money comes into play. The value is stored in such a way that you are then able to exchange it at a later date for other products and services of equal or similar value. Fungibility is a fancy word, a simple concept—and it's hard to imagine living without it.

Try to imagine the world prior to the invention of money. If, for example, you wanted to acquire some of your neighbor's chickens, you needed to swap something of commensurate and agreed-upon value. One solution might be to exchange your goat for eight of his chickens. Another solution would be to create an elaborate barter or accounting system through which you could track a complex series of interrelated transactions. Perhaps your neighbor knew another neighbor owed him a chicken, a friend of his owed you a goat and a friend of yours owed the first friend a watermelon; so if we could get one party to exchange goods with another, while a different party canceled its debt—well, you get the idea. Before you know it the system breaks down because of its inherent complexities and limitations. The ultimate dilemma is the system's inability to store the value of anyone's productive efforts or to foster transactions when the units of value that you have don't match the units of value (or, worse, the perceived units of value) that they have. To wit, what if they already have a goat and don't want another one?

The result is that the fungible storage unit of value was created fairly early in history. In the Bible we encounter references to denari and mites. Florentine merchant banks monopolized the innovation of the instant transportation of money across great distances. The Medici clan had banks all across Europe by A.D. 1470 (Rome, Naples, Geneva, Venice, Pisa, Avignon, Lyons, Milan and Bruges).[2] They enabled you to deposit or borrow money at one of those banks, get a certificate signed by one of the bank executives and then take that certificate to another bank in their system and make a withdrawal from your account. This greatly enhanced commerce across all of Europe and made Florence a great banking powerhouse.

The fungibility attributes mentioned earlier are the reasons that there is a thing called "hard currency." Hard currency is a monetary instrument, like the U.S. dollar or the British pound. These currencies do not radically change in value over the short-term. They are tied to large economies, and the full weight and authority of each respective government and banking system back each currency. In contrast, a weaker currency tends to change its value radically over short periods of time or is not tied to a major economy. Devaluation creates weakened currencies, and weak economies suffer from a higher likelihood of being undermined by currency devaluations.

Portability is another attribute of fungability. Naturally, you want to be able to take this currency, migrate it anywhere in the world and have it recognized as a valuable. As it turns out, there are more $50 and $100 bills outside of the United States than there are inside of the United States because the U.S. currency is considered to be one of the strongest currencies and the most fungible. It's an excellent vehicle for storing value and, as such, in many countries around the world people maintain a small cache of American dollars, typically in the denominations of 50 and 100.

Along with everything else in our world these days the world financial system has become extremely complex and sophisticated. Recently we have seen the creation of pseudocurrencies, which are fungible, currencylike instruments that are not necessarily tied to or backed by a particular government or even recognized by any governmental authority as a form of currency. These exotic currencies go by names such as "eCash," "Cyber Cash," "CyberGold" or couponlike instruments such as Flooz or Beenz.

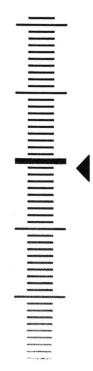

The financial system is extremely complex and sophisticated.

Generally there is an established relationship between the U.S. dollar and these currencies. By tying these pseudocurrencies to a hard currency these new forms of value gain some level of credibility and fungibility. But this is also where we begin to detect abuses and can foresee even further problems. Again, a key attribute of these currencies is that of fungibility—the ability to move in and out of a particular currency at will, currency that is neither detectable nor traceable to the place where the work was originally produced. Now whether or not you think the government deserves to tax its people at the levels that we see today, it does take some level of nominal taxation for a government to conduct its primary functions (e.g., national defense, enforcement of its laws). Modern society requires significant forms of civil service and a large tax base to support it. What happens when taxpayers can receive a significant portion of their income in a form that the government cannot trace and, as such, is incapable of taxing?

This is a big problem for taxing authorities that rely heavily on service or income taxes. It might have a devastating impact particularly on those countries whose tax base is largely tied to the products of knowledge workers. Since knowledge workers can go on-line, enter a marketplace, conduct work and collect income off that work in a form that the government will not be able to identify or trace, the resulting loss of revenues for government operations could devastate an economy and undermine the primary mission of a government.

If this sounds like an academic head game, a pie-in-the-sky absurdity, realize that even today this is not merely a theoretical possibility but an actual reality. It turns out that because of the moratorium on taxes for things bought through the Internet, companies have begun to shift purchases on-line to avoid taxes. Congress has created a tremendous incentive for transacting on-line, handing on-line companies a tremendous competitive advantage. The predictable result is that a large company with any sense purchases an increasing variety of products on-line. Software is a perfect example. A firm with a million-dollar software budget will pay a 7 percent excise tax—unless it purchases its software on-line, in which case it will immediately save $70,000 a year in taxes. Americans are purposefully shifting all kinds of transactions onto the Web. The U.S. government (read the American taxpayer) is subsidizing these purchases through the form of tax-free incentives. Whether this was the intended consequence of the policy or not, that is what is being accomplished.

So we return to our original point regarding electronic money: It has the potential to significantly alter commerce, economic policy and governmental stability throughout the world. We will be able to log on to a computer to deliver or receive legal advice, medical care, accounting, technical writing, programming or a wide range of other services and choose the form and destination of the payment. Why not German marks in a secret account in Barbados?

Why should Christians care? Governmental structures generally tend to be moderating influences, create stability and enable global communications and engagement. Anarchy creates fear and opportunities for exploitation and opens the doors for tyranny. Tax evasion and fraud are illegal and undermine the stability of the government and our culture.

The ultimate issue is integrity. Following God's rules regarding ethical and moral behavior facilitates a safer, saner, more reasonable life. Jesus explained the bottom line in the simplest of terms: Give to Caesar what is Caesar's. If we do not manage our personal and corporate economic responsibilities well, you can be sure that factors such as fear, greed, the potential for violence and the lust for power and control will result in governments and other vulnerable economic entities developing radical solutions to this problem. For example: The government could just insert transaction verification chips in your right hand or forehead. If you don't have a chip you can't transact. Problem solved.

Where Are We Headed?

Financial markets will get larger, stronger and more globally integrated. Paradoxically they will have greater fluctuations caused by rapid adjustments to new information.

- More and more individuals in the U.S. will have stock portfolios because of the growing popularity of 401Ks. The forthcoming explosion of interest in wealth creation will undoubtedly distract many Christians from the aspects of life that they should be focusing upon.
- International debt will increase with the associated pressures on the internal policymaking bodies. Debt fiascoes will be exposed in Russia and other "kleptocracies." A lack of reform could tumble these nations back into some form of dictatorial rule. Realize that the economic chaos that may ensue in those nations could preclude the Church from spreading the gospel in those nations.
- Service economies will continue to grow stronger. Watch for the development of more entertainment-oriented services that offer new forms of escape. Services will be wrapped with more options including that of having them delivered in an entertaining way. Escapist fare will compete with the Church for people's attention and resources. Watch out for the intrusion of "churchatainment," in which religious events replace worship services—events that are all show and no substance, in an effort to maintain the attendance numbers that drive so many ministries. The justification: "We've got to compete with NFL football."

- The patent race has begun. During this decade patents will become even more important to the U.S. and global economies. The U.S. has a distinct advantage over developing countries with regard to the creation of intellectual property. By capturing this knowledge early, the U.S. will earn royalties from the rest of the world. The real battle will start, though, when underdeveloped nations, angry at being aced out again by the superpower, cry "foul play!" and defiantly break global intellectual property laws.

- Electronic money will increase the volatility of world markets by allowing everyone to become day traders with their checking accounts. Forget the lottery; you'll be able to play the financial markets in far more interesting ways. People like you will be betting on all kinds of currencies—e.g., betting on the yen to go up or down, betting on the direction of interest rates, betting on the swing in the Dow Jones average. Who needs to go to Las Vegas when you can use your 401K funds as your chips? In fact, gambling via the Internet is likely to emerge as the nation's next major addiction.

- Watch for electronic money to flow to sophisticated on-line barter exchanges. The sole purpose of this new approach to exchange is to avoid excise and income taxes. You'll hear a loud and rancorous debate in Congress and in state legislatures on this one.

- Electronic pseudomoney will be part of the normal discourse by 2010. Christians will be tempted by the opportunities to under-report true income or by the option to outright avoid income or excise taxes. Keep an eye out for what is happening economically in other nations. Once a country starts down the path of general noncompliance it becomes unstable, as the recent difficulties in Mexico prove. Economic chaos results, with moral anarchy not far behind.

- Hiring employees, contractors or consultants from distant nations will be common, as long as their work can be delivered to the hiring entity through digital means. Paying for those efforts in multiple currencies in electronic form across numerous national boundaries will be no more difficult than balancing your checkbook through a computer program.

What Can You Do?

Christians have the same problems with money and greed that everyone has: We want to live comfortably, we expect to do well financially, and we often overlook inappropriate financial practices that seem morally innocuous. The challenge to us is to not confuse money with true wealth. Jesus spoke more on the issue of money than any other issue during His recorded ministry. And He minced no words on the subject. His admonition was for us to store our wealth in a place where nothing can destroy it—that is, by investing in the love of God, not the paper of man. He called us to recognize that the prevalence of poverty is no excuse for ignoring the needs and suffering of the poor. Wealth is as much a state of mind as a reflection of dollars stored in accounts.

Responsible debt financing to facilitate the structural development of Third World nations is a daunting but important challenge for us to face. Watching as banks line the pockets of corrupt officials to the detriment of the next generation is unacceptable. We must hold the IMF and World Bank accountable for their loans and policies. Support your elected officials in bringing about significant reforms within these institutions.

The advent of new and exciting technologies also provides us with unusual opportunities to help developing countries to build self-reliance and wealth. If believers were willing to take on this opportunity as a mandate to alleviate needless suffering throughout the world and to deliver these new tools of economic progress in tandem with the good news of spiritual freedom, the triple-zero decade could go down in history as one of the greatest eras for the missions movement.

Along those lines, what about using our creative genius to provide education in both life skills and spiritual well-being to people in less developed parts of the world? For example, we have the SCORE program (Service Core Of Retired Executives) in our country. Could we build an equivalent for retired Christian business executives to export economic and spiritual know-how in ways not yet provided?

During this era of greed and insatiable financial accumulation, what a tremendous opportunity we have to provide the world with an obvious and attractive alternative. It may start with something as simple as refusing to engage in tax fraud or even tax avoidance. We don't have to enjoy paying taxes, but we must remain true to our social obligations. If tax evasion becomes rampant everyone will feel the social consequences. As believers, let's be the noticeable minority whose resistance to lowest common denominator behavior causes millions to rethink their inclination to act in their own best interests to the detriment of the national interest.

Without becoming alarmist or carried away, it is prudent to be cautious about letting some of the new economic innovations, such as electronic money, get out of hand. As believers we must pray and think carefully before permitting things such as a single chip tied to your social security number or a national identification number. Be on guard against simple conveniences such as national health cards that contain your vital medical records morphing into national ID cards and financial management cards. All of these may seem like simple, harmless steps that make life easier. Perhaps that's all they will be. But realize that at some point we will have given away so much ground that we will be only one small implant away from control by the Beast.

Most of all, pray that God will grant us the wisdom to discern the implications of the changes that engulf us and to have the courage to resist those transitions that foster immorality and spiritual oppression.

Notes

1. The Old Testament describes a solution to unbearable debt: the "Year of Jubilee." This was a year in which all debts were to be forgiven. It occurred every fiftieth year and was a system designed to avoid the continuous indebtedness and enslavement of people. This concept is known and understood by few world leaders. In the waning years of the 1990s, there was an international movement, led largely by Christians, to facilitate debt forgiveness among underdeveloped nations that were financially in debt way over their heads. The movement has not given up hope of seeing progress, although their efforts, to date, have met with more resistance than openness.
2. James Burke, *Connections* (Boston, MA: Little, Brown and Company, 1995), p. 218.

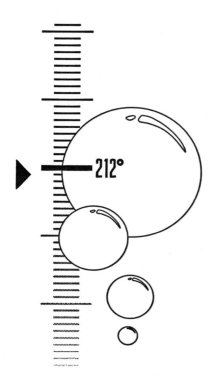

212°

CHAPTER THIRTEEN

INTERNATIONAL POLITICS AND THE ONE-WORLD GOVERNMENT

Future Glimpse

Jill hit the "send" key and watched as her computer e-mailed her ballot to the secretary of state. She had just spent the last hour agonizing over her choices on several dozen initiatives and referenda, as well as a variety of state and local candidates. She always felt remorseful after voting. She knew that she was not an involved, informed voter. Yeah, voting was her right and she exercised it, but mostly to avoid the even more intense guilt of feeling as if she did not participate in the country's hallowed democratic process.

This year's initiatives had been so complex. Antiterrorism policies. Bond issues to fund the purchase of electronic equipment to keep potential criminals under surveillance and to safeguard government computer systems and satellites. The creation of a new regional, multinational alliance for trade and defense policies. The list went on and on. Half the time she just made a blind choice since she did not really understand the issues. At least she was voting. That's more than most Americans could claim.

The cloud of concern that hung over her head, though, regarded the increasing clout of the megacorporations. It seemed as if a dozen companies ruled the world. They bought up small companies, merged with some competitors and drove others out of business. Their influence spanned the globe—and the rumors were that they ran the governments of the nations where they were focused. Sometimes she longed for the days when movie studios produced movies; now, they owned everything from clothing manufacturing plants in Asia, food production companies in South America and electronics giants in North America to airplane manufacturers in Europe and mineral rights in Africa. It all had a vaguely sinister feel to it.

Maybe that was because of the monthly terrorist attacks that seemed to happen like clockwork. Which disenfranchised group would undertake what life-threatening gambit this time? It was one of those anxieties Jill had to ignore; it was just too overwhelming and scary to think about. When would Denver be the target of some nut with a cause?

The blinking icon on her screen snapped her back to reality. The vote was cast. Tomorrow she'd know who'd won and who'd lost, which initiatives passed and which would have to wait until the next election to try again. If there really was a God, she hoped He/She was doing something about those election returns.

National Sovereignty Versus Global Government

As much as we may hate to admit it, we need some form of government. Our natural impulse is to resist being controlled by anyone else. However, several thousand years of human history convincingly prove that unless there is some consensus over the rules and goals of a group—i.e., a government system—then the people undermine their own well-being. The larger a group becomes, the more important its governmental process becomes to retain law and order and purpose. In a world with more than 6 billion people and close to 200 nations, the need for governance is undeniable. The only question is: Who should govern and how?

National governments are like any other organization: Give them a little power and authority, and soon they want more. Sometimes we feel moved to reduce their reach and even wish they did not exist, but we would be worse off for their extinction. National government serves legitimate and necessary functions. One of those is to protect the citizens from physical violence through a national defense system. Another is to maintain and execute the laws of the land to create a sustainable society. A less important function, but one that is clearly evident in the peaceful, industrialized countries, is the promotion of the welfare and the well-being of their national constituencies.

Any one of these functions is required for a nation to experience stability and viability. A sameness begins to take hold of each nation's federal government because of the base needs that any country has in common. You'll see each government create and maintain a sufficient national defense operation to ward off potential invasion or attack. Each government creates and maintains the architecture of the culture and the environment in which the people strive to achieve the quality of life and corporate goals that define the nation. The government is responsible for creating and maintaining police forces, a judicial system, prisons, and just and enforceable laws. Revenue must be generated to finance these activities, so tax systems are created and implemented. These fundamental responsibilities of government cannot be abdicated or transferred. When a government fails any of these responsibilities, the death of the nation is imminent.

Money Takes Priority

One emerging trend is that the economic well-being of people is increasingly co-opting the significance and the viability of the other core responsibilities of a nation's central government. This resulting drive for consistent and even escalating economic growth may eventually undermine the aggregate performance of the government's full range of duties.

The clearest example of this pattern is the recently formed European Union. One of the defining characteristics of this cooperative venture among 12 nations in Europe is the shifting of the central banking responsibility away from a national institution and into the larger collective called the European Union. They have created their own common currency—the euro—and have eliminated many of the trade barriers that used to limit international trading amongst themselves.

But creating such multinational arrangements is not without its pain and potential destruction. The French, as usual, have been the most vocal in opposition to forms of governance that would cause them to lose some form of national autonomy. Understandably, their fear is that France will lose control over its own economy and well-being and potentially be supporting European Union policies that are at odds with their own national policies and self-interest. These are among the very real dangers in the creation of the European Union or any union that shifts the responsibility for some important form of governmental oversight to a larger, pan-national entity.

Perhaps the most interesting insight to be gleaned from the European Union experience is the possibility that in the long run economic needs triumph over other considerations. In a world environment of complexity, competition and the absence of a compelling and cooperative vision, the desire to improve the quality of life supersedes the need to maintain a national identity, a (costly) national defense or even the national sovereignty required to create and maintain laws and jurisdictions unique to the nation. In other words, the quest for material gain becomes the driving force for the creation of a one-world government.

One-World Government

One of the major problems with a global governmental entity, usually referred to as a "one-world government," is encapsulated in the concept of the "tyranny of the majority." This concept describes the tendency of growing political entities to acquiesce to the will of the majority. In the United States, the bastion of democratic politics, this process is especially alluring. You can see the encroachment of this tyranny in our own country over the past quarter century, as more and more key governmental policy and revenue-generating decisions are made by the public through initiatives and referenda. The role of the mass media and even public opinion polls—and, soon to be, instant national opinion communication via voting on the Internet—has also fueled this tyranny. Some see no danger in this process, but rather extol the virtues of a government that is sensitive and responsive to the will of the people it represents.

The problem, however, lies in the strength of the foundation on which the entire system is built. Democracy has worked for two centuries in the U.S. because of the moral consensus that shaped our policies and activities. The consensus was based on a vision of morality and justice defined by absolute moral values, not relative moral values. When the absolutes are pushed aside in favor of relative values, we usher in the rule of the lowest common denominator. Instead of doing what

We do what is convenient and comfortable.

is right, based upon the highest standard of morality and justice (in this case, God's standard, described in the Bible), we do what is convenient or comfortable. In other words, we replace an eternal standard with a personal standard; we substitute selfishness for righteousness.

If you doubt that this grand swap is taking place, look at some of the lightning rod issues in our country. Abortion policy is an example. Many states have a constituency that is intensely opposed to abortion. Yet we have a national system based on pressure politics that imposes its will on the people, making abortion legal. This is an example of the tyranny of the majority. The policy is set by politics, not morality. The question is inevitably asked: But whose morality should rule? The answer that is too infrequently invoked and rarely accepted: God's morality, the basis of our

Constitution and of ultimate truth. Replace that foundation with one based on relativism and rule by feelings and you have LCD policy making— as well as the propensity for societal destruction or (in the case of many underdeveloped nations) moral and political impotence.

In this decade you will see the impact of the European Union transcending mere financial structures and policies to include social and political policies. If it is true that economics wins over national defense requirements or national judicial systems, then we will see an ongoing emergence of quasi-world-government functions that operate independent of national sovereignty. As cultural complexities, globalism and our amnesia regarding history prevail, and as people throughout the world come to accept regional or continental government structures as natural (or inevitable), then it is only a matter of time before we experience a true one-world government. Don't look for it to occur in this decade, but you will see the building blocks toward such a system fall into place.

Global Corporations

Among the building blocks is the growing number of large, global corporations. An ever-increasing number of these entities have more power and influence than many countries do. For example, a 1999 study of 76 nations by the World Bank revealed that 27 of them had an annual gross national product of less than $50 billion. There are dozens of corporations throughout the world, as well as a growing coterie of individuals, whose income far exceeds the GNP of entire nations.

Peter Schwartz, a former executive at Shell Oil, noted that during the tumultuous days of the former Soviet Union, Shell had a better understanding of what was going on inside that country than did the United States government. The CIA and the Department of Defense's views of the political situation inside the Soviet Union were at odds with the understanding that the strategic planning group inside of Shell had developed— and, it turned out, the Shell perspective was more accurate. This should not come as a great surprise given that Shell is a very large, global organization that has built significant partnerships in every major industrialized country in the world. Through those relationships, and its constant monitoring of world events and cultural shifts, Shell has access to information in each country in which it operates; much of that information is not easy for other government agencies to access.

These days the CEOs of the world's largest companies are more powerful, more influential and have a better understanding of the global situation than many government agencies that are responsible for gathering worldwide intelligence or setting international policies. These business leaders also have, in some instances, a greater ability to finance debt and to move enormous quantities of capital from one locale to another. In some cases a corporation's private agenda, through the imposition of its political influence, is able to superimpose that plan upon the national agenda or to substantially influence government policies to favor the operations of the corporation. This is not always at odds with the best interests of the nation, but the potential for such a conflict of interests is certainly ever present.

By many measures, then, these large international corporations can be viewed as quasi-national entities whose internal policies can and will have a tremendous impact on the cultures in which they operate. Imagine the surprise of a general manager, who works for a U.S.-based international conglomerate in Asia (where a significant percentage of the adult males smoke), when the American-led company decides that it is no longer appropriate for its employees to smoke on company property. You can understand the health justifications for this policy, but it is symptomatic of the increasing power of large corporations over their employees and the ability of multinational conglomerates to impact foreign cultures.

It is not stretching the truth to admit that in many instances—especially in nations that are less diverse and complex than the United States—global corporate conglomerates have more influence on social policy development than any other entity. For example, the proclivity of the U.S. and many western European countries to pay domestic-partner health benefits tends to support cohabitation and (sometimes) homosexual or lesbian relationships. This weakens the moral underpinning of these nations, yet our largest employers are exporting U.S. social experimentation and policy around the globe. This is being done ostensibly for competitive reasons, but therein lies the seed of societal destruction. These companies, offering these benefits as a perk or element of added value to their people, are facilitating the moral deterioration of their employees and the culture at large, all for the sake of economic competitiveness.

Also keep in mind that these companies have access to the greatest talent and intellectual horsepower available in the world marketplace. Oftentimes what attracts the best talent is an intellectually challenging and economically rewarding environment, and those environments are being developed and nurtured inside of large corporations. We can easily foresee the day when our best and brightest live and work in large, powerful, influential companies with shareholders as constituents rather than voters. Those individuals will have the power and intellectual capacity to outmaneuver the political structures in which they operate. Such activities raise crucial questions about the moral values and ethical judgments of those organizations, since the choices they make will henceforth influence more than just the base of employees who draw their paycheck from the organization.

Global Policy Development and Enforcement

As we observe both nations and corporations pushing us closer to a one-world government scenario, realize that there are global institutions designed to mimic the product of a national government but on a global scale. The fundamental pieces of such world government are essentially embodied in the combination of the United Nations (defense), the UN's judicial arm at The Hague (international judicial enforcement) and the World Trade Organization (improving the economic well-being of participants).

In recent years the UN has utilized its power and authority primarily as a global defense force trying to create peace, although, in some instances, it also instigates wars. However laudable the goals or outcomes of this global policy body might be, the inescapable reality is that we now have an institution whose territory is the entire world and whose mandate represents a potential threat to the sovereignty of individual nations.

At The Hague (or, more accurately, the International Court of Justice, which is the judicial arm of the UN) international disputes are settled. That is where the terrorists from the Lockerbee plane crash faced justice—not in England, the U.S. or Scotland, but in The Hague.

Meanwhile, a number of organizations have been created in recent years to help improve the economic status of people around the globe. Examples of such entities include the World Trade Organization and trading blocks (e.g., the European Union, the North Atlantic Free Trade Agreement and the Asian equivalent of NAFTA, monikered ASEAN).

All three of the primary functions of a national government are already being pursued on a global basis. Will the world view a global government as a good thing? If the hypothesis is that such decisions are driven by economic outcomes, then the promise of a single worldwide trading block might be the precipitating opportunity. Alternatively, the driver of acceptance could be global instability brought on by significant regional or international conflict. A single governing entity might be embraced in response to seemingly irreconcilable judicial disparities.

Perhaps the most likely scenario is a transition fostered by a combination of these catalysts. While nobody can know what will bring about the shift to a one-world system, we do know that the world will be more integrated and potentially more unstable by 2010 than it is now. Advances in infrastructure and computer technology will increase the database on every individual, facilitating sophisticated, predictive modeling which will further alter how decisions are made and what gets communicated to the people. We have become accustomed to mocking the Orwellian notion of "big brother"—after all, the emergence of omnipresent, oppressive one-world government did not happen by his predicted date, 1984—but things are changing rapidly and fundamentally. Just as the labor pains of childbirth come on quickly, after a period of preparation, so will the creation of a one-world government seem to appear overnight. Many people think that this is the most obvious and logical outcome of an integrated world and look forward to the promise of a single, unified, integrated system of governance.

Global Terrorism

If we are going to understand the big picture, though, we must also keep in mind the spiraling chaos that defines our existence. Changes occur at warp speed and half the time we cannot tell who is responsible, who is in charge or who cares. Moral chaos, economic chaos, relational chaos—it all fuses into one massive experience of disorientation and powerlessness that causes us to throw our hands in the air and say, "Let someone else figure it out; I'm just trying to survive."

But what happens when, in order to advance their own survival agenda, your enemies can hop a plane, visit for a few days, leave a bomb on your doorstep and be back home in less than 12 hours?

Welcome to your worst nightmare: terrorism. Why do we have terrorism? The spiritual answer is rampant sin. The practical answer is that it works.

The primary objective of a terrorist is to gain recognition for his cause—after all, in a highly connected, overstimulated world, the only thing worse than bad publicity is no publicity at all. Unfortunately, the opportunities for marginal players to gain the wherewithal to launch terrorist attacks are rising. The desensitizing nature of our media culture may be feeding already disenchanted thug organizations with young, unstable and unfeeling dupes to carry out their cruelest, attention-grabbing stunts. We are likely to see increasingly frequent eruptions of terrorist activity. There is likely to be a new class of terror created around ultraviolent microcauses. As postmodernist thought worms its way into the global mind and the belief that there is no truth increases, you will see swelling numbers of crusaders use this made-for-TV method to gain an audience for their pet point of view.

One of the more amazing things about the last 10 years is not the number of terrorist acts in the world, but the relative *lack* of terrorist incidents in the U.S. That good fortune is not likely to continue. Intelligence communities are at their wit's end to figure out how to combat "the bad guys," since the tools of technology (and destruction) are so widely available to any and all who seek access to those tools. Without a positive moral compass to guide us, you can expect to see more random acts of violence and terrorist incidents in the U.S. The ease with which a fertilizer bomb can be exploded (like the one in Oklahoma) or a train derailed or poison gas emitted in a subway (as in Japan) gives us reason to pause. The primary line of defense against these weapons and actions in the past has been the strong cultural norms that have fought those evil impulses. Without a moral guidance system there is little holding back waves of evil behavior.

Environmental Realities

Another battleground in the international political arena will be that of the protection and destruction of the environment. As the world's most prolific consumer of natural resources—and most prolific producer of waste materials—the United States will become the target of ever more virulent charges and attacks from outraged citizens of other nations. The more the world becomes one global village, the more we will see foreigners chastising us for our gluttonous lifestyles, believing that, as fellow villagers, it is their right to determine how we behave.

God has not been silent on this issue. In the very first chapter of Scripture, He commanded humans to populate the earth, subdue it and rule over it. Few would disagree that we have made great progress in subduing the earth! Save for the occasional natural disaster (which we call "acts of God") we have taken control of this planet; if anything, maybe we have *over*-subdued it.

God has charged us with the responsibility to manage this planet. Oddly, Christians have been virtually absent from the environmental movement. Somehow, our tree-hugging friends have taken the lead in carrying out this responsibility. Yes, they go too far sometimes because they worship the creation instead of the Creator, but does it seem that in our haste to oppose this idolatry, we have overlooked our own responsibility and focused on the trees rather than the forest? We have a divine mandate to take care of this place. While the environmental picture has become somewhat better in the past quarter century, the progress has been made largely without the assistance of the Christian community. This is to our disgrace and God's disappointment. Responsible environmentalism is a Christian's duty, no less than responsible fiscal behavior or family management. It is time for us to incorporate the protection and responsible use of natural resources into our agenda, and help to shape the environmental movement rather than to be shaped by it.

The handling of the environment is an area where ground has been gained, but there is much more to be accomplished. Consider some of the astounding progress of the past quarter century. In the U.S. alone we can point to the improvements in air pollution (substantial reductions in the

levels of all six of the major air pollutants measured), waste material recovery (more than quadrupled since 1980) and reductions in the release of toxic chemicals (halved since 1985). Even so, the mobility of our culture, the increasing population and our consumption-driven lifestyles continue to raise red flags concerning our care of the planet and, consequently, our consideration of other human beings.

"Conservative conservationist" should be a redundancy, not an oxymoron.

We have honed our ability to spoil and destroy nature and its resources. People are going to live here after we die; we ought to live like we care about their quality of life as much as we care about ours. Our present behavior is reminiscent of the twisted version of Jesus' beatitude about the meek: "The meek will inherit the earth, but only after the rest of us are finished with it." By our very nature, Christians ought to support environmental sustainability. Being a "conservative conservationist" should be redundant, not an oxymoron.

The Quality of Our Air

What is good for global corporations is not necessarily good for the rest of us. We have reduced automobile emissions by 97 percent over the last 30 years, while the oil companies have fought this progress virtually every step of the way. As heartening as the progress has been, our cities still have pollution-caused brown skies on many days. And it's not just the U.S. we need to worry about. We ought to take a careful look at how the Chinese are going to generate an industrial revolution. Thankfully, they have been looking at natural gas and other forms of generating electricity besides burning coal. If they decide to power their revolution by burning coal in plants that lack pollution controls, environmental disaster is inevitable. The disasters that result may include acid rain pouring down on Washington state.

Other issues include the concerns about the greenhouse effect. With all the hype and hysteria, it is hard to tell what is really going on. As God's caretakers of the environment, though, it should not require threats of destruction or an Exxon Valdez to trigger our interest. Perhaps we can start by examining our own consumption patterns, asking tough questions like Do I really need another pair of Nikes? or Does everything have to be disposable? Have you heard the term "new paint disease"? It is a nonlethal but chronic disease that causes those afflicted to buy a new car every year, getting in on the new look (and latest options and enhanced mechanical reliability) before it's too late. When God commanded us to subdue the earth, He probably did not mean extract every possible resource from underground and then pave over everything else.

The Condition of Our Water Supply

Having an ample supply of fresh, potable water is the largest problem for much of the world. Unfortunately, the signs suggest that things are likely to get worse. This is a very significant, fundamental problem. Water is a basic necessity; without it, life does not continue.

Environmental analysts are vitally concerned about the world's water resources. "Competition for water is also increasing between countries, as populations continue to grow rapidly in some of the most water-short regions. In five of the world's hot spots of water dispute—the Aral Sea region, the Ganges, the Jordan, the Nile, and the Tigris-Euphrates—the population of the nations within each basin is projected to climb between 32 percent and 71 percent by 2025. In the absence of water-sharing agreements, this competition could lead to regional instability or even conflict."[1]

Even within the United States we are witnessing regional and interstate squabbles about water rights. (There has even been talk of a split between Northern and Southern California—largely driven by the water rights controversy.) The development of many of our fastest-growing areas—such as Colorado, Nevada, California and Arizona—will largely be determined by the availability of water.

You can expect to see more heated debates regarding who controls water runoff, river flow and ocean access. Expect to experience water shortages and increasing prices for your household water supply.

The State of Agriculture

The good news is that recent advances in food production have made us much more efficient in growing food. In fact, there is no longer any good reason for people to go hungry; we produce enough food to feed the world. The two major stumbling blocks are the distribution of that food and poverty. Political solutions are feasible regarding the distribution dilemma. Poverty is a more vexing issue. With more than 1 billion people living on less than $1 a day, financing the feeding of the world is a challenge to be reckoned with.

Amazingly, we are making progress against starvation in the world. Twenty-six million fewer children were estimated to be underweight in 2000 than in 1980.[2]

UNDERWEIGHT CHILDREN IN DEVELOPING COUNTRIES, 1980 AND 2000

Region	Underweight Children (millions)		Share of Children Who Are Underweight	
	1980	2000	1980	2000
Africa	22	38	26%	29%
Asia	146	108	44%	29%
Latin America & Caribbean	7	3	14%	6%
All developing countries	196	150	37%	27%

Source: United Nations, Administrative Committee on Coordination, Sub-Committee on Nutrition, "Fourth Report on the World Nutrition Situation" (draft) (New York: July 1999).

Just as amazing is that we face real malnutrition in the U.S., not from the lack of food but from the overindulgence of unhealthy food and dietary imbalance. More than half of all Americans are overweight. We could reduce the incidence of cancer by 30 percent to 40 percent and coronary heart disease by 17 percent to 25 percent simply by changing our diet.[3] Some are malnourished because they aren't getting the right balance of nutrients in their meals.

God's people are instructed to feed the hungry and to refrain from gluttony. There is still ample opportunity to do both.

Frankenfood: Read the Label Carefully

Welcome to the future, today. According the Department of Agriculture, one-third of the corn and more than half of the soybeans grown in the U.S. last year were bioengineered. The increasing use of genetically enhanced food is inevitable. The world needs these designer foods to combat a wide range of threats to our global food stocks. We need these foods to continue to effectively feed the world. However, we also need to make sure that appropriate controls and tests are instituted before letting these things out into the wild. They have great potential if handled with care.

It is anticipated that arable land will decrease by as much as 50 percent over the next 50 years. As such, the only way to feed a growing population is through more efficient and effective use of the land that is left in production. Genetics offers one of the ways this can be accomplished.

As mentioned earlier in this book, there is a range of exotic genetic foods in the works. Some of the more exotic versions, like contraceptive corn, should be treated with no less investigation than any serious, synthetic, over-the-counter drug receives. Many of the new foods to which you will be exposed will be marketed as vegetables or food products, but will actually be genetic drugs. Extreme caution is advisable as we wade into an area that we know awfully little about.

Energy Consumption

Watch the unfolding drama over this decade regarding the world's oil supply. On the one hand, we are likely to experience an abundant supply of oil. On the other hand will be the economic and political maneuvering of those who control oil prices and flow. OPEC will probably seek to extend its riches and authority by hiking the price of its treasured resource, perhaps triggering a new oil crisis, maybe even a repeat of the mid-1970s debacle. This will affect the U.S. to a huge extent, since we have become even more automobile-dependent today than we were a quarter century ago.

Fortunately, we have more options available to us today than we did then. Those options include power drawn from the wind, the sun and the water. This provides us some protection against the Middle East holding us hostage at the gas tank, but who wants to fight that battle again? Our increasing per capita gas consumption ought to trigger more circumspection about our fossil fuel usage.

TRENDS IN GLOBAL ENERGY—USE BY SOURCE 1990-97

Energy	Annual Percent Rate of Growth
Wind Power	22
Solar photovoltaics	16
Geothermal power	4
Hydroelectric power	2
Oil	2
Natural Gas	2
Nuclear Power	1
Coal	0

Source: *State of the World 2000,* p. 17

There is some interesting work being conducted on fuel cells, but the challenges are not likely to be overcome within this decade. There have also been some rumblings about "Zero Point" energy, but this breakthrough still resides in the realm of physicists' dreams. If it were found, it would be a fundamental discovery along the lines of fire. Cheap, ubiquitous and unlimited power would surely change the face of the world—but don't hold your breath waiting for it to arrive.

Faustian Bargain

Where does this leave us? We enter the new millennium with a heightened risk of self-destruction. The deal that the Germans cut with Hitler was built on the wretched economic straits of the country at that moment in history. The lessons of history teach us that dictatorship is often perceived to be a reasonable solution to chaos. It may create evil in its own right but many people prefer a predictable evil to uncertainty. Random acts of evil cannot be avoided, understood or prepared for; however, systematic evil with a purpose and method can be understood. This is why some would prefer a despotic but reasonably consistent ruler to chaos. Choosing less liberty to gain security is a Faustian bargain, but one that many people will willingly make.

The foundations for a world government are in the early stages of being laid today. The unsettling economic and moral conditions of our world make the entrance of a global ruler more likely. The need to reduce international friction, poverty and war are powerful inducements to change the prevailing systems. Add the opportunity to improve the economic efficiency for most people in the world and you can make a reasonably persuasive argument for supporting a single, global government to the backward, selfish and restraining national model under which we operate today. Most people will ignore the downsides to gain the benefits promised by the new model.

Where Are We Headed?

In this current moment of prosperity and security in the U.S., it is hard to imagine making radical changes to what seems to be working so well. But remember that these matters move in cycles. Historically speaking, a period of economic decline is inevitable. That period of decline will be a window of opportunity for those who promote a one-world government to strike. Here are some of the outcomes we anticipate happening over the coming decade.

- The European Union will attempt to extend its power and authority beyond its current boundaries. Watch for its policy developments to become political tools for social engineering.
- There will be regional alliances among government units, creating mega-regions whose economic and political power swells in response to the combined resources and united voice the allied nations wield. From those regional alliances will also emerge the political superstars of tomorrow.
- We will continue to see evidence and hints of a one-world government. The initial activities will be in "policing" unpopular despots.

As it becomes more acceptable to have an international body decide who is unpopular and what to do about it, we will see mini-wars conducted by the UN.

- International corporate mergers will blossom. Within most of the culture-setting industries you will see buyouts, mergers, forced takeovers and other forms of co-optation occur. The result will be a smaller field of significant players—each of whom will flex his political and economic muscle in arenas that used to be reserved primarily for career politicians.

- Every year you will read more about subversive terrorist actions. There will be electronic terrorism—e.g., spreading computer virus-es and cracking security codes of government and corporate computer systems. There will be biological terrorism—e.g., spreading of intractable diseases and death through the untraceable releasing of germs and other microbes. There will be traditional, violent terrorism, especially at the hands of extreme religious groups. The desire to have a global stage will cause other groups to use video, satellites and digital technology as conduits to deliver their message. New fortunes will be made by entrepreneurs who exploit people's fears of terrorism by providing food testing products, air and water filtration systems, advanced home security and auto security products, and computer protection devices.

- Many global corporations will create their own extensive, well-financed, "competitive intelligence" systems that incorporate concepts and methods from spy craft. James Bond will be a hotly pursued employee during the decade as corporations strive to protect their economic interests through a variety of stealth measures.

- If you watch the evening news, settle in for a decade in which low-level conflict becomes the norm. Protests, riots and burning cars make for great theater on an otherwise boring and predictable newscast. This "newsworthiness" and the resulting accessibility of the airwaves will not be lost on those who want to make some statement.

- The unprecedented knowledge and information accessed through enormously powerful computers and computer networks will lead some governmental agencies to target segments of society for benefits or punishments.

- Many countries will mandate that their people carry a national identification card.
- Expect to experience cleaner air in the U.S. as people demand industrial compliance with new, higher government standards. At the same time, expect to hear about dirtier air in Asia and Latin America as their industrial revolution continues to move ahead, but at the expense of the environment. Western countries will apply enormous pressure on the developing nations to grow responsibly and will offer realistic alternatives to these emerging nations. The wild card in the process is China.
- Water is likely to be a real problem since the entire world seems to be emptying its underground water reserves at an alarming rate. You will hear more and more about this over the next 10 years. Since we have 20 to 40 years worth of supply this issue will not be solved—or reach a maximum crescendo—during this decade. Toward the tail end of the decade, the debate on this matter will result in improved irrigation techniques. However, regional water disputes will become a dominant political issue.
- Farming, fishing and forestry will continue to represent a shrinking share of the nation's employment base. The individuals who might normally have sought careers in those areas will find jobs in more productive capacities.
- Watch for a high-profile genetic mishap with a food or drug before serious controls are exerted on this exciting yet dangerous area of experimentation. The genetics and biochemical industries will fight such intrusion and regulation with all their might.
- Finally, after 30 years of research and experimentation, we are likely to see some useful alternative fuel opportunities. These may well include wind and photovoltaics. Although the possibilities related to fuel cells will stoke people's imaginations, hybrid products are more likely to emerge than some purely new technology.

• Don't be surprised when political conservatives start to consider engineered sustainability to be an important countervailing concept to the disposable society.

What Can You Do?

When we enter into such frightening realms as one-world government and global terrorism, Christians must be prepared to take some tough, unpopular stands. Think and pray about how God would have you respond to some of the conditions we have described as viable possibilities.

In addition, keep pressure on our government to keep its eye on the ball. Providing strong national defense, a fair and unbiased legal system and an environment in which a market-driven economy can flourish are the primary functions of our government. Supporting democratic movements and strong human rights is consistent with our laws and values and helps to create a more stable and safe world. Creating an environment for a strong economy is crucial, but is not of the same level of priority as the other pair of endeavors.

Prayerfully consider getting involved in local politics, supporting politicians who share your values, voting in elections and voicing an informed opinion to policy makers. By withdrawing from the public debate, the Christian community concedes ground unnecessarily. Take your citizen responsibilities seriously. Staying sequestered in our churches, homes and small groups precludes us from being light in a world of darkness. We must get involved in the community, in the schools and government. Are you active in the PTA? In the chamber of commerce? In your city council or other local policy-making entities? Do you actively support Christians who are candidates for public office,

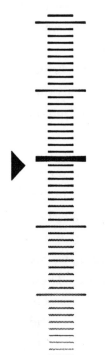

Christians must take some tough, unpopular stands.

through prayer, finances, word of mouth, voting and other forms of assistance?

Be wary of large businesses pushing for Most Favored Nations Status for countries that oppress their people. Those organizations have a duty to their shareholders to maximize their financial return, not to do what is right for society. They have an inherent conflict of interest in those roles.

We need to encourage our national defense leaders to invest in new forms of antiterrorist defense. We are rapidly approaching the time when a graduate student in biotechnology will be able to create a deadly genetically engineered virus. A Japanese cult released poison gas in a Tokyo subway a few years ago. Imagine the devastation they could have caused with the ability to mutate a cold virus into something deadly.

Increasing exposure to violence in all forms of media—news, entertainment, advertising, educational—is desensitizing many youth to truly audacious acts of random violence. This is not entertainment—it is national suicide. Carefully screen the entertainment that you and your family are exposed to. Do your best not to participate in the degradation of society through consumption of this entertainment.

Oppose all threats to U.S. national sovereignty. We must not subjugate ourselves to any external power. There will be incredible pressure to create a one-world government. It may not occur in the next 10 years, but you will continue to see the development of large institutions seeking this type of power.

A long-standing strategy of the Christian community has been nonviolent alternative action. Boycotts, sit-ins, marches, demonstrations, letter writing and the like have proven effective in the past. Perhaps such united action will alter the course of the future in the arenas of political influence and environmentalism, too. Should Christians refuse to work for companies that support or advocate policies that are at odds with biblical principles? Should Christian entrepreneurs form companies that are consistent with our moral stance and compete with those who insist on following the ways of evil? Has God called you to be inside of a company that is at odds with our faith in order to point out the inconsistencies and the problems associated with supporting immorality and tyranny? What believers do you know who really need your encouragement and support as they work from the inside of such organizations to bring about reform?

Support for environmental causes for sustainability would be a new activity for Christians. Focus on areas of policy and action where our message will carry more weight.

We are called to be stewards of the earth. Consequently, we should at least share that calling with our more environmentally driven friends, battling alongside them against the more egregious violations of creation. But don't lose sight of the calling: We are called to be good stewards. There is a subtle but significant difference between saving the whales and worshiping them: It is the difference between stewardship and apostasy.

Go on a short-term mission assignment into the developing world. It can be life-changing. Encourage your children and friends to do the same. A vacation in Europe may be a refreshing time; two weeks in Haiti may be a life-changing experience.

Notes

1. Lester Brown, Christopher Flavin and Hilary French, eds., *State of the World 2000* (New York: The Worldwatch Institute, 2000), pp. 46, 47.
2. Ibid., p. 61.
3. Ibid., p. 69.

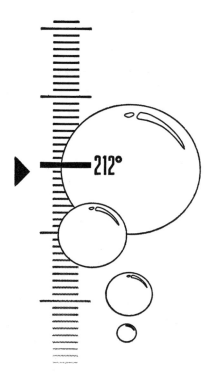

CHAPTER FOURTEEN

MAKING THE MOST OF THE TIMES

Future Glimpse

By now your head may be spinning with news of all the changes that will occur on multiple dimensions within the next 10 years. Without meaning to throw you into a fit of depression, we hope you realize that we have only scratched the surface in terms of the trends that will transform our lives during this decade. Truly, life in the third millennium is not meant for the faint of heart.

If you are like us, you may sit back, scratch your head and wonder: *What does my faith have to do with all of this? Apart from simple tasks, like reading the Bible and going to church, how am I, as a committed follower of Christ, supposed to make sense of all of this and respond in ways that honor Christ and bring His truths to bear on the emerging world?*

Those are exactly the right questions to be asking at this point! There are no easy or right answers to such questions, but let us offer a few thoughts on how you might attempt to arrive at conclusions that enable you to glorify God in an age that questions if that is either possible or desirable.

What the World Wants

Late-night talk-show host David Letterman converted his nightly top-10 lists into a comic staple. In fact, lists have always been intriguing to Americans: the top 40 hit records, the 100 best companies to work for, the 10 most wanted criminals, the 20 largest churches in America, the Fortune 500, the 50 top colleges and universities and so forth. Lists are popular because they help us to understand complex realities and to organize information in ways that facilitate an intelligent reaction. Perhaps a list of the top 10 trends that each of us will have to grapple with during this decade—along with a few suggestions about the perspective needed to artfully do so—will be a useful way of concluding our time together.

Here, then, are 10 trends that we have discussed in this book that will radically reshape or fundamentally define life in this decade. (They are not listed in order of significance; they are all important to understand and address. You may wish to concoct your own list.)

1. The nation's population will grow by another 25 million.
2. Lifestyles will be defined by the complexity of daily opportunities, expectations and behaviors.
3. Personal values will be ever changing and compromised as necessary to get by and feel good about each new choice we make.
4. Selfishness will rule as people strive to make sense of life and maximize their options.
5. New technologies will alter jobs, lifestyles, relationships and business functions.

6. Businesses that provide entertaining experiences will rise to the top.
7. Genetic manipulation will alter medicine and health care.
8. Moral relativism will reign—until replaced by nihilism.
9. Faith will be a study in form without Christian substance.
10. People will embrace new national and international authority structures as regions cooperate economically and politically.

Even if just these 10 trends were to influence the world this decade, life as we now know it would be dramatically different. Of course, there are numerous other trends described in this book that could easily have made the list—generational schisms, killer diseases, freelance employment, biblical ignorance and global terrorism, to name just a few viable candidates—and whose likely unfolding during the decade will further reshape our reality.

Heaven's Response to the World's Top 10

Now let's take a look at how God might be calling us to respond to these trends. The following words from God may help us to understand the most appropriate ways to address the coming changes. To handle these challenges and opportunities appropriately we will have to live strategically. That means we will need the right perspective on the meaning of life; the right focus in our moment-to-moment activities; the right response to emerging trends; the right expectations regarding how the world will react to trends and to us; and the right model to imitate as we strive to be a godly influence on the world. Please take a few extra minutes to read each of these verses and reflect on their meaning in the context of cultural change.

Have the Right Perspective
1 Chronicles 12:32
Men of Issachar, who understood the times and knew what Israel should do—200 chiefs.

John 17:15-18

My prayer is not that you take them out of the world but that you protect them from the evil one. They are not of the world, even as I am not of it. Sanctify them by the truth; your word is truth. As you sent me into the world, I have sent them into the world.

God intends for each of us to use the gifts and abilities He has provided to us. In much the same way that He gave David the men of Issachar to help interpret the times and create strategic responses to the opportunities and challenges of the day, so does He expect you to reflect on your world and use your resources to craft a response that glorifies Him. Keep in mind that even though it would be easier to retreat or to hibernate, He expects us to "fight the good fight of the faith" (1 Tim. 6:12). We are called by God to be in the world yet not of it, to be a light in the darkness. We cannot hope to be a positive force in the lives of others until we are committed to serving God with wisdom and diligence. To do so, we must take the time to analyze our world and conceive intelligent responses to it.

Have the Right Focus

Matthew 22:37-39

"Love the Lord your God with all your heart and with all your soul and with all your mind." This is the first and greatest commandment. And the second is like it: "Love your neighbor as yourself."

Ecclesiastes 12:13

Now all has been heard; here is the conclusion of the matter: Fear God and keep his commandments, for this is the whole duty of man.

Matthew 6:33,34

But seek first his kingdom and his righteousness, and all these things will be given to you as well. Therefore do not worry about tomorrow, for tomorrow will worry about itself. Each day has enough trouble of its own.

Proverbs 3:5,6
Trust in the LORD with all your heart and lean not on your own understanding; in all your ways acknowledge him, and he will make your paths straight.

Proverbs 2:1-5
My son, if you accept my words and store up my commands within you, turning your ear to wisdom and applying your heart to understanding, and if you call out for insight and cry aloud for understanding, and if you look for it as for silver and search for it as for hidden treasure, then you will understand the fear of the LORD and find the knowledge of God.

The purpose of existence is not to achieve earthly success, to gain international fame or to gain comfort and security through our choices and lifestyle. God's words to us make clear that we live for one purpose: to glorify, honor and enjoy Him. Obedience to His commands is critical. Genuine worship of His character and His actions throughout history is necessary. Investing in a growing relationship with Him, made possible through the work of Jesus and the empowerment of the Holy Spirit, is our life's work. When we realize that this life is not about achievement for personal gain or fulfillment but about pursuing God's eternal plans for us, we will be freed from the pressures and anxieties that twist people up in knots. Life is about relating to God, not maximizing our options on this planet. Our energy must be devoted to Him and His ways, not to temporal accomplishments.

Have the Right Response

Genesis 12:3
I will bless those who bless you, and whoever curses you I will curse; and all peoples on earth will be blessed through you.

Romans 12:2
Do not conform any longer to the pattern of this world, but be transformed by the renewing of your mind.

Exodus 20:3,4,7,8,12-17

You shall have no other gods before Me. You shall not make for yourself an idol. You shall not misuse the name of the LORD your God. Remember the Sabbath day by keeping it holy. Honor your father and your mother. You shall not murder. You shall not commit adultery. You shall not steal. You shall not give false testimony against your neighbor. You shall not covet your neighbor's house . . . wife . . . [servants], . . . [livestock], or anything that belongs to your neighbor.

Matthew 28:18-20

Then Jesus came to them and said, "All authority in heaven and on earth has been given to me. Therefore go and make disciples of all nations, baptizing them in the name of the Father and of the Son and of the Holy Spirit, and teaching them to obey everything I have commanded you."

James 2:17,18

In the same way, faith by itself, if it is not accompanied by action, is dead. But someone will say, "You have faith; I have deeds." Show me your faith without deeds, and I will show you my faith by what I do.

Galatians 5:22,23

The fruit of the Spirit is love, joy, peace, patience, kindness, goodness, faithfulness, gentleness and self-control. Against such things there is no law.

Colossians 3:23

Whatever you do, work at it with all your heart, as working for the Lord, not for men.

1 Thessalonians 5:16-18

Be joyful always; pray continually; give thanks in all circumstances, for this is God's will for you in Christ Jesus.

People take their cues from individuals whom they respect. God intends to use us to bless and influence others—especially those who have not chosen to follow Christ. So what should our response be in a world that is undergoing rapid and virtually undirected change?

First, we are called to bless others. It is for this very reason that we have been blessed. We have the ability to bless everyone with whom we have contact, and to do so in a multitude of ways. We can bless them by sharing the good news about Jesus Christ with them. We can bless them by helping them to mature in their relationship with Christ. We can bless them by exemplifying practical faith in action. Once we embrace a desire to bless others, the opportunities to do so become too numerous to count.

Second, we are called to handle life differently than other people might, on the basis of God's instructions and commands to us. Our response will often differ from that of non-Christians because we operate on the basis of different values and divergent goals. Our response will confuse some, anger others and intrigue a few—none of which is important. What matters is that we respond to situations and conditions in ways that are consistent with God's expectations of us.

Third, we are to do all things with excellence and a proper attitude, because we are ultimately serving God, not other people. If we keep in mind that our boss is God, not our employer, our spouse or our government officials, then our efforts will produce greater impact. Quality and demeanor matter. These are part of our witness for Him and our ministry to Him.

Have the Right Expectations

2 Timothy 4:3,4

For the time will come when men will not put up with sound doctrine. Instead, to suit their own desires, they will gather around them a great number of teachers to say what their itching ears want to hear. They will turn their ears away from the truth and turn aside to myths.

Romans 14:10-12

For we will all stand before God's judgment seat. It is written, "As surely as I live," says the Lord, "every knee will bow before me; every tongue will confess to God." So, then, each of us will give an account of himself to God.

Have no misconceptions about what will happen. Jesus warned that as we serve Him we will be despised and exploited by others because of that commitment. Paul tells us that we may expect not only persecution but also that God's truths and principles will be rejected in favor of worldly wisdom. The bottom line is that we must stand firmly behind God's ways. Ultimately, each of us will be held accountable for what we say, do and think. A mark of spiritual maturity is to recognize that God's ways will ignite opposition, but to remain committed to His ways.

Have the Right Model
Matthew 10:38,39
Anyone who does not take his cross and follow me is not worthy of me. Whoever finds his life will lose it, and whoever loses his life for my sake will find it.

Acts 2:42-47
They devoted themselves to the apostles' teaching and to the fellowship, to the breaking of bread and to prayer. Everyone was filled with awe, and many wonders and miraculous signs were done by the apostles. All the believers were together and had everything in common. Selling their possessions and goods, they gave to anyone as he had need. Every day they continued to meet together in the temple courts. They broke bread in their homes and ate together with glad and sincere hearts, praising God and enjoying the favor of all the people. And the Lord added to their number daily those who were being saved.

As a personal role model, we can do no better than Jesus Himself. He exemplified the highest ideals and purest life that has ever been lived. If we strive to live up to those standards, though we will fall short, our efforts will not go unnoticed or unrewarded.

As a corporate model, we must emulate the Early Church. The heart demonstrated by those believers represents a practical, but mind-boggling example for us today. The Church was focused upon the things that matter to God: worship, evangelism, discipleship, fellowship, service and stewardship. They lived in ways that transcended accusations of hypocrisy. The outcome was that they gained the approval of all people—and, most importantly, of God. The Church today ought to emerge as a primary shaping influence on our culture. As trends gain momentum, the reaction of the Church should matter to all people. But our response will not have much bearing or influence until we live as did the Early Church.

Face the Future on Your Knees

What an exciting—and frightening—time the triple-zero decade will be! But there has never been a more important time for Christians to impact the world. Dozens of books have been written in recent years describing the imminent return of the Lord, based upon the fulfillment of biblical prophecies regarding the conditions that point to the Second Coming. Will it be soon? Nobody knows. However, we are told in Scripture that we have no time to lose, since the time could be soon. Are you ready for the closing of the age? What are you doing to prepare yourself, your family and the people with whom you have contact for the return of Christ?

Remember, the people who shape the world are not those who react to changes that have happened, but those who make the changes happen. You have seen our forecast of what is likely to occur during this decade. Does every probable change in our analysis please you? If not, what is your plan to bring about a more palatable platform of change? The Christian Church is potentially one of the most powerful agents of influence in our society, but recent decades have seen the impact of the church wane to almost nothing. In fact, the biggest wild card in estimating the future of our country is the Church. In the midst of moral anarchy and spiritual anarchy, how will God's people respond? How significant a role will believers play in the development of the future? What is the agenda on which Christians can agree and to which they will commit? We have the power—and the divine mandate—to transform the world for the better. But will we? Will you?

The challenges that lie before you are not unlike those that faced Joshua as he prepared to take the Israelites into the Promised Land. The exhortation given to Joshua by God is appropriate as we stand on the edge of the new Promised Land within America.

> Be strong and very courageous. Be careful to obey all the law that my servant Moses gave you; do not turn from it to the right or to the left, that you may be successful wherever you go. Do not let this Book of the Law depart from your mouth; meditate on it day and night, so that you may be careful to do everything written in it. Then you will be prosperous and successful. Have I not commanded you? Be strong and courageous. Do not be terrified; do not be discouraged, for the Lord your God will be with you wherever you go. (Josh. 1:7-9)

IT ONLY TAKES ONE DEGREE

GEORGE BARNA

George Barna is president of Barna Research Group, Ltd., a marketing research firm located in Ventura, California. The company specializes in conducting primary research for Christian ministries and nonprofit organizations. Since its inception in 1984, Barna Research has served several hundred parachurch ministries and numerous churches, in addition to various nonprofit and for-profit organizations.

To date, Barna has written 29 books. His most recent works are *Rechurching the Unchurched, Growing True Disciples, Effective Lay Leadership Teams* and *The Habits of Highly Effective Churches*. Past works include best-sellers such as *The Frog in the Kettle, The Second Coming of the Church, User Friendly Churches, Marketing the Church* and *The Power of Vision*. Several of his books have received national awards. He has also written for numerous periodicals and has published more than two dozen syndicated reports on a variety of topics related to ministry. His work is frequently cited as an authoritative source by the media.

Barna is also widely known for his intensive, research-based seminars for church leaders. He is a popular speaker at ministry conferences around the world and has taught at several universities and seminaries. He has served as a pastor of a large, multiethnic church and has served on several boards of directors. He is the founding director of the Barna Institute, a nonprofit organization dedicated to providing strategic information to ministries.

After graduating summa cum laude in sociology from Boston College, Barna earned two master's degrees from Rutgers University. He also received a doctorate from Dallas Baptist University.

He lives with his wife, Nancy, and their two daughters, Samantha and Corban, in Southern California. He enjoys spending time with his family, writing, reading, playing basketball and guitar, relaxing on the beach and visiting bookstores.

MARK HATCH

Mark Hatch is currently the chief operating officer of Questium, an Internet start-up and subsidiary of Foundation Health Systems, Inc., one of the largest health-care insurance providers in the United States.

Hatch was the vice president of Marketing and Business Development at Ants.com in Santa Barbara, California. Ants.com is a venture-capital-funded e-commerce B2B business-services marketplace. Previously, Hatch was product management director of Computer Services at Kinko's, Inc., where he managed the world's largest fleet of networked, public-access computers. He launched Kinko's first web-based e-commerce offering on Kinkos.com and managed critical alliances with Adobe, Apple, Dell, HP, IBM, Kodak, Microsoft and others.

Hatch spent seven years at Avery Dennison, Inc., where he helped identify and capitalize on trends in computing and Internet technology. Hatch was the director of Electronic Marketing where he created the Electronic Marketing Department and launched Avery.com for Avery's Office Products Group. Another project he started at Avery engaged him in futures research where he worked with renowned futurists at The Institute for the Future, the MIT Media Lab and the Global Business Network (GBN).

Hatch published an article for GBN on electronic commerce, has been quoted in *Wired* and *ComputerWorld,* and has been a presenter at conferences sponsored by the Internet Advertising Bureau and Internet World.

Hatch received his M.B.A. from the Peter F. Drucker School at the Claremont Graduate University and a B.A. in economics from the University of California at Irvine. A veteran of the U.S. Army Special Forces, he has served his country as a member of the elite Green Berets.

He lives with his wife, Cindy, and their two sons, Luke and Christopher, in Northern California. He enjoys time with his family, riding bikes, playing games, reading, and watching for the next adventure that God will bring their way.

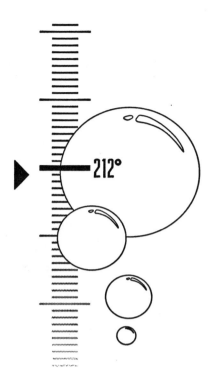

ABOUT BARNA RESEARCH GROUP, LTD.

Barna Research Group, Ltd. (BRG) is a full-service marketing research company located in Ventura, California. BRG has been providing information and analysis regarding cultural trends, ministry practices, marketing and business strategy, fund-raising, worldviews and leadership since 1984. The vision of the company is to provide Christian ministries with current, accurate and reliable information in bite-sized pieces and at affordable prices, to facilitate effective and strategic decision-making.

BRG conducts both quantitative and qualitative research using a variety of data collection methods, with particular emphasis upon the application of the results. The company conducts more research within the Christian community than any other organization in the U.S. and regularly releases reports describing its findings regarding the values, attitudes, lifestyles, religious beliefs and religious practices of adults and teenagers, as well as the current state of churches. That information is also accessible through the seminars, books, website and tapes produced by BRG.

To access many of the findings of BRG, visit the company's website at www.barna.org. You will have access to the free bimonthly reports (*The Barna Update*) published on the site; a data archives that provides current statistics in relation to 40 aspects of ministry and lifestyle; the various resources produced by George Barna and the Barna Research Group; and information about upcoming seminars as well as the firm's research activities. If you wish to receive *The Barna Update* by e-mail every two weeks, you may sign up for that free service on the home page of the site.

To contact Barna Research Group, call 805-658-8885 or write to Barna Research Group, Ltd., 5528 Everglades Street, Ventura, CA 93003.

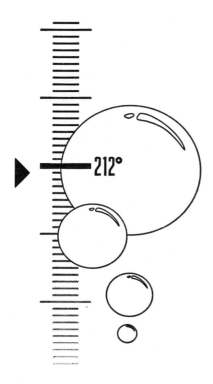

212°

ABOUT THE BARNA INSTITUTE

The Barna Institute (originally named the American Perspectives Institute) was founded as a not-for-profit, 501(c)(3) corporation in 1995. Started by researcher George Barna, the organization was initiated to provide Christian ministries with strategic intelligence that would enhance decision making and ministry activity. By supplying strategic information concerning key issues, conditions and opportunities about which ministries lack necessary insights, The Barna Institute intends to help ministries to be better informed about the culture and people they are seeking to influence, resulting in more productive and life-transforming ministry.

Although various organizations conduct research related to faith issues, the institute provides information that is otherwise unavailable to churches and Christian leaders. This entails focusing either on topics that other researchers have not studied (or have not studied sufficiently) or upon topics that are too large for churches and other ministry organizations to independently fund. The institute is not seeking to compete with other information-providing organizations who seek to help the Church; it strives to complement what those organizations provide to the Body of Christ.

The Barna Institute generates its revenue from Barna Associates (individuals who make an annual donation of $2,000 or more and receive special opportunities to access the institute's findings and resources); through grants and major gifts; and through the sale of resources developed from the institute's research. Past projects have included a study of the role of faith and churches among blacks in America; and the emergence of the cyberchurch and its effects on the nation's faith.

For more information about The Barna Institute or how to become a Barna Associate, call 770-909-0000; write to The Barna Institute, 7657 Briar Crest Court, Riverdale, GA 30296; or e-mail us at barnainstitute@ mindspring.com.

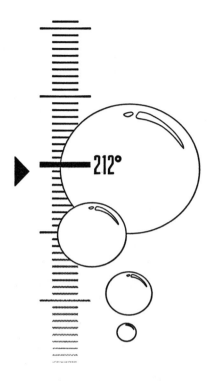

212°

BIBLIOGRAPHY

Alesky, Mark. "Cyborg 1.0." *Wired,* 8.02 (February 2000).

Arquilla, John and David Ronfeldt. *The Advent of Netwar.* Santa Monica, CA: RAND, 1996.

Arthur, W. Brian. *Increasing Returns and Path Dependence in the Economy.* Ann Arbor, MI: University of Michigan Press, 1994.

Barber, Benjamin R. *Jihad vs. McWorld.* New York: Times Books, 1995.

Barna, George. *Re-Churching the Unchurched.* Ventura, CA: Issachar Resources, 2000.

—— *Growing True Disciples.* Ventura, CA: Issachar Resources, 2000.

—— "Third Millennium Teens." Ventura, CA: Barna Research Group, Ltd., 1999.

—— *The Habits of Highly Effective Churches.* Ventura, CA: Regal Books, 1999.

—— *The Second Coming of the Church.* Nashville: Word Books, 1998.

—— *The Frog In the Kettle*. Ventura, CA: Regal Books, 1990.

Brierley, Peter. *Future Church*. London: Monarch Books, 1998.

—— *Steps to the Future*. London: Christian Research, 2000.

Brin, David. *The Transparent Society*. Reading, MA: Addison-Wesley Publishing Company, 1998.

Brockman, John. *Digerati: Encounters with the Cyber Elite*. San Francisco: Hardwired, 1996.

Brown, Lester, Christopher Flavin and Hilary French. *State of the World 1997: A Worldwatch Institute Report on Progress Toward a Sustainable Society*, edited by Linda Starke New York: W. W. Norton and Company, Inc., 1997.

—— *State of the World 2000: A Worldwatch Institute Report On Progress Toward a Sustainable Society*, edited by Linda Starke. New York: W. W. Norton and Company, Inc., 2000.

Brown, Lester, Michael Renner and Christopher Flavin. *Vital Signs 1998: Environmental Trends That Are Shaping Our Future*, edited by Linda Starke. New York: W. W. Norton and Company, Inc. 1998.

Brown, Lester, Michael Renner and Brian Halwell. *Vital Signs 2000: Environmental Trends That Are Shaping Our Future*. New York: W.W. Norton and Company, Inc. 2000.

Burke, James. *Connections*. New York: Little, Brown and Company, 1995.

Canton, James Ph.D. *Technofutures: How Leading-Edge Technology Will Transform Business in the 21st Century*. Carlsbad, CA: Hay House, Inc. 1999.

Colborn, Theo, Diane Dumanoski and John Peterson Meyers. *Our Stolen Future*. New York: Dutton, 1996.

Colson, Charles and Nancy Pearcey. *How Now Shall We Live?* Wheaton, IL: Tyndale House, 1999.

Coase, R. H. *The Firm, the Market and the Law*. Chicago: University of Chicago Press, 1988.

De Callieres, François. *On the Manner of Negotiating with Princes*. New York: Houghton Mifflin, 2000.

De Geus, Arie. *The Living Company*. Boston: Harvard Business School Press, 1997.

Dennet, Daniel C. *Darwin's Dangerous Idea: Evolution and the Meaning of Life*. New York: Simon and Schuster, 1995.

Dertouzos, Michael. *What Will Be*. New York: Harper Collins, 1997.

Diamond, Jared. *Guns, Germs and Steel: The Fates of Human Societies.* New York: W. W. Norton and Company, 1997.

Dichen, Peter. *Global Shift: Transforming the World Economy.* Third ed. New York: Guilford Press, 1998.

Drucker, Peter. *Managing the Future: The 1990s and Beyond.* New York: Truman Talley Books/Dutton, 1992.

Dyson, Esther. *Release 2.0: A Design for Living in the Digital Age.* New York: Broadway Books, 1997.

Dyson, Freeman. *Imagined Worlds.* Cambridge, MA: Harvard University Press, 1997.

Dyson, George B. *Darwin Among the Machines: The Evolution of Global Intelligence.* New York: Helix Books, 1997.

EPM Communications. "Research Alert Yearbook: 2000 Edition." New York: EPM Communications, 2000.

Evans, Philip and Thomas S. Wurster. *Blown to Bits: How the Economics of Information Transformed Strategy.* Boston: Harvard Business School Press, 2000.

Fahey, Liam and Robert M. Randall, eds. *Learning from the Future.* New York: John Wiley and Sons Ltd., 1998.

Farrar, Steve. *Family Survival in the American Jungle.* Portland, OR: Multnomah, 1991.

Gallup, George, Jr. and Timothy Jones. *The Next American Spirituality: Finding God in the Twenty-First Century.* Colorado Springs, CO: Victor Books, 2000.

Gates, Bill. *The Road Ahead.* New York: Viking/Penguin, 1995.

—— *Business @ the Speed of Thought: Using a Digital Nervous System.* New York: Warner Books, 1999.

Gershenfeld, Neil. *When Things Start to Think.* New York: Henry Holt and Company, Inc., 1999.

Gibson, Rowan, ed. *Rethinking the Future.* London: Nicholas Brealey Publishing, 1997.

Gilmore, James H. and B. Joseph Pine II, eds. *Markets of One: Creating Customer-Unique Value Through Mass Customization.* Boston: Harvard Business Review, 1988.

Grantham, Charles. *The Future of Work: The Promise of the New Digital Work Society.* New York: Houghton Mifflin, 2000.

Hafner, Katie and Matthew Lyon. *Where Wizards Stay Up Late: The Origins of the Internet*. New York: Simon and Schuster, 1996.

Hampden-Turner, Charles and Fons Trompenaars. *Mastering the Infinite Game: How East Asian Values Are Transforming Business Practices*. Oxford: Capstone Publishing Ltd., 1997.

Handy, Charles. *Beyond Certainty: The Changing World of Organizations*. Boston: Harvard Business School Press, 1996.

Herman, Arthur. *The Idea of Decline in Western History*. New York: Free Press, 1997.

Hock, Dee. *Birth of the Chaordic Age*. San Francisco: Berrett-Koehler, 1999.

Huntington, Samuel P. *The Clash of Civilizations and the Remaking of World Order*. New York: Simon and Schuster, 1996.

Johansen, Robert and Rob Swigart. *Upsizing the Individual in the Downsized Organization*. Reading, MA: Addison-Wesley Publishing Company, 1994.

Joy, Bill. "Why the Future Doesn't Need Us." *Wired*, 8.04 (April 2000).

Kaplan, Robert D. *The Ends of the Earth: A Journey at the Dawn of the 21st Century*. New York: Random House, 1996.

Katches, Mark, William Heisel and Ronald Campbell. "The Body Brokers." *Orange County Register* (April 16, 2000).

King, Larry. *Future Talk: Conversations about Tomorrow*. New York: Harper Perennial, 1998.

Kolata, Gina. *Clone: The Road to Dolly and the Path Ahead*. New York: William Morrow and Company, Inc., 1998.

Kuegman, Paul. *Pop Internationalism*. Cambridge, MA: MIT Press, 1997.

Kurtzman, Joel, ed. *Thought Leaders: Insights On the Future of Business*. San Francisco: Jossey Bass, 1998.

Kurzwell, Ray. *The Age of Spiritual Machines*. New York: Viking, 1999.

Lessig, Lawrence. *Code and Other Laws of Cyberspace*. New York: Basic Books, 1999.

Lopiano-Misdom, Janine and Joanne DeLuca. *Street Trends: How Today's Alternative Youth Cultures Are Creating Tomorrow's Mainstream Markets*. New York: Harper Collins, 1997.

Mackay, Hugh. *Turning Point: Australians Choosing Their Future*. Sydney, Australia: Macmillan, 1999.

Martin, James. *Cybercorp: The New Business Revolution.* New York: AMA-COM, 1996.

McGrath, Tom. *MTV: The Making of a Revolution.* Philadelphia: Running Press, 1996.

McMichael, A.J. *Planetary Overload: Global Environmental Change and the Health of the Human Species.* Cambridge, MA: Cambridge University Press, 1993.

Michael, Donald N. *Training to Plan and Planning to Learn.* Second ed. Alexandria, VA: Miles River Press, 1997.

Michener, James. *This Noble Land.* New York: Fawcett Columbine, 1996.

Millman, John. *The Other Americans: How Immigrants Renew Our Country, Our Economy and Our Values.* New York: Viking, 1997.

Morrison, Ian. *The Second Curve: Managing the Velocity of Change.* New York: Ballantine Books, 1996.

Naisbitt, John. *Megatrends Asia: Eight Asian Megatrends that Are Changing Our World.* New York: Simon and Schuster, 1996.

—— *High Tech / High Touch: Technology and Our Search for Meaning.* New York: Random House, Inc., 1999.

Neustadt, Richard E. and Earnest R. May. *Thinking in Time: The Uses of History for Decision Makers.* New York: Free Press, 1986.

Occupational Outlook Handbook. Indianapolis: JIST Works, Inc., 2000.

Penenberg, Adam L. "The End of Privacy." *Forbes* 164.13 (Nov. 29, 1999): 182.

Peppers, Don and Martha Rogers. *The One to One Future.* New York: Currency Doubleday, 1993.

Peterson, John L. *Out of the Blue: Wild Cards and Other Big Future Surprises.* Arlington, VA: The Arlington Institute, 1997.

Phillips, Tom. *Revival Signs: Join the New Spiritual Awakening.* Gresham, OR: Vision House, 1995.

Pine, B. Joseph, II and James H. Gilmore. *The Experience Economy.* Boston: Harvard Business School Press, 1999.

Pinker, Steven. *How the Mind Works.* New York: W.W. Norton and Company, Inc., 1997.

Penzias, Arno. *Digital Harmony: Business Technology and Life After Paperwork.* New York: Harper Business, 1995.

Raskin, Jef. *The Humane Interface: New Directions for Designing Interactive Systems.* Reading, MA: Addison-Wesley, Longman, Inc., 2000.

Reingold, Howard. *Tools for Thought: The History and Future of Mind-Expanding Technology*. Cambridge, MA: MIT Press, 1985.

Ringland, Gill. *Scenario Planning*. New York: John Wiley and Sons Ltd., 1998.

Rogers, Everett. *Diffusion of Innovations*. 4th ed. New York: Free Press, 1995.

Rohwer, Jim. *Asia Rising: Why America Will Prosper as Asia's Economies Boom*. New York: Simon and Schuster, 1995.

Rumelt, Richard P., Dan E. Schendel and David J. Teece, eds. *Fundamental Issues in Strategy: A Research Agenda*. Boston: Harvard Business School Press, 1994.

Samuelson, Robert. *The Good Life and Its Discontents: The American Dream in the Age of Entitlement, 1945-1995*. New York: Times Books, 1995.

Schwartz, Evan I. *Webonomics: Nine Essential Principles for Growing Your Business on the World Wide Web*. New York: Broadway Books, 1997.

Schwartz, Peter. *The Art of the Long View: Planning for the Future in an Uncertain World*. New York: Currency Doubleday, 1991.

Shapiro, Andrew L. *The Control Revolution: How the Internet Is Putting Individuals in Charge and Changing the World We Know*. New York: Public Affairs, 1999.

Shapiro, Carl and Hal R. Varian. *Information Rules: A Strategic Guide to the Network Economy*. Boston: Harvard Business School Press, 1999.

Silver, Lee M. *Remaking Eden: Cloning and Beyond in a Brave New World*. New York: Avon Books, 1997.

Sine, Tom. *Mustard Seed Versus McWorld: Reinventing Life and Faith for the Future*. Grand Rapids, MI: Baker Books, 1999.

Smith, J. Walker and Ann Clurman. *Rocking the Ages: The Yankelovich Report on Generational Marketing*. New York: Harper Business, 1997.

Strauss, William and Neil Howe. *The Fourth Turning: An American Prophecy*. New York: Broadway Books, 1997.

Tanner, Edward. *Why Things Bite Back: Technology and the Revenge of the Unintended Consequences*. New York: Alfred A. Knopf, 1996.

Tapscott, Don. *Growing Up Digital: The Rise of the Net Generation*. New York: McGraw-Hill Companies, Inc., 1998.

Tapscott, Don and Art Caston. *Paradigm Shift: The New Promise of Information Technology*. New York: McGraw-Hill, 1993.

Tapscott, Don, David Ticoll and Alex Lowry. *Digital Capital: Harnessing the Power of Business Websites.* Boston: Harvard Business School Press, 2000.

U.S. Bureau of the Census. *Statistical Abstract of the United States, 1999: 119th edition.* Washington, DC: 1999.

Van Creveld, Martin. *The Transformation of War.* New York: Free Press, 1991.

Van Der Heijden, Kees. *Scenarios: The Art of Strategic Conversation.* West Sussex, UK: John Wiley and Sons Ltd., 1996.

Von Weizsäcker, Ernst, Amory B. Lovins and L. Hunter Lovins. *Factor Four: Doubling Wealth, Halving Resources.* London: Earthscan Publications Ltd., 1997.

Wacker, Watts and Jim Taylor. *The 500 Year Delta.* New York: Harper Collins, 1997.

Weiners, Brad and David Pescovitz. *Reality Check.* San Francisco: Hardwired, 1996.

Wheelwright, Jeff. *Degrees of Disaster: Prince William Sound: How Nature Reels and Rebounds.* New York: Simon and Schuster, 1994.

Yergin, Daniel and Joseph Stanislaw. *The Commanding Heights.* New York: Simon and Schuster, 1998.

More of the Best of Barna

The Habits of Highly Effective Churches
Being Strategic in Your God-Given Ministry
George Barna
Paperback
ISBN 08307.18605

Real Teens
A Contemporary Snapshot of Youth Culture
George Barna
Paperback
ISBN 08307.26632

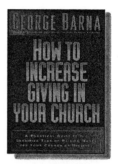

How to Increase Giving in Your Church
A Practical Guide to the Sensitive Task of Raising Money for Your Church or Ministry
George Barna
Paperback
ISBN 08307.19210

Grow from the Outside In
Understanding the Unchurched and How to Reach Them
George Barna
Paperback
ISBN 08307.30877

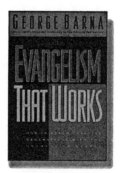

Evangelism That Works
How to Reach Changing Generations with the Unchanging Gospel
George Barna
Paperback
ISBN 08307.17765

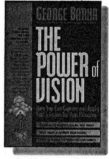

The Power of Vision
How You Can Capture and Apply God's Vision for Your Ministry
George Barna
Paperback
ISBN 08307.16017

Great Reading for Leaders

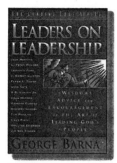

Leaders on Leadership
Wisdom, Advice and Encouragement
on the Art of Leading God's People
George Barna
Paperback
ISBN 08307.18621

Turning Vision into Action
Defining and Putting into Practice
the Unique Vision God Has for
Your Ministry
George Barna
Paperback
ISBN 08307.18664

**The Measure
of a Man**
20 Attributes of a Godly Man
Gene Getz
Paperback
ISBN 08307.17560

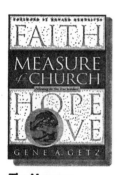

**The Measure
of a Church**
Does Your Church Meet
the Mark?
Gene Getz
Paperback
ISBN 08307.27744

Friends
The Key to Reaching Generation X
Ralph Moore
Paperback
ISBN 08307.28570

**Turnaround
Churches**
How to Overcome Barriers
to Growth and Bring New
Life to an Established
Church
George Barna
Paperback
ISBN 08307.16572

Regal
God's Word for Your World SM
Available at your local Christian bookstore.
www.regalbooks.com

043736